UNIVERSITY CASEBOOK SER

2014 SUPPLEMENT

EMPLOYMENT LAW

CASES AND MATERIALS

CONCISE AND UNABRIDGED SEVENTH EDITIONS

by

MARK A. ROTHSTEIN
Herbert F. Boehl Chair of Law and Medicine
University of Louisville

LANCE M. LIEBMAN
William S. Beinecke Professor of Law
Columbia University

KIMBERLY A. YURACKO
Professor of Law
Northwestern University

FOUNDATION
PRESS

University Casebook Series is a trademark registered in the U.S. Patent and Trademark Office.

© 2008–2010, 2012 THOMSON REUTERS/FOUNDATION PRESS
© 2013 LEG, Inc. d/b/a West Academic Publishing
© 2014 LEG, Inc. d/b/a West Academic
    444 Cedar Street, Suite 700
    St. Paul, MN 55101
    1-877-888-1330

Printed in the United States of America

ISBN: 978-1-62810-139-3

Mat #41655218

TABLE OF CONTENTS

UNABRIDGED VERSION

PART I. BACKGROUND

PART II. ESTABLISHING THE EMPLOYMENT RELATIONSHIP

PART III. TERMS AND CONDITIONS OF EMPLOYMENT

TABLE OF CASES

The principal cases are in bold type.

UNIVERSITY CASEBOOK SERIES®

2014 SUPPLEMENT

EMPLOYMENT LAW

CASES AND MATERIALS

CONCISE AND UNABRIDGED SEVENTH EDITIONS

PART I

BACKGROUND

CHAPTER 1

WORK AND LAW

A. WORK AND SOCIETY

Page 8. Please delete the Greenhouse reading and replace with the following:

Nicholas Kristof, It's Now the Canadian Dream*

New York Times, May 15, 2014, A25.

It was in 1931 that the historian James Truslow Adams coined the phrase "the American dream."

The American dream is not just a yearning for affluence, Adams said, but also for the chance to overcome barriers and social class, to become the best that we can be. Adams acknowledged that the United States didn't fully live up to that ideal, but he argued that America came closer than anywhere else.

Adams was right at the time, and for decades. When my father, an eastern European refugee, reached France after World War II, he was determined to continue to the United States because it was less class bound, more meritocratic and offered more opportunity.

Yet today the American dream has derailed, partly because of growing inequality. Or maybe the American dream has just swapped citizenship, for now it is more likely to be found in Canada or Europe—and a central issue in this year's political campaigns should be how to repatriate it.

A report last month in The Times by David Leonhardt and Kevin Quealy noted that the American middle class is no longer the richest in the world, with Canada apparently pulling ahead in median after-tax income. Other countries in Europe are poised to overtake us as well.

In fact, the discrepancy is arguably even greater. Canadians receive essentially free health care, while Americans pay for part of their health care costs with after-tax dollars. Meanwhile, the American worker toils, on average, 4.6 percent more hours than a Canadian worker, 21 percent more hours than a French worker and an astonishing 28 percent more hours than a German worker, according to data from the Organization for Economic Cooperation and Development.

Canadians and Europeans also live longer, on average, than Americans do. Their children are less likely to die than ours. American women are twice as likely to die as a result of pregnancy or childbirth as Canadian women. And, while our universities are still the best in the world, children in other industrialized countries, on average, get a better education than ours. Most sobering of all: A recent O.E.C.D.

---

report found that for people aged 16 to 24, Americans ranked last among rich countries in numeracy and technological proficiency.

Economic mobility is tricky to measure, but several studies show that a child born in the bottom 20 percent economically is less likely to rise to the top in America than in Europe. A Danish child is twice as likely to rise as an American child.

When our futures are determined to a significant extent at birth, we've reverted to the feudalism that our ancestors fled.

"Equality of opportunity—the 'American dream'—has always been a cherished American ideal," Joseph Stiglitz, the Nobel-winning economist at Columbia University, noted in a recent speech. "But data now show that this is a myth: America has become the advanced country not only with the highest level of inequality, but one of those with the least equality of opportunity."

Consider that the American economy has, over all, grown more quickly than France's. But so much of the growth has gone to the top 1 percent that the bottom 99 percent of French people have done better than the bottom 99 percent of Americans.

Three data points:

- The top 1 percent in America now own assets worth more than those held by the entire bottom 90 percent.

- The six Walmart heirs are worth as much as the bottom 41 percent of American households put together.

- The top six hedge fund managers and traders averaged more than $2 billion each in earnings last year, partly because of the egregious "carried interest" tax break. President Obama has been unable to get financing for universal prekindergarten; this year's proposed federal budget for pre-K for all, so important to our nation's future, would be a bit more than a single month's earnings for those six tycoons.

* * *

It's time to bring the American dream home from exile.

NOTES AND QUESTIONS

1.   The current level of income and wealth inequality in the United States is comparable to the period at the beginning of the twentieth century, before enactment of the federal income tax, the Fair Labor Standards Act and state minimum wage laws, Social Security and income support for the elderly, unionization and collective bargaining, the G.I. Bill and widespread access to higher education, and other laws and policies that fostered development of the middle class. One of the rationalizations for American laissez-faire capitalism and its "rugged individualism" social policy has been that, even though there are wide gaps between the "haves" and "have nots," there is vertical social mobility. In other words, through talent and hard work, in a few years or a few generations (especially for immigrants), an individual or his or her children can go from the bottom to the top of the income ladder. What effect does the new "locked in" nature of socioeconomic position have on America's social narrative?

2. Among the recent scholarship on the issue of economic inequality are Thomas Piketty, Capital in the Twenty-first Century (2014) and Joseph E. Stigletz, The Price of Inequality: How Today's Divided Society Endangers Our Future (2013).

3. For the purposes of this course, there are two related questions. First, how, if at all, have labor and employment laws contributed to the rising inequality? Second, how, if at all, have labor and employment laws been affected by the rising inequality?

CHAPTER 2

THE DEVELOPMENT OF EMPLOYMENT LAW

A. THE FOUNDATIONS OF EMPLOYMENT LAW

2. EMPLOYER—EMPLOYEE

Page 27.   Please add the following at the end of the first full paragraph.

In Mayo Fdn. for Med. Educ. & Research v. United States, 131 S.Ct. 704 (2011), the Supreme Court held that the Treasury Department's rule that treats medical residents as full-time employees, and therefore not exempt from the payment of payroll taxes, is a valid interpretation of federal law.

B. SOURCES OF MODERN EMPLOYMENT LAW

2. COLLECTIVE BARGAINING

Page 52.   Please add the following note.

4. Union density continues to decline. In 2013, 6.6% of private sector employees, 35.3% of public sector employees, and 11.3% of all employees belonged to a union. See U.S. Dep't of Labor, Bureau of Labor Statistics, Union Members Summary, 2013 (2014), www.bls.gov/news.release/union2.nro.htm.

6. ARBITRATION

Page 62.   Please add the following to the end of note 1.

See also Marzette v. Anheuser-Busch, Inc., 371 S.W.3d 49 (Mo. Ct. App. 2012) (signature on the bottom of employment application insufficient consideration for agreement to arbitrate all employment claims in the event of being hired).

Page 63.   Please add the following to the end of note 6.

In Oxford Health Plans LLC v. Sutter, 133 S.Ct. 2064 (2013), an arbitrator construed a collective bargaining agreement to permit class actions. Supreme Court held that the arbitrator did not exceed his powers because his holding was an interpretation of language in the contract.

PART II

ESTABLISHING THE EMPLOYMENT RELATIONSHIP

CHAPTER 3

THE HIRING PROCESS

B. THE LABOR POOL

1. UNDOCUMENTED ALIENS

Page 104.   Please add the following to note 7.

In Staff Mgmt. v. Jimenez, 839N.W.2d 640 (Iowa 2013), the Iowa Supreme Court distinguished *Hoffman* and held that undocumented workers are entitled to state workers' compensation benefits. Cf. New York Hosp. Med. Ctr. of Queens v. Microtech Contracting Corp., 5 N.E.3d 993 (N.Y. 2014) (immigration status of employees does not affect employer's protection from third-party lawsuits contained in "exclusive remedy" provision of workers' compensation law).

Page 105.   Please add the following case before Residency Requirements.

Chamber of Commerce v. Whiting
131 S.Ct. 1968 (2011).

■ CHIEF JUSTICE ROBERTS delivered the opinion of the Court, except as to Parts II–B and III–B.

Federal immigration law expressly preempts "any State or local law imposing civil or criminal sanctions (other than through licensing and similar laws) upon those who employ . . . unauthorized aliens." 8 U.S.C. § 1324a(h)(2). A recently enacted Arizona statute—the Legal Arizona Workers Act—provides that the licenses of state employers that knowingly or intentionally employ unauthorized aliens may be, and in certain circumstances must be, suspended or revoked. The law also requires that all Arizona employers use a federal electronic verification system to confirm that the workers they employ are legally authorized workers. The question presented is whether federal immigration law preempts those provisions of Arizona law. Because we conclude that the State's licensing provisions fall squarely within the federal statute's savings clause and that the Arizona regulation does not otherwise conflict with federal law, we hold that the Arizona law is not preempted.

I.

A.

In 1952, Congress enacted the Immigration and Nationality Act (INA). That statute established a "comprehensive federal statutory scheme for regulation of immigration and naturalization" and set "the terms and conditions of admission to the country and the subsequent treatment of aliens lawfully in the country." De Canas v. Bica, 424 U.S. 351, 353, 359 (1976).

In the years following the enactment of the INA, several States took action to prohibit the employment of individuals living within state borders who were not lawful residents of the United States.

* * *

We first addressed the interaction of federal immigration law and state laws dealing with the employment of unauthorized aliens in *De Canas*. In that case, we recognized that the "[p]ower to regulate immigration is unquestionably . . . a federal power." At the same time, however, we noted that the "States possess broad authority under their police powers to regulate the employment relationship to protect workers within the State," that "prohibit[ing] the knowing employment . . . of persons not entitled to lawful residence in the United States, let alone to work here, is certainly within the mainstream of [the State's] police power," and that the Federal Government had "at best" expressed a peripheral concern with [the] employment of illegal entrants at that point in time. As a result, we declined to hold that a state law assessing civil fines for the employment of unauthorized aliens was preempted by federal immigration law.

Ten years after *De Canas*, Congress enacted the Immigration Reform and Control Act (IRCA). IRCA makes it "unlawful for a person or other entity . . . to hire, or to recruit or refer for a fee, for employment in the United States an alien knowing the alien is an unauthorized alien." 8 U.S.C. § 1324a(a)(1)(A). IRCA defines an "unauthorized alien" as an alien who is not "lawfully admitted for permanent residence" or not otherwise authorized by the Attorney General to be employed in the United States.

* * *

IRCA also restricts the ability of States to combat employment of unauthorized workers. The Act expressly preempts "any State or local law imposing civil or criminal sanctions (other than through licensing and similar laws) upon those who employ, or recruit or refer for a fee for employment, unauthorized aliens." Under that provision, state laws imposing civil fines for the employment of unauthorized workers like the one we upheld in *De Canas* are now expressly preempted.

* * *

B.

Acting against this statutory and historical background, several States have recently enacted laws attempting to impose sanctions for the employment of unauthorized aliens through, among other things, "licensing and similar laws." Arizona is one of them. The Legal Arizona Workers Act of 2007 allows Arizona courts to suspend or revoke the licenses necessary to do business in the State if an employer knowingly or intentionally employs an unauthorized alien.

Under the Arizona law, if an individual files a complaint alleging that an employer has hired an unauthorized alien, the attorney general or the county attorney first verifies the employee's work authorization with the Federal Government pursuant to 8 U.S.C. § 1373(c). Section 1373(c) provides that the Federal Government "shall respond to an inquiry by a" State "seeking to verify or ascertain the citizenship or immigration status of any individual . . . by providing the requested verification or status information." The Arizona law expressly prohibits state, county, or local officials from attempting "to independently make a final determination on whether an alien is authorized to work in the United States." If the § 1373(c) inquiry reveals that a worker is an unauthorized alien, the attorney general or the county attorney must notify United States Immigration and Customs Enforcement officials, notify local law enforcement, and bring an action against the employer.

When a complaint is brought against an employer under Arizona law, "the court shall consider only the federal government's determination pursuant to" 8 U.S.C. § 1373(c) in "determining whether an employee is an unauthorized alien." Good-faith compliance with the federal I–9 process provides employers prosecuted by the State with an affirmative defense.

A first instance of "knowingly employ[ing] an unauthorized alien" requires that the court order the employer to terminate the employment of all unauthorized aliens and file quarterly reports on all new hires for a probationary period of three years. The court may also "order the appropriate agencies to suspend all licenses . . . that are held by the employer for [a period] not to exceed ten business days." A second knowing violation requires that the adjudicating court "permanently revoke all licenses that are held by the employer specific to the business location where the unauthorized alien performed work."

For a first intentional violation, the court must order the employer to terminate the employment of all unauthorized aliens and file quarterly reports on all new hires for a probationary period of five years. The court must also suspend all the employer's licenses for a minimum of 10 days. A second intentional violation requires the permanent revocation of all business licenses.

With respect to both knowing and intentional violations, a violation qualifies as a "second violation" only if it occurs at the same business location as the first violation, during the time that the employer is already on probation for a violation at that location.

The Arizona law also requires that "every employer, after hiring an employee, shall verify the employment eligibility of the employee" by using E-Verify. "[P]roof of verifying the employment authorization of an employee through the e-verify program creates a rebuttable presumption that an employer did not knowingly employ an unauthorized alien."

C.

* * *

The Court of Appeals affirmed the District Court in all respects, holding that Arizona's law was a " 'licensing and similar law[ ]' " falling within IRCA's savings clause and that none of the state law's challenged provisions was "expressly or impliedly preempted by federal policy."

II.

The Chamber of Commerce argues that Arizona's law is expressly preempted by IRCA's text and impliedly preempted because it conflicts with federal law. We address each of the Chamber's arguments in turn.

A.

* * *

IRCA expressly preempts States from imposing "civil or criminal sanctions" on those who employ unauthorized aliens, "other than through licensing and similar laws." The Arizona law, on its face, purports to impose sanctions through licensing laws. The state law authorizes state courts to suspend or revoke an employer's business licenses if that employer knowingly or intentionally employs an unauthorized alien. The Arizona law defines "license" as "any agency permit, certificate, approval, registration, charter or similar form of authorization that is required by law and that is issued by any agency for the purposes of operating a business in" the State. That definition largely parrots the definition of "license" that Congress codified in the Administrative Procedure Act.

Apart from that general definition, the Arizona law specifically includes within its definition of license documents such as articles of incorporation, certificates of partnership, and grants of authority to foreign companies to transact business in the State. These examples have clear counterparts in the APA definition just quoted.

A license is "a right or permission granted in accordance with law . . . to engage in some business or occupation, to do some act, or to engage in some transaction which but for such license would be unlawful." Webster's Third New International Dictionary 1304 (2002). Articles of incorporation and certificates of partnership allow the formation of legal entities and permit them as such to engage in business and transactions "which but for such" authorization "would be unlawful." As for state-issued authorizations for foreign businesses to operate within a State, we have repeatedly referred to those as "licenses." Moreover, even if a law regulating articles of incorporation, partnership certificates, and the like is not itself a "licensing law," it is at the very least "similar" to a licensing law, and therefore comfortably within the savings clause.

The Chamber and the United States as amicus argue that the Arizona law is not a "licensing" law because it operates only to suspend and revoke licenses rather than to grant them. Again, this construction of the term runs contrary to the definition that Congress itself has codified. It is also contrary to common sense. There is no basis in law, fact, or logic for deeming a law that grants licenses a licensing law, but a law that suspends or revokes those very licenses something else altogether.

* * *

B.

As an alternative to its express preemption argument, the Chamber contends that Arizona's law is impliedly preempted because it conflicts with federal law. At its broadest level, the Chamber's argument is that Congress "intended the federal system to be exclusive," and that any state system therefore necessarily conflicts with federal law. But Arizona's procedures simply implement the sanctions that Congress expressly allowed Arizona to pursue through licensing laws. Given that Congress specifically preserved such authority for the States, it stands to reason that Congress did not intend to prevent the States from using appropriate tools to exercise that authority.

And here Arizona went the extra mile in ensuring that its law closely tracks IRCA's provisions in all material respects. The Arizona law begins by adopting the federal definition of who qualifies as an "unauthorized alien."

Not only that, the Arizona law expressly provides that state investigators must verify the work authorization of an allegedly unauthorized alien with the Federal Government, and "shall not attempt to independently make a final determination on whether an alien is authorized to work in the United States." What is more, a state court "shall consider only the federal government's determination" when deciding "whether an employee is an unauthorized alien." As a result, there can by definition be no conflict between state and federal law as to worker authorization, either at the investigatory or adjudicatory stage.

* * *

The Chamber and JUSTICE BREYER assert that employers will err on the side of discrimination rather than risk the " 'business death penalty' " by "hiring unauthorized workers." That is not the choice. License termination is not an available sanction simply for "hiring unauthorized workers." Only far more egregious violations of the law trigger that consequence. The Arizona law covers only knowing or intentional violations. The law's permanent licensing sanctions do not come into play until a second knowing or intentional violation at the same business location, and only if the second violation occurs while the employer is still on probation for the first. These limits ensure that licensing sanctions are imposed only when an employer's conduct fully justifies them. An employer acting in good faith need have no fear of the sanctions.

As the Chamber points out, IRCA has its own anti-discrimination provisions, Arizona law certainly does nothing to displace those. Other federal laws, and Arizona anti-discrimination laws, provide further protection against employment discrimination—and strong incentive for employers not to discriminate.

All that is required to avoid sanctions under the Legal Arizona Workers Act is to refrain from knowingly or intentionally violating the employment law. Employers enjoy safe harbors from liability when they use the I–9 system and E-Verify—as Arizona law requires them to do. The most rational path for employers is to obey the law—both the law barring the employment of unauthorized aliens and the law prohibiting discrimination—and there is no reason to suppose that Arizona employers will choose not to do so.

As with any piece of legislation, Congress did indeed seek to strike a balance among a variety of interests when it enacted IRCA. Part of that balance, however, involved allocating authority between the Federal Government and the States. The principle that Congress adopted in doing so was not that the Federal Government can impose large sanctions, and the States only small ones. IRCA instead preserved state authority over a particular category of sanctions—those imposed "through licensing and similar laws."

* * *

III.

* * *

Because Arizona's unauthorized alien employment law fits within the confines of IRCA's savings clause and does not conflict with federal immigration law, the judgment of the United States Court of Appeals for the Ninth Circuit is affirmed.

It is so ordered.

JUSTICE KAGAN took no part in the consideration or decision of this case.

JUSTICE BREYER, with whom JUSTICE GINSBURG joins, dissenting.

* * *

Arizona calls its state statute a "licensing law," and the statute uses the word "licensing." But the statute strays beyond the bounds of the federal licensing exception, for it defines "license" to include articles of incorporation and partnership certificates, indeed virtually every state-law authorization for any firm, corporation, or partnership to do business in the State. Congress did not intend its "licensing" language to create so broad an exemption, for doing so would permit States to eviscerate the federal Act's pre-emption provision, indeed to subvert the Act itself, by undermining Congress' efforts (1) to protect lawful workers from national-origin-based discrimination and (2) to protect lawful employers against erroneous prosecution or punishment.

* * *

First, the state statute seriously threatens the federal Act's antidiscriminatory objectives by radically skewing the relevant penalties. For example, in the absence of the Arizona statute, an Arizona employer who intentionally hires an unauthorized alien for the second time would risk a maximum penalty of $6,500. But the Arizona statute subjects that same employer (in respect to the same two incidents) to mandatory, permanent loss of the right to do business in Arizona—a penalty that Arizona's Governor has called the "business death penalty." At the same time, the state law leaves the other side of the punishment balance—the antidiscrimination side—unchanged.

This is no idle concern. Despite the federal Act's efforts to prevent discriminatory practices, there is evidence that four years after it had become law, discrimination was a serious problem. In 1990, the General Accounting Office identified "widespread discrimination . . . as a result of" the Act. Sixteen percent of employers in Los Angeles admitted that they applied the I–9 requirement "only to foreign-looking or foreign-sounding persons," and 22 percent of Texas employers reported that they "began a practice to (1) hire only persons born in the United States or (2) not hire persons with temporary work eligibility documents" because of the Act. If even the federal Act (with its carefully balanced penalties) can result in some employers discriminating, how will employers behave when erring on the side of discrimination leads only to relatively small fines, while erring on the side of hiring unauthorized workers leads to the "business death penalty"?

Second, Arizona's law subjects lawful employers to increased burdens and risks of erroneous prosecution. In addition to the Arizona law's severely burdensome sanctions, the law's procedures create enforcement risks not present in the federal system. The federal Act creates one centralized enforcement scheme, run by officials versed in immigration law and with access to the relevant federal documents. The upshot is an increased likelihood that federal officials (or the employer) will discover whether adverse information flows from an error-prone source and that they will proceed accordingly, thereby diminishing the likelihood that burdensome proceedings and liability reflect documentary mistakes.

Contrast the enforcement system that Arizona's statute creates. Any citizen of the State can complain (anonymously or otherwise) to the state attorney general (or any county attorney), who then "shall investigate," and, upon a determination that that the "complaint is not false and frivolous . . . shall notify the appropriate county attorney to bring an action." This mandatory language, the lower standard ("not frivolous" instead of "substantial"), and the removal of immigration officials from the state screening process (substituting numerous, elected county attorneys) increase the likelihood that suspicious circumstances will lead to prosecutions and liability of employers—even where more careful investigation would have revealed that there was no violation.

Why would Congress, after deliberately limiting ordinary penalties to the range of a few thousand dollars per illegal worker, want to permit far more drastic state penalties that would directly and mandatorily destroy entire businesses? Why would Congress, after carefully balancing sanctions to avoid encouraging discrimination, want to allow States to destroy that balance? Why would Congress, after creating detailed procedural protections for employers, want to allow States to undermine them? Why would Congress want to write into an express pre-emption provision—a provision designed to prevent States from undercutting federal statutory objectives—an exception that could so easily destabilize its efforts? The answer to these questions is that Congress would not have wanted to do any of these things. And that fact indicates that the majority's reading of the licensing exception—a reading that would allow what Congress sought to forbid—is wrong.

JUSTICE SOTOMAYOR, dissenting.

* * *

Congress made explicit its intent that IRCA be enforced uniformly. IRCA declares that "[i]t is the sense of the Congress that . . . the immigration laws of the United States should be enforced vigorously and uniformly." Congress structured IRCA's provisions in a number of ways to accomplish this goal of uniform enforcement.

First, and most obviously, Congress expressly displaced the myriad state laws that imposed civil and criminal sanctions on employers who hired unauthorized aliens. Congress could not have made its intent to preempt state and local laws imposing civil or criminal sanctions any more " 'clear [or] manifest.' "

Second, Congress centralized in the Federal Government enforcement of IRCA's prohibition on the knowing employment of unauthorized aliens. IRCA instructs the Attorney General to designate a specialized federal agency unit whose "primary duty" will be to prosecute violations of IRCA. IRCA also instructs the Attorney General to establish procedures for receiving complaints, investigating complaints having "a substantial probability of validity," and investigating other violations.

* * *

Third, Congress provided persons "adversely affected" by an agency order with a right of review in the federal courts of appeals. In this way, Congress ensured that administrative orders finding violations of IRCA would be reviewed by federal judges with experience adjudicating immigration-related matters.

Fourth, Congress created a uniquely federal system by which employers must verify the work authorization status of new hires. Under this system, an employer must attest under penalty of perjury on a form designated by the Attorney General (the I–9 form) that it has examined enumerated identification documents to verify that a new hire is not an unauthorized alien. Good-faith compliance with this verification requirement entitles an employer to an affirmative defense if charged with violating IRCA. Notably, however, IRCA prohibits use of the I–9 form for any purpose other than enforcement of IRCA and various provisions of federal criminal law. Use of the I–9 form is thus limited to federal proceedings, as the majority acknowledges.

Finally, Congress created no mechanism for States to access information regarding an alien's work authorization status for purposes of enforcing state prohibitions on the employment of unauthorized aliens. The relevant sections of IRCA make no provision for the sharing of work authorization information between federal and state authorities even though access to that information would be critical to a State's ability to determine whether an employer has employed an unauthorized alien. In stark contrast, a separate provision in the same title of IRCA creates a verification system by which States can ascertain the immigration status of aliens applying for benefits under programs such as Medicaid and the food stamp program.

* * *

NOTES

1.   In a related case, Arizona v. United States, 132 S.Ct. 2492 (2012), the Supreme Court declared unconstitutional three provisions of another Arizona immigration law, the Support Our Law Enforcement and Safe

Neighborhoods Act. The Court held that federal law preempted the following provisions: (1) making it a sate misdemeanor to fail to comply with federal alien-registration requirements; (2) making it a state misdemeanor for an unauthorized alien to seek or engage in work in the state; and (3) authorizing state and local officers to arrest without a warrant a person the office has probable cause to believe has committed an act that makes the person "removable" from the United States. The Court reversed an injunction prohibiting enforcement of a provision requiring officers making a stop, detention, or arrest to verify the person's immigration status.

2. Not surprisingly, the *Whiting* decision has been subject to scholarly criticism. See, e.g., Keith Cunningham-Parmeter, Forced Federalism: States as Laboratories of Immigration Reform, 62 Hastings L.J. 1673 (2011); Kevin R. Johnson, Immigration and Civil Rights: State and Local Efforts to Regulate Immigration, 46 Ga. L. Rev. 609 (2012).

3. In 2013, California enacted a law that makes it illegal for employers to report or threaten to report a worker's immigration status, or the status of family members, in retaliation for a worker exercising such employment rights as complaining about unsafe working conditions or sexual harassment. Employers that violate the law are subject to revocation of their business licenses and civil penalties up to $10,000 per violation. Cal. Bus. & Prof. Code § 494.6; Cal. Lab. Code §§ 98.6, 244. Should an unauthorized worker make a daily complaint about some working condition to keep from being reported by his or her employer?

3. EMPLOYMENT OF VETERANS

Page 110. Please add the following before Applications, Interviews, and References.

In Staub v. Proctor Hospital, 131 S.Ct. 1186 (2011), an Army reservist brought an action under USERRA to challenge his discharge. The case turned on the burden of proving that hostility to an individual's military status was a "motivating factor" in an adverse employment action. At issue was the "cat's paw" theory, under which the plaintiff seeks to hold an employer liable for the animus of a supervisor who was not responsible for the ultimate employment decision. The Court held that discriminatory actions of a supervisor leading an unbiased decision maker to take an adverse action could establish liability. For a further discussion of the "cat's paw" theory, see Chapter 4.

4. HIRING THE UNEMPLOYED

According to the Bureau of Labor Statistics, as of April 2014, the mean duration of unemployment in the United States was 35.1 weeks, and the percentage of individuals unemployed for 27 or more weeks was 35.3%. www.bls.gov/news.release/pdf/empsit.pdf. The figures vary according to several demographic factors, including gender, race, and age. For example, workers age 55–64 have a much higher duration of unemployment.

Long-term unemployed workers (those out of work 27 or more weeks) have a more difficult time obtaining interviews or job offers for various reasons. Individuals who have been out of the work force for an extended period of time may lose some of their skills, lose touch with their network of contacts, or may fail to interview well because of numerous prior rejections. There are also some employers that simply refuse to consider any long-term unemployed individuals. According to one review of job vacancy postings on Monster.com, CareerBuilder, and Craigslist, hundreds of employers said they would only consider or "strongly prefer" currently employed or recently unemployed individuals. Catherine Rampell, The Help-Wanted Sign Comes With a Frustrating Asterisk, N.Y. Times July 26, 2011, at B1. Apparently, these employers believe that individuals out of work for extended periods of time are less capable, productive, or desirable.

Under current law, the most likely legal challenges to such employer practices would be "disparate impact" claims for age or race discrimination, under the ADEA and Title VII, but these types of cases are difficult to prove. See Chapter 4. At the state level, New Jersey was the first state to prohibit employment notices that bar unemployed workers from applying. At the federal level, the Obama Administration's "jobs bill" would have prohibited employers with 15 or more employees from discriminating against job applicants because they are unemployed. No action was taken on the bill.

Legislation has been introduced at the federal, state, and local levels to address this issue. At the federal level, the Fair Employment Opportunity Act of 2011, S. 1471, H.R. 2501, would have prohibited employers with 15 or more employees from discriminating against job applicants because they are unemployed. At the state level, legislation has been enacted in New Jersey, Oregon, and the District of Columbia prohibiting employers from listing "current employment" as a requirement in a job advertisement. In California, Governor Brown vetoed similar legislation because he was unhappy with certain amendments to the bill. At the city level, the New York City Council enacted legislation in 2013, over the veto of Mayor Bloomberg, that permits unemployed individuals who believe they were subject to discrimination because they were out of work to sue prospective employers for compensatory and punitive damages, and to obtain attorney fees.

In New Jersey Dep't of Labor & Workforce Dev. v. Craig Ultrasonics, 82 A.3d 258 (N.J. Super. Ct. App. Div. 2014), an employer challenged the constitutionality of the New Jersey law that imposed a $1000 fine on employers that publish an advertisement stating that a job applicant must be currently employed in order to be considered. The court rejected the employer's argument that the law violated the First Amendment. "Because the statute only prohibits an employer from stating in its ads that current employment is a prerequisite to the acceptance of an applicant's materials, . . . [it] is no more extensive than necessary to serve the government's asserted interest." 82 A.3d at 272.

C. APPLICATIONS, INTERVIEWS, AND REFERENCES

1. APPLICATIONS

Page 120.   Please add the following case after note 9.

NASA v. Nelson
131 S.Ct. 746 (2011).

■ JUSTICE ALITO delivered the opinion of the Court.

In two cases decided more than 30 years ago, this Court referred broadly to a constitutional privacy "interest in avoiding disclosure of personal matters." Whalen v. Roe, 429 U.S. 589, 599–600 (1977); Nixon v. Administrator of General Services, 433 U.S. 425, 457 (1977). Respondents in this case, federal contract employees at a Government laboratory, claim that two parts of a standard employment background investigation violate their rights under *Whalen* and *Nixon*. Respondents challenge a section of a form questionnaire that asks employees about treatment or counseling for recent illegal-drug use. They also object to certain open-ended questions on a form sent to employees' designated references.

We assume, without deciding, that the Constitution protects a privacy right of the sort mentioned in *Whalen* and *Nixon*. We hold, however, that the challenged portions of the Government's background check do not violate this right in the present case. The Government's interests as employer and proprietor in managing its internal operations, combined with the protections against public dissemination provided by the Privacy Act of 1974, 5 U.S.C. § 552a, satisfy any "interest in avoiding disclosure" that may "arguably ha[ve] its roots in the Constitution."

The National Aeronautics and Space Administration (NASA) is an independent federal agency charged with planning and conducting the Government's "space activities." NASA's workforce numbers in the tens of thousands of employees. While many of these workers are federal civil servants, a substantial majority are employed directly by Government contractors. Contract employees play an important role in NASA's mission, and their duties are functionally equivalent to those performed by civil servants.

One NASA facility, the Jet Propulsion Laboratory (JPL) in Pasadena, California, is staffed exclusively by contract employees. NASA owns JPL, but the California Institute of Technology (Cal Tech) operates the facility under a Government contract. JPL is the lead NASA center for deep-space robotics and communications. Most of this country's unmanned space missions—from the Explorer 1 satellite in 1958 to the Mars Rovers of today—have been developed and run by JPL. JPL scientists contribute to NASA earth-observation and technology-development projects. Many JPL employees also engage in pure scientific research on topics like "the star formation history of the universe" and "the fundamental properties of quantum fluids."

Twenty-eight JPL employees are respondents here. Many of them have worked at the lab for decades, and none has ever been the subject of a Government background investigation. At the time when respondents were hired, background checks were standard only for federal civil servants. In some instances, individual contracts required background checks for the employees of federal contractors, but no blanket policy was in place.

The Government has recently taken steps to eliminate this two-track approach to background investigations. In 2004, a recommendation by the 9/11 Commission prompted the President to order new, uniform identification standards for "[f]ederal employees," including "contractor employees." The Department of Commerce implemented this directive by mandating that contract employees with long-term access to federal facilities complete a standard background check, typically the National Agency Check with Inquiries (NACI).

An October 2007 deadline was set for completion of these investigations. In January 2007, NASA modified its contract with Cal Tech to reflect the new background-check requirement. JPL management informed employees that anyone failing to complete the NACI process by October 2007 would be denied access to JPL and would face termination by Cal Tech.

The NACI process has long been the standard background investigation for prospective civil servants. The process begins when the applicant or employee fills out a form questionnaire. Employees who work in "non-sensitive" positions (as all respondents here do) complete Standard Form 85 (SF–85).

Most of the questions on SF–85 seek basic biographical information: name, address, prior residences, education, employment history, and personal and professional references. The form also asks about citizenship, selective-service registration, and military service. The last question asks whether the employee has "used, possessed, supplied, or manufactured illegal drugs" in the last year. If the answer is yes, the employee must provide details, including information about "any treatment or counseling received." A "truthful response," the form notes, cannot be used as evidence against the employee in a criminal proceeding. The employee must certify that all responses on the form are true and must sign a release authorizing the Government to obtain personal information from schools, employers, and others during its investigation.

Once a completed SF–85 is on file, the "agency check" and "inquiries" begin. The Government runs the information provided by the employee through FBI and other federal-agency databases. It also sends out form questionnaires to the former employers, schools, landlords, and references listed on SF–85. The particular form at issue in this case—the Investigative Request for Personal Information, Form 42—goes to the employee's former landlords and references.

Form 42 is a two-page document that takes about five minutes to complete. It explains to the reference that "[y]our name has been provided by" a particular employee or applicant to help the Government determine that person's "suitability for employment or a security clearance." After several preliminary questions about the extent of the reference's associations with the employee, the form asks if the reference has "any reason to question" the employee's "honesty or trustworthiness." It also asks if the reference knows of any "adverse information" concerning the employee's "violations of the law," "financial integrity," "abuse of alcohol and/or drugs," "mental or emotional stability," "general behavior or conduct," or "other matters." If "yes" is checked for any of these categories, the form calls for an explanation in the space below. That space is also available for providing "additional information" ("derogatory" or "favorable") that may bear on "suitability for government employment or a security clearance."

All responses to SF–85 and Form 42 are subject to the protections of the Privacy Act. The Act authorizes the Government to keep records pertaining to an individual only when they are "relevant and necessary" to an end "required to be accomplished" by law. Individuals are permitted to access their records and request amendments to them. Subject to certain exceptions, the Government may not disclose records pertaining to an individual without that individual's written consent.

About two months before the October 2007 deadline for completing the NACI, respondents brought this suit, claiming, as relevant here, that the background-check process violates a constitutional right to informational privacy. The District Court denied respondents' motion for a preliminary injunction, but the Ninth Circuit granted an injunction pending appeal, and later reversed the District Court's order. The court held that portions of both SF–85 and Form 42 are likely unconstitutional and should be preliminarily enjoined.

* * *

As noted, respondents contend that portions of SF–85 and Form 42 violate their "right to informational privacy." This Court considered a similar claim in *Whalen*, which concerned New York's practice of collecting "the names and addresses of all persons" prescribed dangerous drugs with both "legitimate and illegitimate uses." In discussing that claim, the Court said that "[t]he cases sometimes characterized as protecting 'privacy'" actually involved "at least two different kinds of interests": one, an "interest in avoiding disclosure of personal matters"; the other, an interest in "making certain kinds of important decisions" free from government interference. The patients who brought suit in *Whalen* argued that New York's statute "threaten[ed] to impair" both their "nondisclosure" interests and their interests in making healthcare decisions independently. The Court, however, upheld the statute as a reasonable exercise of New York's broad police powers.

Whalen acknowledged that the disclosure of "private information" to the State was an "unpleasant invasion of privacy," but the Court pointed out that the New York statute contained "security provisions" that protected against "public disclosure" of patients' information. This sort of "statutory or regulatory duty to avoid unwarranted disclosures" of "accumulated private data" was sufficient, in the Court's view, to protect a privacy interest that "arguably ha[d] its roots in the Constitution." The Court thus concluded that the statute did not violate any right or liberty protected by the Fourteenth Amendment.

Four months later, the Court referred again to a constitutional "interest in avoiding disclosure." Former President Nixon brought a challenge to the Presidential Recordings and Materials Preservation Act, a statute that required him to turn over his presidential papers and tape recordings for archival review and screening. In a section of the opinion entitled "Privacy," the Court addressed a combination of claims that the review required by this Act violated the former President's "Fourth and Fifth Amendmen[t]" rights. The Court rejected those challenges after concluding that the Act at issue, like the statute in *Whalen*, contained protections against "undue dissemination of private materials." Indeed, the Court observed that the former President's claim was "weaker" than the one "found wanting . . . in *Whalen*," as the Government was required to return immediately all "purely private papers and recordings" identified by the archivists. Citing Fourth Amendment precedent, the Court also stated that the public interest in preserving presidential papers outweighed any "legitimate expectation of privacy" that the former President may have enjoyed.

The Court announced the decision in *Nixon* in the waning days of October Term 1976. Since then, the Court has said little else on the subject of an "individual interest in avoiding disclosure of personal matters." A few opinions have mentioned the concept in passing and in other contexts. But no other decision has squarely addressed a constitutional right to informational privacy.

As was our approach in *Whalen*, we will assume for present purposes that the Government's challenged inquiries implicate a privacy interest of constitutional significance. We hold, however, that, whatever the scope of this interest, it does not prevent the Government from asking reasonable questions of the sort included on SF–85 and Form 42 in an employment background investigation that is subject to the Privacy Act's safeguards against public disclosure.

As an initial matter, judicial review of the Government's challenged inquiries must take into account the context in which they arise. When the Government asks respondents and their references to fill out SF–85 and Form 42, it does not exercise its sovereign power "to regulate or license." Rather, the Government conducts the challenged background checks in its capacity "as proprietor" and manager of its "internal operation." Time and again our cases have recognized that the Government has a much freer hand in dealing "with citizen employees than it does when it brings its sovereign power to bear on citizens at large." This distinction is grounded on the "common-sense realization" that if every "employment decision became a constitutional matter," the Government could not function.

* * *

Respondents argue that, because they are contract employees and not civil servants, the Government's broad authority in managing its affairs should apply with diminished force. But the Government's interest as "proprietor" in managing its operations, the fact that respondents' direct employment relationship is with Cal Tech—which operates JPL under a Government contract—says very little about the interests at stake in this case. The record shows that, as a "practical matter," there are no "[r]elevant distinctions" between the duties performed by NASA's civil-service workforce and its contractor workforce. The two classes of employees perform "functionally equivalent duties," and the extent of employees' "access to NASA . . . facilities" turns not on formal status but on the nature of "the jobs they perform."

At JPL, in particular, the work that contract employees perform is critical to NASA's mission. Respondents in this case include "the lead trouble-shooter for . . . th[e] $568 [million]" Kepler space observatory, the leader of the program that "tests . . . all new technology that NASA will use in space," and one of the lead "trajectory designers for . . . the Galileo Project and the Apollo Moon landings." This is important work, and all of it is funded with a multibillion dollar investment from the American taxpayer. The Government has a strong interest in conducting basic background checks into the contract employees minding the store at JPL.

With these interests in view, we conclude that the challenged portions of both SF–85 and Form 42 consist of reasonable, employment-related inquiries that further the Government's interests in managing its internal operations. As to SF–85, the only part of the form challenged here is its request for information about "any treatment or counseling received" for illegal-drug use within the previous year. The "treatment or counseling" question, however, must be considered in context. It is a follow-up to SF–85's inquiry into whether the employee has "used, possessed, supplied, or manufactured illegal drugs" during the past year. The Government has good reason to ask employees about their recent illegal-drug use. Like any employer, the Government is entitled to have its projects staffed by reliable, law-abiding persons who will " 'efficiently and effectively' " discharge their duties. Questions about illegal-drug use are a useful way of figuring out which persons have these characteristics.

In context, the follow-up question on "treatment or counseling" for recent illegal-drug use is also a reasonable, employment-related inquiry. The Government, recognizing that illegal-drug use is both a criminal and a medical issue, seeks to separate out those illegal-drug users who are taking steps to address and overcome their problems. The Government thus uses responses to the "treatment or counseling" question as a mitigating factor in determining whether to grant contract employees long-term access to federal facilities.

This is a reasonable, and indeed a humane, approach, and respondents do not dispute the legitimacy of the Government's decision to use drug treatment as a mitigating factor in its contractor credentialing decisions. Respondents' argument is that, if drug treatment is only used to mitigate, then the Government should change the mandatory phrasing of SF–85—"Include [in your answer] any treatment or counseling received"—so as to make a response optional. As it stands, the mandatory "treatment or counseling" question is unconstitutional, in respondents' view, because it is "more intrusive than necessary to satisfy the government's objective."

We reject the argument that the Government, when it requests job-related personal information in an employment background check, has a constitutional burden to demonstrate that its questions are "necessary" or the least restrictive means of furthering its interests. So exacting a standard runs directly contrary to *Whalen*. The patients in

Whalen, much like respondents here, argued that New York's statute was unconstitutional because the State could not "demonstrate the necessity" of its program. The Court quickly rejected that argument, concluding that New York's collection of patients' prescription information could "not be held unconstitutional simply because" a court viewed it as "unnecessary, in whole or in part."

That analysis applies with even greater force where the Government acts, not as a regulator, but as the manager of its internal affairs. SF–85's "treatment or counseling" question reasonably seeks to identify a subset of acknowledged drug users who are attempting to overcome their problems. The Government's considered position is that phrasing the question in more permissive terms would result in a lower response rate, and the question's effectiveness in identifying illegal-drug users who are suitable for employment would be "materially reduced." That is a reasonable position, falling within the " 'wide latitude' " granted the Government in its dealings with employees.

* * *

In light of the protection provided by the Privacy Act's nondisclosure requirement, and because the challenged portions of the forms consist of reasonable inquiries in an employment background check, we conclude that the Government's inquiries do not violate a constitutional right to informational privacy.

* * *

For these reasons, the judgment of the Court of Appeals is reversed, and the case is remanded for further proceedings consistent with this opinion.

It is so ordered.

JUSTICE KAGAN took no part in the consideration or decision of this case.

JUSTICE SCALIA, with whom JUSTICE THOMAS joins, concurring in the judgment.

* * *

In sum, I would simply hold that there is no constitutional right to "informational privacy." Besides being consistent with constitutional text and tradition, this view has the attractive benefit of resolving this case without resort to the Court's exegesis on the Government's legitimate interest in identifying contractor drug abusers and the comfortingly narrow scope of NASA's "routine use" regulations. I shall not fill the U.S. Reports with further explanation of the incoherence of the Court's "substantive due process" doctrine in its many manifestations, since the Court does not play the substantive-due-process card. Instead, it states that it will "assume, without deciding" that there exists a right to informational privacy.

The Court's sole justification for its decision to "assume, without deciding" is that the Court made the same mistake before—in two 33-year-old cases, Whalen v. Roe, 429 U.S. 589 (1977) and Nixon v. Administrator of General Services, 433 U.S. 425 (1977). But stare decisis is simply irrelevant when the pertinent precedent assumed, without deciding, the existence of a constitutional right.

NOTES AND QUESTIONS

1. Although the background investigation in this case involved current employees, most background investigations take place before hiring. For a discussion of other privacy issues involving current employees, see Chapter 7.

2. Should the same privacy standards apply to private employers, private employers at government facilities, government employers, and government in its non-employer role? What does Justice Alito say?

3. In the three Supreme Court cases that assumed without deciding there is a constitutional right to informational privacy, *Whalen, Nixon,* and *Nelson,* the Court upheld the challenged government action. Similarly, virtually all of the lower courts have upheld information disclosure requirements. Therefore, merely recognizing a constitutional right may be insufficient to provide meaningful protection. See Mark A. Rothstein, Constitutional Right to Informational Health Privacy in Critical Condition, 39 J.L. Med. & Ethics 280 (2011).

4. In another recent privacy case, FAA v. Cooper, 132 S.Ct. 1441 (2012), a licensed pilot failed to disclose his HIV status to the Federal Aviation Administration (FAA) to maintain his flight medical certificate. At the same time, he applied for and received Social Security Disability Income (SSDI) benefits due to his HIV status. When the Department of Transportation (the FAA's parent agency) and the Social Security Administration (SSA) launched an investigation into FAA certification of medically unfit individuals, Cooper's name appeared on a list of pilots receiving SSDI. His license was revoked and he was fined and sentenced to probation for making false statements to a government agency. He then sued alleging a violation of the Privacy Act, claiming that the disclosure of confidential medical information by the SSA to DOT caused him mental and emotional distress. The Supreme Court, five-to-three, in an opinion by Justice Alito, held that "actual damages" recoverable under the Privacy Act are limited to pecuniary loss and therefore damages for mental and emotional distress are not recoverable. Justice Sotomayor's dissenting opinion asserted that the majority opinion "allows a swath of government violations to go unremedied."

3.   REFERENCES

Page 130.   Please add the following note.

3A. A surgeon sought references from a prior employer in order to obtain another job. Does a former employer's failure to respond to a prospective employer's "credentialing questionnaire" in a timely manner constitute implied defamation? See Schmitt v. Meritcare Health Sys., 834 N.W.2d 627 (N.D. 2013) (held: no).

Page 132.   Please add the following note.

12. Retailers estimate that about 44 percent of missing merchandise is attributable to employee theft. In an attempt to prevent hiring individuals who are likely to steal from them, some major retailers, including Target,

CVS, and Family Dollar, use commercial databases that aggregate the names of employees reported by their prior employers as being untrustworthy. Once in one of the databases, it is very difficult to get out of it or to get a job at another retailer using the database company. Reportedly, lawsuits challenging these practices are on the rise. See Stephanie Clifford & Jessica Silver-Greenberg, Retailers Track Employee Thefts in Vast Databases, N.Y. Times, April 3, 2013, at 1.

D. TRUTH DETECTING DEVICES AND PSYCHOLOGICAL AND PERSONALITY TESTING

2. OTHER TRUTH DETECTING DEVICES AND PSYCHOLOGICAL AND PERSONALITY TESTS

Page 148.   Please add the following note.

8.   Because of high unemployment a job posting may result in the employer being inundated with hundreds or even thousands of on-line applicants. One method employers are increasingly using to screen applicants is psychological and personality testing. According to one estimate, the use of such tests is increasing by 20 percent a year, especially in the food service, retail, and hospitality industries. McDonald's 35 questions for applicants include a mix of general and specific questions. Here are some samples.

- *While you are on a break, a customer spills a large drink in a busy area of the restaurant. Cleaning the floors is the job of another team member, but he is taking a customer's order. What would you do?*

- *I am sometimes unkind to others.*

- *I often lose my patience with others.*

- *I dislike having several things to do on the same day.*

Eve Tahmincioglu, Employers Turn to Tests to Weed Out Job Seekers, www.msnbc.com/id/44120975/ns/business-personal_finance. What possible legal issues are raised by the use of these types of questions?

Page 155.   Please add the following note.

4A. According to a 2011 poll conducted by the Society for Human Resource Management, 18% of 495 randomly selected human resource professionals said they used some kind of personality test in the hiring or promotion process. Of those using such tests, 71% said the tests can be useful in predicting job-related behavior or organizational fit.

F. DRUG TESTING AND OTHER LABORATORY PROCEDURES

1. DRUG TESTING

Page 182.   Please add the following note.

9A. There has been a resurgence of efforts to require drug screening of various federal and state employees. Broad drug testing policies lacking a governmental need or purpose are likely to be held unconstitutional. For example, in National Federation of Federal Employees-IAM v. Vilsack, 681 F.3d 483 (D.C. Cir. 2012), the D.C. Circuit held unconstitutional the random drug testing of all employees working at Job Corp Civilian Conservation Centers operated by the U.S. Forest Service. According to the court, the policy did not come within the narrow exception for constitutionally permissible, suspicionless searches.

2. GENETIC DISCRIMINATION

a. THE PROBLEM

Page 186.   Please add the following to note 4.

See generally Elizabeth Pendo, Race, Sex, and Genes at Work: Uncovering the Lessons of *Norman-Bloodsaw*, 10 Hous. J. Health L. & Pol'y 227 (2010).

G. NEGLIGENT HIRING

Page 194.   Please add the following to note 3, at the end of the first paragraph.

See also C.A. v. William S. Hart Union High Sch. Dist., 270 P.3d 699 (Cal. 2012) (school district vicariously liable for negligent hiring by administrators or supervisors after school employee sexually harassed and abused student).

Page 195.   Please add the following notes.

3A. Whether an employer has a duty to conduct a preemployment background check depends on the nature of the job. For example, after the Deepwater Horizon drilling rig exploded in the Gulf of Mexico contractors were hired to help with the cleanup. A general laborer whose job it was to manually remove tar balls from the coast was raped by another employee after driving her home. Although the perpetrator had a long criminal record, the contractor and its subcontractor failed to perform any background check. In holding there was no cause of action for negligent hiring under Mississippi law, the Fifth Circuit noted, among other things, that the legislature mandated criminal background checks for certain employees, such as substitute teachers and health care facility employees. Thus, there was a "strong inference" that it did not intend to mandate them for all employees. See Keen v. Miller Environmental Group, Inc., 702 F.3d 239 (5th Cir. 2012).

7A. The plaintiff must prove a causal relationship between the employer's act of negligence and a subsequent injury. In one case, a customer brought an action for negligent hiring against a restaurant for injuries allegedly caused by a broil cook's intentional placement of a human hair in her steak. The broil cook had a prior criminal record and was fired by another restaurant for drinking on the job. The Wisconsin Court of Appeals held there was no causal connection between the employer's negligent failure to discover the cook's background and the injury sustained by the customer. Hansen v. Texas Roadhouse, Inc., 827 N.W.2d 99 (Wis. Ct. App. 2012), petition for review denied, 827 N.W.2d 376 (Wis. 2013). Do you agree with the court? How closely do the prior and subsequent acts of misconduct have to align?

7B. The plaintiff's husband contracted with a temporary labor supplier to provide two workers to assist his wife in pulling weeds in the yard of their home. Two men were dispatched, each of whom had completed an employment application in which they denied having any criminal convictions, medical conditions, mental illness, or disabilities. One of the men, however, purposely failed to disclose that he had been diagnosed and treated for schizophrenia and that he had not been taking his medicine to control his condition. In the course of work, he became agitated and attacked the plaintiff, for which he eventually pled guilty to aggravated assault. In an action for negligent hiring, did the temporary labor supplier have a duty to verify the elements of the employment applications? See Drury v. Harris Ventures, Inc., 691 S.E.2d 356 (Ga. Ct. App. 2010) (held: no).

Page 197.   Please add the following note.

12. Each year, more than 700,000 Americans are released from state and federal prisons. If arrests are added to the number of convictions, almost 65 million Americans have some type of criminal record. With high unemployment and little legal prohibition on discrimination based on criminal background, it is small wonder there is a widespread refusal to consider former arrestees and offenders. According to a 2012 survey by the Society for Human Resources Management, 69% of companies surveyed, most of them large employers, said they conducted criminal background checks on some or all job candidates. Of the organizations that conduct criminal background checks, 52% responded that reducing legal liability for negligent hiring was a primary reason for doing the background checks. http://www.shrm.org/Research/SurveyFindings/Documents/072612_research_criminal.pdf.

For a discussion of discrimination against individuals with arrest records, see EEOC Enforcement Guidance on the Consideration of Arrest and Conviction Records in Employment Decisions under Title VII of the Civil Rights Act of 1964 (2012), available at http://eeoc.gov/laws/guidance/arrest_conviction.cfm.

CHAPTER 4

DISCRIMINATION

A. DISCRIMINATION ON THE BASIS OF RACE OR SEX

2. WHAT IS UNLAWFUL DISCRIMINATION?

a. DISPARATE TREATMENT

Page 210.   Please add after last sentence of note 1.

In Coleman v. Donohue, 667 F.3d 835 (7th Cir. 2012), the Seventh Circuit made clear that evidence of a similarly situated comparator may serve not only as an element of the plaintiff's prima facie case under *McDonnell Douglas* but also as evidence that the employer's legitimate nondiscriminatory reason was pretextual.

Page 210.   Please delete Note 6 and replace with the following.

Wal-Mart Stores, Inc. v. Dukes
131 S.Ct. 2541 (2011).

■ JUSTICE SCALIA delivered the opinion of the Court.

We are presented with one of the most expansive class actions ever. The District Court and the Court of Appeals approved the certification of a class comprising about one and a half million plaintiffs, current and former female employees of petitioner Wal-Mart who allege that the discretion exercised by their local supervisors over pay and promotion matters violates Title VII by discriminating against women. In addition to injunctive and declaratory relief, the plaintiffs seek an award of backpay. We consider whether the certification of the plaintiff class was consistent with Federal Rules of Civil Procedure 23(a) and (b)(2).

Petitioner Wal-Mart is the Nation's largest private employer. It operates four types of retail stores throughout the country: Discount Stores, Supercenters, Neighborhood Markets, and Sam's clubs. Those stores are divided into seven nationwide divisions, which in turn comprise 41 regions of 80 to 85 stores apiece. Each store has between 40 and 53 separate departments and 80 to 500 staff positions. In all, Wal-Mart operates approximately 3,400 stores and employs more than one million people.

Pay and promotion decisions at Wal-Mart are generally committed to local managers' broad discretion, which is exercised "in a largely subjective manner." Local store managers may increase the wages of hourly employees (within limits) with only limited corporate oversight. As for salaried employees, such as store managers and their deputies, higher corporate authorities have discretion to set their pay within preestablished ranges.

Promotions work in a similar fashion. Wal-Mart permits store managers to apply their own subjective criteria when selecting candidates as "support managers," which is the first step on the path to management. Admission to Wal-Mart's management training program, however, does require that a candidate meet certain objective criteria, including an above-average performance rating, at least one year's tenure in the applicant's current position, and a willingness to relocate. But except for those requirements, regional and district managers have discretion to use their own judgment when selecting candidates for management training. Promotion to higher office—e.g., assistant manager, co-manager, or store manager—is similarly at the discretion of the employee's superiors after prescribed objective factors are satisfied.

The named plaintiffs in this lawsuit, representing the 1.5 million members of the certified class, are three current or former Wal-Mart employees who allege that the company discriminated against them on the basis of their sex by denying them equal pay or promotions, in violation of Title VII of the Civil Rights Act of 1964.

Betty Dukes began working at a Pittsburgh, California, Wal-Mart in 1994. She started as a cashier, but later sought and received a promotion to customer service manager. After a series of disciplinary violations, however, Dukes was demoted back to cashier and then to greeter. Dukes concedes she violated company policy, but contends that the disciplinary actions were in fact retaliation for invoking internal complaint procedures and that male employees have not been disciplined for similar infractions. Dukes also claims two male greeters in the Pittsburgh store are paid more than she is.

Christine Kwapnoski has worked at Sam's Club stores in Missouri and California for most of her adult life. She has held a number of positions, including a supervisory position. She claims that a male manager yelled at her frequently and screamed at female employees, but not at men. The manager in question "told her to 'doll up,' to wear some makeup, and to dress a little better."

The final named plaintiff, Edith Arana, worked at a Wal-Mart store in Duarte, California, from 1995 to 2001. In 2000, she approached the store manager on more than one occasion about management training, but was brushed off. Arana concluded she was being denied opportunity for advancement because of her sex. She initiated internal complaint procedures, whereupon she was told to apply directly to the district manager if she thought her store manager was being unfair. Arana, however, decided against that and never applied for management training again. In 2001, she was fired for failure to comply with Wal-Mart's timekeeping policy.

These plaintiffs, respondents here, do not allege that Wal-Mart has any express corporate policy against the advancement of women. Rather, they claim that their local managers' discretion over pay and promotions is exercised disproportionately in favor of men, leading to an unlawful disparate impact on female employees. And, respondents say, because Wal-Mart is aware of this effect, its refusal to cabin its managers' authority amounts to disparate treatment. Their complaint seeks injunctive and declaratory relief, punitive damages, and backpay. It does not ask for compensatory damages.

Importantly for our purposes, respondents claim that the discrimination to which they have been subjected is common to all Wal-Mart's female employees. The basic theory of their case is that a strong and uniform "corporate culture" permits bias against women to infect, perhaps subconsciously, the discretionary decisionmaking of each one of Wal-Mart's thousands of managers—thereby making every woman at the company the victim of one common discriminatory practice. Respondents therefore wish to litigate the Title VII claims of all female employees at Wal-Mart's stores in a nationwide class action.

* * *

The class action is "an exception to the usual rule that litigation is conducted by and on behalf of the individual named parties only." In order to justify a departure from that rule, "a class representative must be part of the class and 'possess the same interest and suffer the same injury' as the class members." Rule 23(a) ensures that the named plaintiffs are appropriate representatives of the class whose claims they wish to litigate. The Rule's four requirements—numerosity, commonality, typicality, and adequate representation—"effectively 'limit the class claims to those fairly encompassed by the named plaintiff's claims.'"

The crux of this case is commonality—the rule requiring a plaintiff to show that "there are questions of law or fact common to the class." That language is easy to misread, since "[a]ny competently crafted class complaint literally raises common 'questions.'" For example: Do all of us plaintiffs indeed work for Wal-Mart? Do our managers have discretion over pay? Is that an unlawful employment practice? What remedies should we get? Reciting these questions is not sufficient to obtain class certification. Commonality requires the plaintiff to demonstrate that the class members "have suffered the same injury," This does not mean merely that they have all suffered a violation of the same provision of law. Title VII, for example, can be violated in many ways—by intentional discrimination, or by hiring and promotion criteria that result in disparate impact, and by the use of these practices on the part of many different superiors in a single company. Quite obviously, the mere claim by employees of the same company that they have suffered a Title VII injury, or even a disparate-impact Title VII injury, gives no cause to believe that all their claims can productively be litigated at once. Their claims must depend upon a common contention—for example, the assertion of discriminatory bias on the part of the same supervisor. That common contention, moreover, must be of such a nature that it is capable of classwide resolution—which means that determination of its truth or falsity will resolve an issue that is central to the validity of each one of the claims in one stroke.

"What matters to class certification . . . is not the raising of common 'questions'—even in droves—but, rather the capacity of a classwide proceeding to generate common answers apt to drive the resolution of the litigation. Dissimilarities within the proposed class are what have the potential to impede the generation of common answers."

* * *

In this case, proof of commonality necessarily overlaps with respondents' merits contention that Wal-Mart engages in a pattern or practice of discrimination. That is so because, in resolving an individual's Title VII claim, the crux of the inquiry is "the reason for a particular employment decision." Here respondents wish to sue about literally millions of employment decisions at once. Without some glue holding the alleged reasons for all those decisions together, it will be impossible to say that examination of all the class members' claims for relief will produce a common answer to the crucial question why *was I disfavored*.

* * *

The second manner of bridging the gap requires "significant proof" that Wal-Mart "operated under a general policy of discrimination." That is entirely absent here. Wal-Mart's announced policy forbids sex discrimination, and as the District Court recognized the company imposes penalties for denials of equal employment opportunity. The only evidence of a general policy of discrimination respondents produced was the testimony of Dr. William Bielby, their sociological expert. Relying on "social framework" analysis, Bielby testified that Wal-Mart has a "strong corporate culture," that makes it " 'vulnerable' " to "gender bias". He could not, however, determine with any specificity how regularly stereotypes play a meaningful role in employment decisions at Wal-Mart. At his deposition . . . Dr. Bielby conceded that he could not calculate whether 0.5 percent or 95 percent of the employment decisions at Wal-Mart might be determined by stereotyped thinking.

The only corporate policy that the plaintiffs' evidence convincingly establishes is Wal-Mart's "policy" of allowing discretion by local supervisors over employment matters. On its face, of course, that is just the opposite of a uniform employment practice that would provide the commonality needed for a class action; it is a policy against having uniform employment practices. It is also a very common and presumptively reasonable way of doing business—one that we have said "should itself raise no inference of discriminatory conduct."

To be sure, we have recognized that, "in appropriate cases," giving discretion to lower-level supervisors can be the basis of Title VII liability under a disparate-impact theory—since "an employer's undisciplined system of subjective decisionmaking [can have] precisely the same effects as a system pervaded by impermissible intentional discrimination." But the recognition that this type of Title VII claim "can" exist does not lead to the conclusion that every employee in a company using a system of discretion has such a claim in common. To the contrary, left to their own devices most managers in any corporation—and surely most managers in a corporation that forbids sex discrimination—would select sex-neutral, performance-based criteria for hiring and promotion that produce no actionable disparity at all. Others may choose to reward various attributes that produce disparate impact—such as scores on general aptitude tests or educational achievements. And still other managers may be guilty of intentional discrimination that produces a sex-based disparity. In such a company, demonstrating the invalidity of one manager's use of discretion will do nothing to demonstrate the invalidity of another's. A party seeking to certify a nationwide class will be unable to show that all the employees' Title VII claims will in fact depend on the answers to common questions.

Respondents have not identified a common mode of exercising discretion that pervades the entire company—aside from their reliance on Dr. Bielby's social frameworks analysis that we have rejected. In a company of Wal-Mart's size and geographical scope, it is quite unbelievable that all managers would exercise their discretion in a common way without some common direction. Respondents attempt to make that showing by means of statistical and anecdotal evidence, but their evidence falls well short.

The statistical evidence consists primarily of regression analyses performed by Dr. Richard Drogin, a statistician, and Dr. Marc Bendick, a labor economist. Drogin conducted his analysis region-by-region, comparing the number of women promoted into management positions with the percentage of women in the available pool of hourly workers. After considering regional and national data, Drogin concluded that "there are statistically significant disparities between men and women at Wal-Mart . . . [and] these disparities . . . can be explained only by gender discrimination." Bendick compared work-force data from Wal-Mart and competitive retailers and concluded that Wal-Mart "promotes a lower percentage of women than its competitors."

Even if they are taken at face value, these studies are insufficient to establish that respondents' theory can be proved on a classwide basis.

* * *

There is another, more fundamental, respect in which respondents' statistical proof fails. Even if it established (as it does not) a pay or promotion pattern that differs from the nationwide figures or the regional figures in all of Wal-Mart's 3,400 stores, that would still not demonstrate that commonality of issue exists. Some managers will claim that the availability of women, or qualified women, or interested women, in their stores' area does not mirror the national or regional statistics. And almost all of them will claim to have been applying some sex-neutral, performance-based criteria—whose nature and effects will differ from store to store. In the landmark case of ours which held that giving discretion to lower-level supervisors can be the basis of Title VII liability under a disparate-impact theory, the plurality opinion conditioned that holding on the corollary that merely proving that the discretionary system has produced a racial or sexual disparity is not enough. "[T]he plaintiff must begin by identifying the specific employment practice that is challenged." That is all the more necessary when a class of plaintiffs is sought to be certified. Other than the bare existence of delegated discretion, respondents have identified no "specific employment practice"—much less one that ties all their 1.5 million claims together. Merely showing that Wal-Mart's policy of discretion has produced an overall sex-based disparity does not suffice.

Respondents' anecdotal evidence suffers from the same defects, and in addition is too weak to raise any inference that all the individual, discretionary personnel decisions are discriminatory.

* * *

In sum, we agree with Chief Judge Kozinski that the members of the class:

> "held a multitude of different jobs, at different levels of Wal-Mart's hierarchy, for variable lengths of time, in 3,400 stores, sprinkled across 50 states, with a kaleidoscope of supervisors (male and female), subject to a variety of regional policies that all differed. . . . Some thrived while others did poorly. They have little in common but their sex and this lawsuit."

* * *

. . . Wal-Mart is entitled to individualized determinations of each employee's eligibility for backpay. Title VII includes a detailed remedial scheme. If a plaintiff prevails in showing that an employer has discriminated against him in violation of the statute, the court "may enjoin the respondent from engaging in such unlawful employment practice, and order such affirmative action as may be appropriate, [including] reinstatement or hiring of employees, with or without backpay or any other equitable relief as the court deems appropriate." But if the employer can show that it took an adverse employment action against an employee for any reason other than discrimination, the court cannot order the "hiring, reinstatement, or promotion of an individual as an employee, or the payment to him of any backpay."

We have established a procedure for trying pattern-or-practice cases that gives effect to these statutory requirements. When the plaintiff seeks individual relief such as reinstatement or backpay after establishing a pattern or practice of discrimination, "a district court must usually conduct additional proceedings . . . to determine the scope of individual relief." At this phase, the burden of proof will shift to the company, but it will have the right to raise any individual affirmative defenses it may have, and to "demonstrate that the individual applicant was denied an employment opportunity for lawful reasons."

The Court of Appeals believed that it was possible to replace such proceedings with Trial by Formula. A sample set of the class members would be selected, as to whom liability for sex discrimination and the backpay owing as a result would be determined in depositions supervised by a master. The percentage of claims determined to be valid would then be applied to the entire remaining class, and the number of (presumptively) valid claims thus derived would be multiplied by the average backpay award in the sample set to arrive at the entire class recovery—without further individualized proceedings. We disapprove that novel project. Because the Rules Enabling Act forbids interpreting Rule 23 to "abridge, enlarge or modify any substantive right," a class cannot be certified on the premise that Wal-Mart will not be entitled to litigate its statutory defenses to individual claims. And because the necessity of that litigation will prevent backpay from being "incidental" to the classwide injunction, respondents' class could not be certified even assuming, arguendo, that "incidental" monetary relief can be awarded to a 23(b)(2) class.

* * *

The judgment of the Court of Appeals is reversed.

JUSTICE GINSBURG, with whom JUSTICE BREYER, JUSTICE SOTOMAYOR, and JUSTICE KAGAN join, concurring in part and dissenting in part.

The class in this case, I agree with the Court, should not have been certified under Federal Rule of Civil Procedure 23(b)(2). The plaintiffs, alleging discrimination in violation of Title VII, seek monetary relief that is not merely incidental to any injunctive or declaratory relief that might be available. A putative class of this type may be certifiable under Rule 23(b)(3), if the plaintiffs show that common class questions "predominate" over issues affecting individuals—e.g., qualification for, and the amount of, backpay or compensatory damages—and that a class action is "superior" to other modes of adjudication.

Whether the class the plaintiffs describe meets the specific requirements of Rule 23(b)(3) is not before the Court, and I would reserve that matter for consideration and decision on remand. The Court, however, disqualifies the class at the starting gate, holding that the plaintiffs cannot cross the "commonality" line set by Rule 23(a)(2). In so ruling, the Court imports into the Rule 23(a) determination concerns properly addressed in a Rule 23(b)(3) assessment.

Rule 23(a)(2) establishes a preliminary requirement for maintaining a class action: "[T]here are questions of law or fact common to the class." The Rule "does not require that all questions of law or fact raised in the litigation be common," indeed, "[e]ven a single question of law or fact common to the members of the class will satisfy the commonality requirement."

* * *

The District Court certified a class of "[a]ll women employed at any Wal-Mart domestic retail store at any time since December 26, 1998." The named plaintiffs, led by Betty Dukes, propose to litigate, on behalf of the class, allegations that Wal-Mart discriminates on the basis of gender in pay and promotions. They allege that the company "[r]eli[es] on gender stereotypes in making employment decisions such as . . . promotion[s][and] pay." Wal-Mart permits those prejudices to infect personnel decisions, the plaintiffs contend, by leaving pay and promotions in the hands of "a nearly all male managerial workforce" using "arbitrary and subjective criteria." Further alleged barriers to the advancement of female employees include the company's requirement, "as a condition of promotion to management jobs, that employees be willing to relocate." Absent instruction otherwise, there is a risk that managers will act on the familiar assumption that women, because of their services to husband and children, are less mobile than men.

Women fill 70 percent of the hourly jobs in the retailer's stores but make up only "33 percent of management employees." "[T]he higher one looks in the organization the lower the percentage of women." The plaintiffs' "largely uncontested descriptive statistics" also show that women working in the company's stores "are paid less than men in every region" and "that the salary gap widens over time even for men and women hired into the same jobs at the same time."

The District Court identified "systems for . . . promoting in-store employees" that were "sufficiently similar across regions and stores" to conclude that "the manner in which these systems affect the class raises issues that are common to all class members." The selection of employees for promotion to in-store management "is fairly characterized as a 'tap on the shoulder' process," in which managers have discretion about whose shoulders to tap. Vacancies are not regularly posted; from among those employees satisfying minimum qualifications, managers choose whom to promote on the basis of their own subjective impressions.

Wal-Mart's compensation policies also operate uniformly across stores, the District Court found. The retailer leaves open a $2 band for every position's hourly pay rate. Wal-Mart provides no standards or criteria for setting wages within that band, and thus does nothing to counter unconscious bias on the part of supervisors.

Wal-Mart's supervisors do not make their discretionary decisions in a vacuum. The District Court reviewed means Wal-Mart used to maintain a "carefully constructed ... corporate culture," such as frequent meetings to reinforce the common way of thinking, regular transfers of managers between stores to ensure uniformity throughout the company, monitoring of stores "on a close and constant basis," and "Wal-Mart TV," "broadcas[t] . . . into all stores."

The plaintiffs' evidence, including class members' tales of their own experiences, suggests that gender bias suffused Wal-Mart's company culture. Among illustrations, senior management often refer to female associates as "little Janie Qs."

* * *

The District Court's identification of a common question, whether Wal-Mart's pay and promotions policies gave rise to unlawful discrimination, was hardly infirm. The practice of delegating to supervisors large discretion to make personnel decisions, uncontrolled by formal standards, has long been known to have the potential to produce disparate effects. Managers, like all humankind, may be prey to biases of which they are unaware. The risk of discrimination is heightened when those managers are predominantly of one sex, and are steeped in a corporate culture that perpetuates gender stereotypes.

* * *

The plaintiffs' allegations state claims of gender discrimination in the form of biased decisionmaking in both pay and promotions. The evidence reviewed by the District Court adequately demonstrated that resolving those claims would necessitate examination of particular policies and practices alleged to affect, adversely and globally, women employed at Wal-Mart's stores. Rule 23(a)(2), setting a necessary but not a sufficient criterion for class-action certification, demands nothing further.

* * *

Wal-Mart's delegation of discretion over pay and promotions is a policy uniform throughout all stores. The very nature of discretion is that people will exercise it in various ways. A system of delegated discretion, is a practice actionable under Title VII when it produces discriminatory outcomes. A finding that Wal-Mart's pay and promotions practices in fact violate the law would be the first step in the usual order of proof for plaintiffs seeking individual remedies for company-wide discrimination. That each individual employee's unique circumstances will ultimately determine whether she is entitled to backpay or damages, should not factor into the Rule 23(a)(2) determination.

Page 221.   Please add before the last sentence of the first paragraph of note 7.

For a recent lucid account of the burdens and remedies under mixed motive law, see Harris v. City of Santa Monica, 56 Cal. 4th 203 (2013).

Page 221.   Please delete last paragraph of note 7 and replace with the following.

Direct evidence of discrimination is no longer required for a plaintiff to prevail in a mixed-motive Title VII case. The plaintiff can succeed by proving his or her case by a preponderance of the evidence using direct or circumstantial evidence. Desert Palace, Inc. v. Costa, 539 U.S. 90 (2003). After *Desert Palace*, courts have struggled to decide when a case should be analyzed at the pretrial stage using the *McDonnell Douglas* framework and when it should be analyzed using the mixed motives framework from *Price Waterhouse*. See Coleman v. Donohue, 667 F.3d 835 (7th Cir. 2012) (Wood, J., concurring) (arguing that the two tests should be collapsed at the pretrial stage of a case, as they have been at the trial stage of a case, and the plaintiff should simply be required to present evidence showing that "the employer took . . . adverse action on account of her protected class"). In University of Texas Southwestern Medical Center v. Nassar, 133 S.Ct. 2517, 2530 (2013), the Supreme Court in dicta suggested that such a collapse of the two evidentiary frameworks was appropriate when it explained that the mixed-motive evidentiary framework "is not itself a substantive bar on discrimination. Rather, it is a rule that establishes the causation standard for proving a violation defined elsewhere in Title VII."

Page 227.   Please add at end of the note that begins on page 226.

The Court's focus in *Gross* was on the evidentiary burden born by the plaintiff at trial with the Court making clear that the plaintiff retains the burden of proving "but-for" causation in ADEA claims. *Gross* did not address the evidentiary framework applicable to a motion for summary judgment. In Shelly v. Green, 666 F.3d 599 (9th Cir. 2012), the Ninth Circuit held that it was appropriate for courts to continue using the *McDonnell Douglas* burden shifting framework, as they had prior to *Gross*, to decide summary judgment motions in ADEA cases. The court rejected the district court's conclusion that because *Gross* required a plaintiff to prove "but-for" causation to win at trial, the *McDonnell Douglas* burden shifting framework was no longer appropriate at summary judgment.

Page 229.   Please add at the end of note 2.

May a male employer terminate a female employee because the employer's wife finds the employee to be a threat to their marriage even in the absence of any inappropriate behavior on the part of the employee? See Nelson v. Knight, 2012 WL 6652747 (Iowa, Dec. 21, 2012) (finding no sex discrimination but noting that "[i]f an employer repeatedly took adverse employment actions against persons of a particular gender because of alleged personal relationship issues, it might well be possible to infer that gender and not the relationship was a motivating factor").

Page 238.   Please delete note 2 and replace with the following.

2.   Courts have held that the PDA does not require employers to accommodate pregnant employees. "This is because the PDA does not require an employer to provide special accommodations to its pregnant employees; instead, the PDA only ensures that pregnant employees are given the same opportunities and benefits as *nonpregnant* employees who are similarly limited in their ability to work." Nelson v. Chattahoochee Valley Hosp. Soc., 731 F. Supp.2d 1217, 1230 (M.D. Ala. 2010). Indeed, the PDA does not require an employer to accommodate a worker even if the desired accommodation is provided to employees injured on the job or those disabled within the meaning of the ADA. An employer may, without running afoul of the PDA, accommodate certain employees but not pregnant workers who are otherwise similar in their ability or inability to work. According to the Fourth Circuit, the PDA does not grant pregnant employees a "most favored nation" status among those similar in their ability or inability to work. Young v. United Parcel Service, 707 F.3d 437 (4th Cir. 2013), cert. granted 134 S.Ct. 2898 (2014). State law may provide pregnant workers with greater protection. In 2014, New Jersey amended its Law Against Discrimination to not only explicitly prohibit discrimination against pregnant women but also to require employers to make reasonable accommodations available to pregnant workers. N.J. Stat. Ann. § 10:5–12. However, should an employer choose to provide special accommodations to pregnant employees, they may not necessarily be able to force the employees to accept the accommodations. This is particularly relevant when accommodations involve a reduction in hours or responsibilities resulting in a lower salary. In U.S. EEOC v. Catholic Healthcare W., 530 F.Supp.2d 1096 (C.D. Cal. 2008), a federal district court applied the BFOQ test to Catholic Healthcare's unsolicited transfer of a pregnant radiology technologist to a different area of work. Catholic Healthcare's transfer was found to be discriminatory.

Page 239.   Please delete the final sentence of note 4 and replace with the following.

Recent decisions by courts have generally allowed a similar distinction between work-related disabilities and pregnancy. See Serednyj v. Beverly Healthcare, LLC, 656 F.3d 540 (7th Cir. 2011); Urbano v. Continental Airlines, Inc., 138 F.3d 204 (5th Cir. 1998), cert. denied, 525 U.S. 1000 (1998); Young v. United Parcel Serv., Inc., 2011 WL 665321 (D. Md. Feb. 14, 2011); Brophy v. Day & Zimmerman Hawthorne Corp., 799 F. Supp. 2d 1185 (D. Nev. 2011); Cunningham v. Dearborn Bd. of Educ., 246 Mich. App. 621, 633 N.W.2d 481 (2001).

Page 239.   Please delete note 6 and replace with the following.

6.   In the case of religious institutions, pregnant women may be terminated not for the pregnancy itself but rather for premarital sex. In 1996, Leigh Cline's teaching contract with the Catholic Diocese of Toledo was not renewed because Cline's due date was only five months after her wedding. The court of appeals reversed an award of summary judgment for the defendant. By engaging in premarital sex, Cline violated her duties to uphold the school's religious teachings; however, "a school cannot use the mere observation or knowledge of pregnancy as its sole method of detecting violations of its premarital sex policy." Cline v. Catholic Diocese of Toledo, 206 F.3d 651, 667 (6th Cir. 2000). In a similar case, Jarretta Hamilton was fired from Southland Christian School after informing the school administrator that she had engaged in premarital sex. In 2012, the court of appeals reversed an award of summary judgment for the school, finding "a genuine issue of material fact about the reason that Southland fired her." Hamilton v. Southland Christian Sch., Inc., 680 F.3d 1316 (11th Cir. 2012).

Page 240.   **Please add the following note.**

12. The PDA has generally not been interpreted to extend protection to women who seek to breastfeed at work. See, e.g., Wallace v. Pyro Mining Co., 951 F.2d 351 (6th Cir. 1991) (PDA did not give employee right to breastfeed at work because doing so was not a medical necessity); Barrash v. Bowen, 846 F.2d 927, 931 (4th Cir. 1988) (plaintiff could not establish disparate impact claim based on denial of breastfeeding leave because the PDA applied only to incapacitating illnesses). Recently, the Fifth Circuit held that lactation was a related medical condition of pregnancy for purposes of the PDA and that discrimination against a woman because she is lactating or expressing breast milk violates Title VII and the PDA. Importantly, however, the plaintiff in the case did not seek any accommodation to breastfeed and was allegedly fired simply for raising the issue of breastfeeding at work with her employer. See EEOC v. Houston Funding II, 2013 WL 2360114 (5th Cir., May 30, 2013). The Patient Protection and Affordable Care Act, H.R. 3590, which President Obama signed into law on March 23, 2010, does provide some limited protection to breastfeeding mothers. The Act amended the Fair Labor Standards Act of 1938 (29 U.S.C. § 207) to require an employer to provide reasonable break time for a non exempt employee to express breast milk for one year after a child's birth. As of 2014, twenty-five states also have laws providing some protection for breastfeeding in the workplace. See National Conference of State Legislatures, available at http://www.ncsl.org/issues-research/health/breastfeeding-state-laws.aspx (last visited July 30, 2014).

b.   DISPARATE IMPACT/ADVERSE IMPACT

Page 246.   **Please add as note 9.**

9. Since a race-based disparate impact claim requires proof that those of a particular race are disproportionately excluded by a particular practice, plaintiffs must have some way of identifying or determining the race of those individuals who are and are not excluded by the challenged practice. In EEOC v. Kaplan Higher Education Corp., 748 F.3d 749 (6th Cir. 2014), the Sixth Circuit dismissed the EEOC's disparate impact challenge to Kaplan's credit check policy for new employees on the grounds that the testimony presented by the EEOC's expert regarding racially disparate impact, which was based on a visual race rating of applicants, was inadmissible under Daubert v. Merrell Dow Pharmaceuticals, Inc., 509 U.S. 579 (1993). Without such expert testimony, the EEOC could not show race based impact. How could the EEOC have established the race of the relevant applicants so as to establish its disparate impact claim?

3. THE BONA FIDE OCCUPATIONAL QUALIFICATION DEFENSE

Page 272.   Please add to the end of note 5.

Particularly in cases involving touching or viewing of naked bodies, however, courts have regularly deferred to customer preferences for privacy and held sex to be a BFOQ. See Backus v. Baptist Medical Center, 510 F. Supp. 1191 (E.D. Ark. 1981) (sex a BFOQ in hiring of hospital obstetrics and gynecology nurses); Jones v. Hinds Gen. Hosp., 666 F. Supp. 933, 935 (S.D. Miss. 1987) (finding sex a BFOQ for hiring female nurse assistants and male orderlies since such jobs often required the employee to "view or touch the private parts of their patients"); Fesel v. Masonic Home of Del., Inc., 447 F. Supp. 1346 (D. Del. 1978) (finding sex a BFOQ in hiring nurse to care for elderly female residents of retirement home). See generally Kimberly A. Yuracko, Private Nurses and Playboy Bunnies: Explaining Permissible Sex Discrimination, 92 Cal. L. Rev. 147 (2004) (explaining that courts are far more deferential to employer BFOQ claims responding to customer privacy preferences than to those responding to customer preferences for sexual titillation).

B. PROCEDURE

3. PROVING DISCRIMINATION

Page 286.   Please replace *Staub v. Proctor Hospital* with the Supreme Court decision.

Staub v. Proctor Hospital
131 S.Ct. 1186 (2011).

■ JUSTICE SCALIA, delivered the opinion of the Court.

We consider the circumstances under which an employer may be held liable for employment discrimination based on the discriminatory animus of an employee who influenced, but did not make, the ultimate employment decision.

Petitioner Vincent Staub worked as an angiography technician for respondent Proctor Hospital until 2004, when he was fired. Staub and Proctor hotly dispute the facts surrounding the firing, but because a jury found for Staub in his claim of employment discrimination against Proctor, we describe the facts viewed in the light most favorable to him.

While employed by Proctor, Staub was a member of the United States Army Reserve, which required him to attend drill one weekend per month and to train full time for two to three weeks a year. Both Janice Mulally, Staub's immediate supervisor, and Michael Korenchuk, Mulally's supervisor, were hostile to Staub's military obligations. Mulally scheduled Staub for additional shifts without notice so that he would " 'pa[y] back the department for everyone else having to bend over backwards to cover [his] schedule for the Reserves.' " She also informed Staub's co-worker, Leslie Sweborg, that Staub's " 'military duty had been a strain on th[e] department,' " and asked Sweborg to help her " 'get rid of him.' " Korenchuk referred to Staub's military obligations as " 'a b[u]nch of smoking and joking and [a] waste of taxpayers['] money.' " He was also aware that Mulally was " 'out to get' " Staub.

In January 2004, Mulally issued Staub a "Corrective Action" disciplinary warning for purportedly violating a company rule requiring him to stay in his work area whenever he was not working with a patient. The Corrective Action included a directive requiring Staub to report to Mulally or Korenchuk " 'when [he] ha[d] no patients and [the angio] cases [we]re complete[d].' " According to Staub, Mulally's justification for the Corrective Action was false for two reasons: First, the company rule invoked by Mulally did not exist; and second, even if it did, Staub did not violate it.

On April 2, 2004, Angie Day, Staub's co-worker, complained to Linda Buck, Proctor's vice president of human resources, and Garrett McGowan, Proctor's chief operating officer, about Staub's frequent unavailability and abruptness. McGowan directed Korenchuk and Buck to create a plan that would solve Staub's " 'availability' problems." But three weeks later, before they had time to do so, Korenchuk informed Buck that Staub had left his desk without informing a supervisor, in violation of the January Corrective Action. Staub now contends this accusation was false: he had left Korenchuk a voice-mail notification that he was leaving his desk. Buck relied on Korenchuk's accusation, however, and after reviewing Staub's personnel file, she decided to fire him. The termination notice stated that Staub had ignored the directive issued in the January 2004 Corrective Action.

Staub challenged his firing through Proctor's grievance process, claiming that Mulally had fabricated the allegation underlying the Corrective Action out of hostility toward his military obligations. Buck did not follow up with Mulally about this claim. After discussing the matter with another personnel officer, Buck adhered to her decision.

Staub sued Proctor under the Uniformed Services Employment and Reemployment Rights Act of 1994, claiming that his discharge was motivated by hostility to his obligations as a military reservist. His contention was not that Buck had any such hostility but that Mulally and Korenchuk did, and that their actions influenced Buck's ultimate employment decision. A jury found that Staub's "military status was a motivating factor in [Proctor's] decision to discharge him," and awarded $57,640 in damages.

The Seventh Circuit reversed, holding that Proctor was entitled to judgment as a matter of law. The court observed that Staub had brought a " 'cat's paw' case," meaning that he sought to hold his employer liable for the animus of a supervisor who was not charged with making the ultimate employment decision.[1] It explained that under Seventh Circuit precedent, a "cat's paw" case could not succeed unless the nondecisionmaker exercised such " 'singular influence' " over

---

[1]   The term "cat's paw" derives from a fable conceived by Aesop, put into verse by La Fontaine in 1679, and injected into United States employment discrimination law by Posner in 1990. In the fable, a monkey induces a cat by flattery to extract roasting chestnuts from the fire. After the cat has done so, burning its paws in the process, the monkey makes off with the chestnuts and leaves the cat with nothing. A coda to the fable (relevant only marginally, if at all, to employment law) observes that the cat is similar to princes who, flattered by the king, perform services on the king's behalf and receive no reward.

the decisionmaker that the decision to terminate was the product of "blind reliance." It then noted that "Buck looked beyond what Mulally and Korenchuk said," relying in part on her conversation with Day and her review of Staub's personnel file. The court "admit[ted] that Buck's investigation could have been more robust," since it "failed to pursue Staub's theory that Mulally fabricated the write-up." But the court said that the " 'singular influence' " rule "does not require the decisionmaker to be a paragon of independence": "It is enough that the decisionmaker is not wholly dependent on a single source of information and conducts her own investigation into the facts relevant to the decision." Because the undisputed evidence established that Buck was not wholly dependent on the advice of Korenchuk and Mulally, the court held that Proctor was entitled to judgment.

* * *

The Uniformed Services Employment and Reemployment Rights Act (USERRA) provides in relevant part as follows:

"A person who is a member of . . . or has an obligation to perform service in a uniformed service shall not be denied initial employment, reemployment, retention in employment, promotion, or any benefit of employment by an employer on the basis of that membership, . . . or obligation."

It elaborates further:

"An employer shall be considered to have engaged in actions prohibited . . . under subsection (a), if the person's membership . . . is a motivating factor in the employer's action, unless the employer can prove that the action would have been taken in the absence of such membership."

The statute is very similar to Title VII, which prohibits employment "discrimination because of . . . race, color, religion, sex, or national origin" and states that such discrimination is established when one of those factors "was a motivating factor for any employment practice, even though other factors also motivated the practice."

The central difficulty in this case is construing the phrase "motivating factor in the employer's action." When the company official who makes the decision to take an adverse employment action is personally acting out of hostility to the employee's membership in or obligation to a uniformed service, a motivating factor obviously exists. The problem we confront arises when that official has no discriminatory animus but is influenced by previous company action that is the product of a like animus in someone else.

* * *

Staub contends that the fact that an unfavorable entry on the plaintiff's personnel record was caused to be put there, with discriminatory animus, by Mulally and Korenchuk, suffices to establish the tort, even if Mulally and Korenchuk did not intend to cause his dismissal. But discrimination was no part of Buck's reason for the dismissal; and while Korenchuk and Mulally acted with discriminatory animus, the act they committed—the mere making of the reports—was not a denial of "initial employment, reemployment, retention in employment, promotion, or any benefit of employment," as liability under USERRA requires. If dismissal was not the object of Mulally's and Korenchuk's reports, it may have been their result, or even their foreseeable consequence, but that is not enough to render Mulally or Korenchuk responsible.

Here, however, Staub is seeking to hold liable not Mulally and Korenchuk, but their employer. Perhaps, therefore, the discriminatory motive of one of the employer's agents (Mulally or Korenchuk) can be aggregated with the act of another agent (Buck) to impose liability on Proctor. When a decision to fire is made with no unlawful animus on the part of the firing agent, but partly on the basis of a report prompted (unbeknownst to that agent) by discrimination, discrimination might perhaps be called a "factor" or a "causal factor" in the decision; but it seems to us a considerable stretch to call it a motivating factor.

Proctor, on the other hand, contends that the employer is not liable unless the de facto decisionmaker (the technical decisionmaker or the agent for whom he is the "cat's paw") is motivated by discriminatory animus. This avoids the aggregation of animus and adverse action, but it seems to us not the only application of general tort law that can do so. Animus and responsibility for the adverse action can both be attributed to the earlier agent (here, Staub's supervisors) if the adverse action is the intended consequence of that agent's discriminatory conduct. So long as the agent intends, for discriminatory reasons, that the adverse action occur, he has the scienter required to be liable under USERRA. And it is axiomatic under tort law that the exercise of judgment by the decisionmaker does not prevent the earlier agent's action (and hence the earlier agent's discriminatory animus) from being the proximate cause of the harm. Proximate cause requires only "some direct relation between the injury asserted and the injurious conduct alleged," and excludes only those "link[s] that are too remote, purely contingent, or indirect." We do not think that the ultimate decisionmaker's exercise of judgment automatically renders the link to the supervisor's bias "remote" or "purely contingent." The decisionmaker's exercise of judgment is also a proximate cause of the employment decision, but it is common for injuries to have multiple proximate causes. Nor can the ultimate decisionmaker's judgment be deemed a superseding cause of the harm. A cause can be thought "superseding" only if it is a "cause of independent origin that was not foreseeable."

Moreover, the approach urged upon us by Proctor gives an unlikely meaning to a provision designed to prevent employer discrimination. An employer's authority to reward, punish, or dismiss is often allocated among multiple agents. The one who makes the ultimate decision does so on the basis of performance assessments by other supervisors. Proctor's view would have the improbable consequence that if an employer isolates a personnel official from an employee's supervisors, vests the decision to take adverse employment actions in that official, and asks that official to review the employee's personnel file before taking the adverse action, then the employer will be effectively shielded from discriminatory acts and recommendations of supervisors that were designed and intended to produce the adverse action. That seems to us an implausible meaning of the text, and one that is not compelled by its words.

Proctor suggests that even if the decisionmaker's mere exercise of independent judgment does not suffice to negate the effect of the prior discrimination, at least the decisionmaker's independent investigation (and rejection) of the employee's allegations of discriminatory animus ought to do so. We decline to adopt such a hard-and-fast rule. As we have already acknowledged, the requirement that the biased supervisor's action be a causal factor of the ultimate employment action incorporates the traditional tort-law concept of proximate cause. Thus, if the employer's investigation results in an adverse action for reasons unrelated to the supervisor's original biased action (by the terms of USERRA it is the employer's burden to establish that), then the employer will not be liable. But the supervisor's biased report may remain a causal factor if the independent investigation takes it into account without determining that the adverse action was, apart from the supervisor's recommendation, entirely justified. We are aware of no principle in tort or agency law under which an employer's mere conduct of an independent investigation has a claim-preclusive effect. Nor do we think the independent investigation somehow relieves the employer of "fault." The employer is at fault because one of its agents committed an action based on discriminatory animus that was intended to cause, and did in fact cause, an adverse employment decision.

We therefore hold that if a supervisor performs an act motivated by antimilitary animus that is intended by the supervisor to cause an adverse employment action, and if that act is a proximate cause of the ultimate employment action, then the employer is liable under USERRA.

Applying our analysis to the facts of this case, it is clear that the Seventh Circuit's judgment must be reversed. Both Mulally and Korenchuk were acting within the scope of their employment when they took the actions that allegedly caused Buck to fire Staub. A "reprimand . . . for workplace failings" constitutes conduct within the scope of an agent's employment. As the Seventh Circuit recognized, there was evidence that Mulally's and Korenchuk's actions were motivated by hostility toward Staub's military obligations. There was also evidence that Mulally's and Korenchuk's actions were causal factors underlying Buck's decision to fire Staub. Buck's termination notice expressly stated that Staub was terminated because he had "ignored" the directive in the Corrective Action. Finally, there was evidence that both Mulally and Korenchuk had the specific intent to cause Staub to be terminated. Mulally stated she was trying to " 'get rid of' " Staub, and Korenchuk was aware that Mulally was " 'out to get' " Staub. Moreover, Korenchuk informed Buck, Proctor's personnel officer responsible for terminating employees, of Staub's alleged noncompliance with Mulally's Corrective Action, and Buck fired Staub immediately thereafter; a reasonable jury could infer that Korenchuk intended that Staub be fired. The Seventh Circuit therefore erred in holding that Proctor was entitled to judgment as a matter of law.

C. RETALIATION

Page 303.   Please delete the Note and add the following.

NOTE

In University of Texas Southwestern Medical Center v. Nassar, 570 U.S. ___, 113 S.Ct. 2517 (2013) the Supreme Court held that plaintiffs bringing retaliation claims under Title VII were required to prove that the desire to retaliate was the "but for" cause of the challenged employment action.   Such plaintiffs could not rely on the mixed-motive framework available for status-based discrimination claims. In explaining the different causation standards, the Court emphasized that Title VII's antiretaliation provision appears in a different section from its status-based discrimination ban and that the retaliation provision uses the same critical "because" language used in the ADEA, which the Court in Gross v. FBL Fin. Servs., Inc., 557 U.S. 167 (2009) had interpreted as requiring but for causation.

E. DISCRIMINATION BASED ON FACTORS OTHER THAN RACE OR SEX

1. RELIGION

Page 333.   Please add the following notes.

14A.   In Walden v. CDC, 669 F.3d 1277 (11th Cir. 2012), the plaintiff worked as an Employee Assistance Program (EAP) counselor for Computer Sciences Corporation (CSC), a contractor supplying EAP services to the CDC. The plaintiff is a devout Christian who believes it is immoral to engage in same-sex relationships. After she refused to provide relationship counseling to a CDC employee engaged in a same-sex relationship, a CDC official asked CSC to remove the plaintiff from the contract, and the CSC did so by placing the plaintiff on layoff status pending reassignment. Affirming summary judgment for the defendants on the plaintiff's Title VII religious discrimination claim, the Eleventh Circuit held that "CSC reasonably accommodated Ms. Walden when it encouraged her to obtain new employment with the company and offered her assistance in obtaining a new position."

14B.   What must an employee do to trigger an employer's duty to accommodate her religion? In EEOC v. Abercrombie & Fitch Stores, Inc., 731 F.3d 1106 (10th Cir. 2013), the Tenth Circuit placed the burden squarely on the applicant or employee to notify an employer that a particular   practice   was   religiously   motivated   and   would   require accommodation.   In the case, the EEOC presented evidence showing that the employer refused to hire the applicant because she wore a headscarf to the interview. The Tenth Circuit nonetheless reversed the district court's award   of   summary   judgment   for   the   EEOC   and   granted   summary judgment for Abercrombie & Fitch on the ground that the applicant had not made clear during her interview that she wore the headscarf for religious reasons. As the court noted: "During the course of the interview, [the applicant] never informed [the employer] that she was Muslim, never brought up the subject of her headscarf, and never indicated that she wore the headscarf for religious reasons and that she felt obliged to do so, and thus would need an accommodation to address the conflict between her religious practice and Abercrombie's clothing policy." 731 F.3d at 1113. But see Adeyeye v. Heartland Sweeteners, LLC, 721 F.3d 444 (7th Cir. 2013), in which the Seventh Circuit held that an employee's request to take unpaid leave to attend the funeral ceremonies of his father in Nigeria was sufficient to put the employer on notice of the religious nature of the request. The court explained that even though the plaintiff's religious beliefs and practices were unfamiliar to most Americans, his request for leave gave sufficient notice of the religious nature of the leave by referring to "a 'funeral ceremony,' a 'funeral rite,' and animal sacrifice." Id. at 450–51. Moreover, the court explained that "[i]f the managers who considered the request had questions about whether the request was religious, nothing would have prevented them from asking Adeyeye to explain a little more about the nature of his request. . . ." Id. at 451.

Page 334.   Please add the following after note 17.

Hosanna-Tabor Evangelical Lutheran Church & School v. EEOC
132 S.Ct. 694 (2012).

■ CHIEF JUSTICE ROBERTS delivered the opinion of the Court.

Certain employment discrimination laws authorize employees who have been wrongfully terminated to sue their employers for reinstatement and damages. The question presented is whether the Establishment and Free Exercise Clauses of the First Amendment bar such an action when the employer is a religious group and the employee is one of the group's ministers.

Petitioner Hosanna-Tabor Evangelical Lutheran Church and School is a member congregation of the Lutheran Church-Missouri Synod, the second largest Lutheran denomination in America. Hosanna-Tabor operated a small school in Redford, Michigan, offering a Christ-centered education to students in kindergarten through eighth grade.

The Synod classifies teachers into two categories: "called" and "lay." "Called" teachers are regarded as having been called to their vocation by God through a congregation. To be eligible to receive a call from a congregation, a teacher must satisfy certain academic requirements. One way of doing so is by completing a "colloquy" program at a Lutheran college or university. The program requires candidates to take eight courses of theological study, obtain the endorsement of their local Synod district, and pass an oral examination by a faculty committee. A teacher who meets these requirements may be called by a congregation. Once called, a teacher receives the formal title "Minister of Religion, Commissioned." A commissioned minister serves for an open-ended term; at Hosanna-Tabor, a call could be rescinded only for cause and by a supermajority vote of the congregation.

"Lay" or "contract" teachers, by contrast, are not required to be trained by the Synod or even to be Lutheran. At Hosanna-Tabor, they were appointed by the school board, without a vote of the congregation, to one-year renewable terms. Although teachers at the school generally performed the same duties regardless of whether they were lay or called, lay teachers were hired only when called teachers were unavailable.

Respondent Cheryl Perich was first employed by Hosanna-Tabor as a lay teacher in 1999. After Perich completed her colloquy later that school year, Hosanna-Tabor asked her to become a called teacher. Perich accepted the call and received a "diploma of vocation" designating her a commissioned minister.

Perich taught kindergarten during her first four years at Hosanna-Tabor and fourth grade during the 2003–2004 school year. She taught math, language arts, social studies, science, gym, art, and music. She also taught a religion class four days a week, led the students in prayer and devotional exercises each day, and attended a weekly school-wide chapel service. Perich led the chapel service herself about twice a year.

Perich became ill in June 2004 with what was eventually diagnosed as narcolepsy. Symptoms included sudden and deep sleeps from which she could not be roused. Because of her illness, Perich began the 2004–2005 school year on disability leave. On January 27, 2005, however, Perich notified the school principal, Stacey Hoeft, that she would be able to report to work the following month. Hoeft responded that the school had already contracted with a lay teacher to fill Perich's position for the remainder of the school year. Hoeft also expressed concern that Perich was not yet ready to return to the classroom.

On January 30, Hosanna-Tabor held a meeting of its congregation at which school administrators stated that Perich was unlikely to be physically capable of returning to work that school year or the next. The congregation voted to offer Perich a "peaceful release" from her call, whereby the congregation would pay a portion of her health insurance premiums in exchange for her resignation as a called teacher. Perich refused to resign and produced a note from her doctor stating that she would be able to return to work on February 22. The school board urged Perich to reconsider, informing her that the school no longer had a position for her, but Perich stood by her decision not to resign.

On the morning of February 22—the first day she was medically cleared to return to work—Perich presented herself at the school. Hoeft asked her to leave but she would not do so until she obtained written documentation that she had reported to work. Later that afternoon, Hoeft called Perich at home and told her that she would likely be fired. Perich responded that she had spoken with an attorney and intended to assert her legal rights.

Following a school board meeting that evening, board chairman Scott Salo sent Perich a letter stating that Hosanna-Tabor was reviewing the process for rescinding her call in light of her "regrettable" actions. Salo subsequently followed up with a letter advising Perich that the congregation would consider whether to rescind her call at its next meeting. As grounds for termination, the letter cited Perich's "insubordination and disruptive behavior" on February 22, as well as the damage she had done to her "working relationship" with the school by "threatening to take legal action." The congregation voted to rescind Perich's call on April 10, and Hosanna-Tabor sent her a letter of termination the next day.

Perich filed a charge with the Equal Employment Opportunity Commission, alleging that her employment had been terminated in violation of the Americans with Disabilities Act. The ADA prohibits an employer from discriminating against a qualified individual on the basis of disability. It also prohibits an employer from retaliating "against any individual because such individual has opposed any act or practice made unlawful by [the ADA] or because such individual made a charge, testified, assisted, or participated in any manner in an investigation, proceeding, or hearing under [the ADA]."

The EEOC brought suit against Hosanna-Tabor, alleging that Perich had been fired in retaliation for threatening to file an ADA lawsuit. Perich intervened in the litigation, claiming unlawful retaliation under both the ADA and the Michigan Persons with Disabilities Civil Rights Act. The EEOC and Perich sought Perich's reinstatement to her former position (or frontpay in lieu thereof), along with backpay, compensatory and punitive damages, attorney's fees, and other injunctive relief.

Hosanna-Tabor moved for summary judgment. Invoking what is known as the "ministerial exception," the Church argued that the suit was barred by the First Amendment because the claims at issue concerned the employment relationship between a religious institution and one of its ministers. According to the Church, Perich was a minister, and she had been fired for a religious reason—namely, that her threat to sue the Church violated the Synod's belief that Christians should resolve their disputes internally.

The District Court agreed that the suit was barred by the ministerial exception and granted summary judgment in Hosanna-Tabor's favor.

* * *

The Court of Appeals for the Sixth Circuit vacated and remanded, directing the District Court to proceed to the merits of Perich's retaliation claims.

* * *

We granted certiorari.

The First Amendment provides, in part, that "Congress shall make no law respecting an establishment of religion, or prohibiting the free exercise thereof." We have said that these two Clauses "often exert conflicting pressures," and that there can be "internal tension . . . between the Establishment Clause and the Free Exercise Clause." Not so here. Both Religion Clauses bar the government from interfering with the decision of a religious group to fire one of its ministers.

* * *

It was against this background that the First Amendment was adopted. Familiar with life under the established Church of England, the founding generation sought to foreclose the possibility of a national church. By forbidding the "establishment of religion" and guaranteeing the "free exercise thereof," the Religion Clauses ensured that the new Federal Government—unlike the English Crown—would have no role in filling ecclesiastical offices. The Establishment Clause prevents the Government from appointing ministers, and the Free Exercise Clause prevents it from interfering with the freedom of religious groups to select their own.

* * *

Until today, we have not had occasion to consider whether this freedom of a religious organization to select its ministers is implicated by a suit alleging discrimination in employment. The Courts of Appeals, in contrast, have had extensive experience with this issue. Since the passage of Title VII of the Civil Rights Act of 1964 and other employment discrimination laws, the Courts of Appeals have uniformly recognized the existence of a "ministerial exception," grounded in the First Amendment, that precludes application of such legislation to claims concerning the employment relationship between a religious institution and its ministers.

We agree that there is such a ministerial exception. The members of a religious group put their faith in the hands of their ministers. Requiring a church to accept or retain an unwanted minister, or punishing a church for failing to do so, intrudes upon more than a mere employment decision. Such action interferes with the internal governance of the church, depriving the church of control over the selection of those who will personify its beliefs. By imposing an unwanted minister, the state infringes the Free Exercise Clause, which protects a religious group's right to shape its own faith and mission through its appointments. According the state the power to determine which individuals will minister to the faithful also violates the Establishment Clause, which prohibits government involvement in such ecclesiastical decisions.

The EEOC and Perich acknowledge that employment discrimination laws would be unconstitutional as applied to religious groups in certain circumstances. They grant, for example, that it would violate the First Amendment for courts to apply such laws to compel the ordination of women by the Catholic Church or by an Orthodox Jewish seminary. According to the EEOC and Perich, religious organizations could successfully defend against employment discrimination claims in those circumstances by invoking the constitutional right to freedom of association—a right "implicit" in the First Amendment. The EEOC and Perich thus see no need—and no basis—for a special rule for ministers grounded in the Religion Clauses themselves.

We find this position untenable. The right to freedom of association is a right enjoyed by religious and secular groups alike. It follows under the EEOC's and Perich's view that the First Amendment analysis should be the same, whether the association in question is the Lutheran Church, a labor union, or a social club. That result is hard to square with the text of the First Amendment itself, which gives special solicitude to the rights of religious organizations. We cannot accept the remarkable view that the Religion Clauses have nothing to say about a religious organization's freedom to select its own ministers.

The EEOC and Perich also contend that our decision in Employment Div., Dept. of Human Resources of Ore. v. Smith, 494 U.S. 872 (1990), precludes recognition of a ministerial exception. In *Smith*, two members of the Native American Church were denied state unemployment benefits after it was determined that they had been fired from their jobs for ingesting peyote, a crime under Oregon law. We held that this did not violate the Free Exercise Clause, even though the peyote had been ingested for sacramental purposes, because the "right of free exercise does not relieve an individual of the obligation to comply with a valid and neutral law of general applicability on the ground that the law proscribes (or prescribes) conduct that his religion prescribes (or proscribes)."

It is true that the ADA's prohibition on retaliation, like Oregon's prohibition on peyote use, is a valid and neutral law of general applicability. But a church's selection of its ministers is unlike an individual's ingestion of peyote. Smith involved government regulation of only outward physical acts. The present case, in contrast, concerns government interference with an internal church decision that affects the faith and mission of the church itself. The contention that Smith forecloses recognition of a ministerial exception rooted in the Religion Clauses has no merit.

Having concluded that there is a ministerial exception grounded in the Religion Clauses of the First Amendment, we consider whether the exception applies in this case. We hold that it does.

Every Court of Appeals to have considered the question has concluded that the ministerial exception is not limited to the head of a religious congregation, and we agree. We are reluctant, however, to adopt a rigid formula for deciding when an employee qualifies as a minister. It is enough for us to conclude, in this our first case involving the ministerial exception, that the exception covers Perich, given all the circumstances of her employment.

To begin with, Hosanna-Tabor held Perich out as a minister, with a role distinct from that of most of its members. When Hosanna-Tabor extended her a call, it issued her a diploma of vocation according her the title "Minister of Religion, Commissioned." She was tasked with performing that office "according to the Word of God and the confessional standards of the Evangelical Lutheran Church as drawn from the Sacred Scriptures." The congregation prayed that God "bless [her] ministrations to the glory of His holy name, [and] the building of His church." In a supplement to the diploma, the congregation undertook to periodically review Perich's "skills of ministry" and "ministerial responsibilities," and to provide for her "continuing education as a professional person in the ministry of the Gospel."

* * *

Perich held herself out as a minister of the Church by accepting the formal call to religious service, according to its terms. She did so in other ways as well. For example, she claimed a special housing allowance on her taxes that was available only to employees earning their compensation " 'in the exercise of the ministry.' " In a form she submitted to the Synod following her termination, Perich again indicated that she regarded herself as a minister at Hosanna-Tabor, stating: "I feel that God is leading me to serve in the teaching ministry. . . . I am anxious to be in the teaching ministry again soon."

Perich's job duties reflected a role in conveying the Church's message and carrying out its mission. Hosanna-Tabor expressly charged her with "lead[ing] others toward Christian maturity" and "teach[ing] faithfully the Word of God, the Sacred Scriptures, in its truth and purity and as set forth in all the symbolical books of the Evangelical Lutheran Church." In fulfilling these responsibilities, Perich taught her students religion four days a week, and led them in prayer three times a day. Once a week, she took her students to a school-wide chapel service, and—about twice a year—she took her turn leading it, choosing the liturgy, selecting the hymns, and delivering a short message based on verses from the Bible. During her last year of teaching, Perich also led her fourth graders in a brief devotional exercise each morning. As a source of religious instruction, Perich performed an important role in transmitting the Lutheran faith to the next generation.

In light of these considerations—the formal title given Perich by the Church, the substance reflected in that title, her own use of that title, and the important religious functions she performed for the Church—we conclude that Perich was a minister covered by the ministerial exception.

* * *

Although the Sixth Circuit did not adopt the extreme position pressed here by the EEOC, it did regard the relative amount of time Perich spent performing religious functions as largely determinative. The issue before us, however, is not one that can be resolved by a stopwatch. The amount of time an employee spends on particular activities is relevant in assessing that employee's status, but that factor cannot be considered in isolation, without regard to the nature of the religious functions performed and the other considerations discussed above.

* * *

The EEOC and Perich foresee a parade of horribles that will follow our recognition of a ministerial exception to employment discrimination suits. According to the EEOC and Perich, such an exception could protect religious organizations from liability for retaliating against employees for reporting criminal misconduct or for testifying before a grand jury or in a criminal trial. What is more, the EEOC contends, the logic of the exception would confer on religious employers "unfettered discretion" to violate employment laws by, for example, hiring children or aliens not authorized to work in the United States.

Hosanna-Tabor responds that the ministerial exception would not in any way bar criminal prosecutions for interfering with law enforcement investigations or other proceedings. Nor, according to the Church, would the exception bar government enforcement of general laws restricting eligibility for employment, because the exception applies only to suits by or on behalf of ministers themselves. Hosanna-Tabor also notes that the ministerial exception has been around in the lower courts for 40 years.

The case before us is an employment discrimination suit brought on behalf of a minister, challenging her church's decision to fire her.

Today we hold only that the ministerial exception bars such a suit. We express no view on whether the exception bars other types of suits, including actions by employees alleging breach of contract or tortious conduct by their religious employers. There will be time enough to address the applicability of the exception to other circumstances if and when they arise.

* * *

The interest of society in the enforcement of employment discrimination statutes is undoubtedly important. But so too is the interest of religious groups in choosing who will preach their beliefs, teach their faith, and carry out their mission. When a minister who has been fired sues her church alleging that her termination was discriminatory, the First Amendment has struck the balance for us. The church must be free to choose those who will guide it on its way.

The judgment of the Court of Appeals for the Sixth Circuit is reversed.

It is so ordered.

JUSTICE THOMAS, concurring.

I join the Court's opinion. I write separately to note that, in my view, the Religion Clauses require civil courts to apply the ministerial exception and to defer to a religious organization's good-faith understanding of who qualifies as its minister. As the Court explains, the Religion Clauses guarantee religious organizations autonomy in matters of internal governance, including the selection of those who will minister the faith. A religious organization's right to choose its ministers would be hollow, however, if secular courts could second-guess the organization's sincere determination that a given employee is a "minister" under the organization's theological tenets. Our country's religious landscape includes organizations with different leadership structures and doctrines that influence their conceptions of ministerial status. The question whether an employee is a minister is itself religious in nature, and the answer will vary widely. Judicial attempts to fashion a civil definition of "minister" through a bright-line test or multi-factor analysis risk disadvantaging those religious groups whose beliefs, practices, and membership are outside of the "mainstream" or unpalatable to some.

JUSTICE ALITO, with whom JUSTICE KAGAN joins, concurring.

I join the Court's opinion, but I write separately to clarify my understanding of the significance of formal ordination and designation as a "minister" in determining whether an "employee" of a religious group falls within the so-called "ministerial" exception. The term "minister" is commonly used by many Protestant denominations to refer to members of their clergy, but the term is rarely if ever used in this way by Catholics, Jews, Muslims, Hindus, or Buddhists. In addition, the concept of ordination as understood by most Christian churches and by Judaism has no clear counterpart in some Christian denominations and some other religions. Because virtually every religion in the world is represented in the population of the United States, it would be a mistake if the term "minister" or the concept of ordination were viewed as central to the important issue of religious autonomy that is presented in cases like this one. Instead, courts should focus on the function performed by persons who work for religious bodies.

NOTE

Relying on *Hosanna-Tabor*, the Fifth Circuit in Cannata v. Catholic Diocese of Austin, 700 F.3d 169 (5th Cir. 2012), held that the ministerial exception barred an ADEA claim by the church's music director because by playing the piano during services he "furthered the mission of the church and helped convey its message to the congregants." Id. at 177. The court emphasized that in determining when the ministerial exception applies "the *Hosanna-Tabor* Court engaged in a fact-intensive inquiry and explicitly rejected the adoption of a 'rigid formula' or bright-line test." Id. at 176.

2. NATIONAL ORIGIN

Page 342.   Please add the following note.

7A. In Cortezano v. Salin Bank & Trust Co., 680 F.3d 936 (7th Cir. 2012), the plaintiff alleged she was discharged because she was married to a Mexican citizen and therefore this was national origin discrimination in violation of Title VII. The court disagreed. "[A]ny discrimination . . . was not based on [her husband's] race or national origin, but rather his status as an alien who lacked permission to be in the country."

3. AGE

Page 348.   Please add before last sentence of note 2.

However, an exception exists that allows state and local governments to set mandatory retirement ages for firefighters and law enforcement officers. See Sadi v. City of Cleveland, 2013 WL 2476729 (6th Cir., June 11, 2013) (finding no ADEA violation when police officers were forced to retire pursuant to mandatory retirement law).

Page 348.   Please add at end of note 4.

Liquidated damages in the amount of backpay are available in cases in which an employer's violation of the Act is "willful." 29 U.S.C. § 626(b). See Miller v. Raytheon Co., 2013 WL 1845586 at *4 (5th Cir., May 2, 2013) ("A violation of the ADEA is willful, and liquidated damages may be awarded, when an employer must have 'kn[own] or show[n] reckless disregard for the matter of whether its conduct was prohibited by the ADEA.' ").

Page 348.   Please add at the end of note 5.

The ADEA may not, however, be the exclusive remedy for workers alleging age discrimination. In Levin v. Madigan, 692 F.3d 607 (7th Cir. 2012), the Seventh Circuit permitted a state employee to bring an equal protection claim for age discrimination under 42 U.S.C. § 1983. While several district courts have ruled similarly, the other circuit courts to consider the issue have held that the ADEA is the exclusive remedy for age discrimination claims. Compare Shapiro v. N.Y. City Dep't of Educ, 561 F.Supp.2d 413 (S.D.N.Y. 2008) (ADEA does not preclude a 1983 claim) and Mustafa v. State of Neb. Dep't of Corr. Servs., 196 F.Supp.2d 945

(D.Neb.2002) (same) with Zombro v. Baltimore City Police Dep't, 868 F.2d 1364 (4th Cir. 1989) (ADEA is the exclusive remedy for age discrimination claims); Ahlmeyer v. Nev. Sys. Of Higher Ed., 555 F.3d 1051 (9th Cir. 2009) (same); Tapia-Tapia v. Potter, 322 F.3d 742 (1st Cir. 2003) (same); Lafleur v. Tex. Dep't of Health, 126 F.3d 758 (5th Cir. 1997) (same); Chennareddy v. Bowsher, 935 F.2d 315 (D.C. Cir. 1991) (same). The Supreme Court accepted cert in Madigan v. Levin for the 2013 term, but then dismissed it as improvidently granted, 134 S. Ct. 2 (2013).

Page 349.   Please add the following note.

6A. Only a few of the circuits have explicitly ruled on whether a claim for hostile work environment is cognizable under the ADEA. In Dediol v. Best Chevrolet, Inc., 655 F.3d 435 (5th Cir. 2011), the Fifth Circuit recognized such an action. Adopting the reasoning of the Sixth Circuit in Crawford v. Medina Gen. Hosp., 96 F.3d 830 (6th Cir. 1996), the Fifth Circuit said that an employee-plaintiff must prove that (1) the employee is 40 or older; (2) the employee was subjected to harassment based on age, either through words or actions; (3) the harassment created an objectively intimidating, hostile, or offensive work environment; and (4) there exists some basis for liability on the part of the employer.

4. DISABILITY

Page 357.   Please add the following at the end of Major Life Activity.

In Norton v. Assisted Living Concepts, Inc., 786 F. Supp.2d 1173 (E.D. Tex. 2011), the court held that under the ADAAA cancer at any stage substantially limits the major life activity of cell growth. The case illustrates the effect of the amendments, as pre-ADAAA numerous cases had held that various plaintiffs with cancer were not covered under the ADA because they did not have a substantial limitation of a major life activity.

Page 357.   Please add the following at the end of *Minor and transitory impairments.*

Nonetheless, in Summers v. Altarum Institute Corp., 740 F.3d 325 (4th Cir. 2014), the Fourth Circuit held that a temporary impairment, albeit one lasting more than six months, was not excluded from the definition of disability under the ADAAA.

Page 365.   Please add the following note.

4.   To be actionable discrimination under the ADA an individual with a disability must suffer an "adverse employment action" because of the disability. In EEOC v. C.R. England, Inc., 644 F.3d 1028 (10th Cir. 2011), the plaintiff worked as a driver-trainer for a trucking company. Because he was HIV-positive the employer required employees training with the plaintiff to sign an acknowledgment of the trainer's HIV status. The Tenth Circuit held that on the present record the plaintiff did not prove that any of his employment opportunities were limited and thus there was no violation of the ADA. The court stated it was not sanctioning a "co-worker preference" defense and that under different facts an employer's use of a co-worker consent policy could be actionable.

Page 370.   Please add at the end of note 4.

The Seventh Circuit has interpreted *Barnett* as contradicting its prior precedent regarding reassignments under the ADA. In EEOC v. Humiston-Keeling, 227 F.3d 1024 (7th Cir. 2000), the Seventh Circuit had held that a competitive transfer policy did not violate the ADA. In EEOC v. United Airlines, 693 F.3d 760 (7th Cir. 2012), the Seventh Circuit held that *Humiston-Keeling* could not survive *Barnett* and ruled that the ADA does "mandate that an employer appoint employees with disabilities to vacant positions for which they are qualified, provided that such accommodations would be ordinarily reasonable and would not present an undue hardship to that employer." Id. at 761.

Page 370.   Please add at the end of note 5.

Ongoing technological advancements may, however, make such an accommodation seem more reasonable to courts in the future. See Core v. Champaign County Bd. of County Com'rs, 2012 WL 3073418 (S.D. Ohio 2012). As the Sixth Circuit explained in EEOC v. Ford Motor Co., 2014 WL 1584674 (6th Cir. 2014): "When we first developed the principle that attendance is an essential requirement of most jobs, technology was such that the workplace and an employer's brick-and-mortar location were synonymous. However, as technology has advanced in the intervening decades, and an ever-greater number of employers and employees utilize remote work arrangements, attendance at the workplace can no longer be assumed to mean attendance at the employer's physical location." 2014 WL 1584674 at *6.

Page 370.   Please add after the first sentence of note 6.

What is an essential function of a job varies, of course, depending on the context. In Samper v. Providence St. Vincent Medical Ctr., 675 F.3d 1233 (9th Cir. 2013), the Ninth Circuit held that a neonatal intensive care unit nurse who could not meet her employer's attendance requirements, even with accommodation, was not a qualified individual under the ADA because "on-site regular attendance is an essential job function" for such a position.

Page 371.   Please add after note 7.

8.   Following the Supreme Court's ruling in Gross v. FBL Fin. Servs., Inc., 557 U.S. 167 (2009), in which the Supreme Court held that the mixed motives framework did not apply to ADEA claims, the Seventh Circuit has held that the mixed motives framework similarly does not apply to ADA claims. See Serwatka v. Rockwell Automation, Inc., 591 F.3d 957, 962 (7th Cir. 2010) (explaining that "in the absence of a cross-reference to Title VII's mixed-motive liability language or comparable stand-alone language in the ADA itself, a plaintiff complaining of discriminatory discharge under the ADA must show that his or her employer would not have fired him but for his actual or perceived disability; proof of mixed motives will not suffice").

5.   SEXUAL ORIENTATION

Page 381.   Please delete note 10 and replace with the following:

10. Traditionally, discrimination based on an individual's transsexualism was not prohibited under Title VII. The Seventh Circuit explained the reason for such exclusion in blunt terms in Ulane v. Eastern Airlines, 742 F.2d 1081 (7th Cir. 1984). According to the court, "The phrase in Title VII prohibiting discrimination based on sex, in its plain meaning, implies that it is unlawful to discriminate against women because they are women and against men because they are men. The words of Title VII do not outlaw discrimination against a person who has a sexual identity disorder." Id. at 1085. In recent years, however, courts have increasingly held that discrimination against transsexual workers who are transitioning from one sex to the other violates the prohibition on sex stereotyping articulated by the Supreme Court in *Price Waterhouse*. The first circuit court to provide such protection was the Sixth Circuit in Smith v. City of Salem, 378 F.3d 566 (6th Cir. 2004). *Smith* involved a biologically male lieutenant in the Salem Fire Department who was disciplined after he began to express a more feminine appearance at work. In reversing the district court's dismissal of Smith's claims, the Sixth Circuit explained that after *Price Waterhouse*, "employers who discriminate against men because they do wear dresses and makeup, or otherwise act femininely, are also engaging in sex discrimination because the discrimination would not occur but for the victim's sex." Id. at 574. See also Glenn v. Brumby, 663 F.3d 1312 (11th Cir. 2011) (holding that discriminating against someone on the basis of his or her gender non-conformity constitutes sex-based discrimination under the Equal Protection Clause).

Such protection has not, however, extended to transsexual workers' use of the bathroom of their choice. Transsexual workers continue to lose claims asserting a right to use the bathroom associated with their gender identity rather than their biological sex. For example, Etsitty v. Utah Transit Auth., 502 F.3d 1215 (10th Cir. 2007) involved a bus driver who informed her employer that she was transsexual and would begin to present as female at work and use female restrooms while on her route. Her employer terminated her because it was unable to accommodate her restroom needs. The Tenth Circuit held that Etsitty was not entitled to protection under Title VII because the employer's concern about potential liability stemming from her use of female restrooms, while still biologically male, was a legitimate business justification for burdening the plaintiff's gender expression. See also Kastle v. Maricopa County Community College District, 325 Fed. Appx. 492 (9th Cir. 2009) (explaining that "after *Hopkins* and *Schwenk*, it is unlawful to discriminate against a transgender (or any other person) because he or she does not behave in accordance with an employer's expectations for men or women," but holding that employer's ban on transsexual plaintiff's use of women's restroom for safety reasons did not constitute sex discrimination). Transgendered individuals have also been held to be protected under at least one state sex discrimination law. See, e.g., Enriquez v. West Jersey Health Sys., 777 A.2d 365 (N.J.App.Div.2001), cert. denied, 785 A.2d 439 (N.J.2001). See generally Ann C. McGinley, Erasing Boundaries: Masculinities, Sexual Minorities, and Employment Discrimination, 43 U. Mich. J. L Reform 713 (2010).

11. In Macy v. Holder, Appeal No. 0120120821, 2012 WL 1435995 (EEOC April 20, 2012), the EEOC held that discrimination against transgendered individuals constitutes sex discrimination under Title VII. The case involved a forensics technician who was offered a job by the Bureau of Alcohol, Tobacco, Firearms, and Explosives. When she later mentioned that she was transitioning from male to female, she was told that the job had been cut for budget reasons. She later learned that the job was not cut, but it was offered to someone else who is not transgender. The EEOC ruling extends protection to federal government employees, but it is not clear how the courts will view the actions.

12. As of 2012, 21 states ban discrimination in employment based on sexual orientation and 16 states ban employment discrimination based on gender identity or expression.

PART III

TERMS AND CONDITIONS OF EMPLOYMENT

CHAPTER 5

WAGES AND HOURS

A. FEDERAL AND STATE WAGE AND HOUR REGULATION

1. FEDERAL WAGE AND HOUR REGULATION: THE FAIR LABOR STANDARDS ACT

b. BASIC PROVISIONS OF THE FAIR LABOR STANDARDS ACT

(i) Minimum Wage

Page 393. **Please delete the first paragraph under STATE MINIMUM WAGE LAWS and replace with the following note.**

In all, 27 states have minimum wages higher than that required by federal law, and five of them are phasing in hourly minimums of $10 or more: California ($10); Connecticut, Hawaii and Maryland ($10.10); and Vermont ($10.50). This year, eight states and the District of Columbia have increased their minimums. In several more states and municipalities, voters will decide on minimum wage increases in November.

c. COVERAGE

(i) Who Is a Covered Employer?

Page 397. **Please add the following note after Note 3:**

4. In Thompson v. Real Estate Mortgage Network, 748 F.3d 142 (3d Cir. 2014), the Third Circuit determined for the first time that a successor-employer may be held financially accountable for its predecessor's wage-and-hour violations under the FLSA. Instead of applying the New Jersey state law test for determining whether successor liability applied, the court applied the federal common law test, which allowed for a lower bar to relief. It requires consideration of the following factors in determining whether successor liability should be imposed: "(1) continuity in operations and work force of the successor and predecessor employers; (2) notice to the successor-employer of its predecessor's legal obligations; and (3) ability of the predecessor to provide adequate relief directly." By contrast, under New Jersey law, successor companies are considered legally distinct from their predecessors and do not assume any debts or obligations of the successor unless: (1) the successor agrees to assume such liabilities; (2) the transaction amounts to a consolidation or merger of the buyer and seller; (3) the purchasing company is merely a "continuation" of the selling company; or (4) the transaction was consummated to fraudulently escape its liabilities and debts.

(ii) Who Is a Covered Employee?

a. WHO IS AN EMPLOYEE?

Page 405. Add the following to Note 4 after the sentence beginning "See Patel v. Quality Inn South...":

Congress's purposes in enacting the FLSA and the IRCA are in harmony. The IRCA unambiguously prohibits hiring unauthorized aliens, and the FLSA unambiguously requires that any unauthorized aliens—hired in violation of federal immigration law—be paid minimum and overtime wages. Holding employers that violate federal immigration law and federal employment law liable for both violations advances the purpose of federal immigration policy by deterring employers from hiring undocumented aliens for their most attractive quality: their willingness to work for less than the minimum wage. Lucas v. Jerusalem Café, LLC, 721 F.3d 927 (8th Cir. 2013).

Page 407. In the paragraph on that runs over from 406, replace "The Wage and Hour Division (WHD) of the Department Of Labor has derived a 6 factor test from the Walling decision" with the following sentence and then continue with the rest of the paragraph.

The Wage and Hour Division of the Department of Labor derived a 6-factor test from the *Walling* decision that provides guidance about the legality of trainee programs and in 2010 it extended that test to unpaid internships.

Page 407. Replace all of Note 7 after its first paragraph with:

Circuit courts split on the interpretation of the FLSA in the context of training programs. Some courts apply *Walling* or the six factors the DOL derived from *Walling*. See, e.g., Donovan v. Am. Airlines, Inc., 686 F.2d 267 (5th Cir. 1982) (relying on *Walling* to determine whether airline trainees were employees for the purposes of the FLSA); Hawkins v. Securitas Sec. Services USA, 2013 WL 1337158 (N.D. Ill. 2013) ("A trainee's entitlement to wages for time spent in training is governed by a six-part test developed by the Department of Labor and derived from Walling v. Portland Terminal Co."). Others consider the "economic realities" of the situation and look at the totality of the circumstances, sometimes considering the DOL guidelines. See, e.g., Kaplan v. Code Blue Billing & Coding, Inc., 504 Fed. Appx. 831, 834–35 (11th Cir. 2013) (stating that to determine whether a trainee is an employee a court "must consider "the economic realities of the relationship, including whether a person's work confers an economic benefit on the entity for whom they are working" and considering the DOL guidelines as "guidance"). Still others apply the primary benefit test, in which they ask whether the employer or the trainees principally benefited from the work the trainees did. See, e.g., Solis v. Laurelbrook Sanitarium & Sch., Inc., 642 F.3d 518 (6th Cir. 2011) ("the proper approach for determining whether an employment relationship exists in the context of a training or learning situation is to ascertain which party derives the primary benefit from the relationship"). The Ninth Circuit has developed its own approach in which it considers whether the putative employer received an advantage from the trainee's activities and whether there was an agreement for compensation. Nance v. May Trucking Co., 2014 WL 199136 (D. Or. 2014) (to determine whether a trainee is an employee a court "consider[s] (1) whether Defendant received an immediate advantage from Plaintiffs' work at the orientation and (2) whether there was an express or implied agreement for compensation").

In the Southern District of New York, two judges applied the totality of the circumstances test to determine whether unpaid interns are employees and came to differing conclusions. Compare Xuedan Wang v. Hearst Corp., 293 F.R.D. 489, 493 (S.D.N.Y. 2013) motion to certify appeal granted, 2013 WL 3326650 (S.D.N.Y. 2013) (stating that "the Supreme

Court in *Walling* looked to the totality of circumstances of the training program to determine whether the plaintiffs were 'employees' under the FLSA," using the DOL's six factor test as a "framework for . . . analysis" and determining that there was a genuine issue of material fact about whether the interns were employees), with Glatt v. Fox Searchlight Pictures Inc., 293 F.R.D. 516, 532–34 (S.D.N.Y. 2013) on reconsideration in part, 2013 WL 4834428 (S.D.N.Y. 2013), 2013 WL 5405696 (S.D.N.Y. 2013) (applying the totality of the circumstances test, considering the DOL factors, and concluding that unpaid interns were employees for purposes of the FLSA). As a result, the questions of what test applies and whether unpaid interns are employees are currently before the Second Circuit.

The *Glatt* and *Wang* lawsuits are part of a flood of lawsuits from unpaid interns seeking back wages. These lawsuits could have significant consequences for unpaid internships. A pending lawsuit has already led magazine publisher Condé Nast to end its internship program entirely. Cara Buckley, *Sued Over Pay, Condé Nast Ends Internship Program*, N.Y. Times (Oct. 23, 2013).

The uncertain legality of unpaid internships is problematic. The problems are exacerbated by the large number of students who intern during college. The consulting company Accenture found that 72% of students who graduated from college in 2011 and 2012 had interned at some point during college. More than half of those internships were unpaid, Accenture, 2013 College Graduate Employment Survey 5. See also Busk v. Integrity Staffing Solutions, 713 F.3d 525 (9th Cir. 2013), cert. granted, 134 S.Ct. 1490 (2014). Plaintiffs worked for a company that provides warehouse space to clients such as Amazon. They brought federal and Nevada state class actions saying that they had been denied legally required compensation for the time it took them to pass through security clearance at the end of their shifts and also for the time spent walking to the cafeteria for lunch. One issue the Supreme Court may address is whether a federal court can hear a state-law claim for which the state's opt-out class action procedure controls given that the federal FLSA law allows only opt-in class actions.

Page 408.   Please add the following to note 7.

See Glatt v. Fox Searchlight Pictures, Inc., 293 F.R.D. 516 (S.D.N.Y. 2013), permitting a class action against Fox alleging violations of federal, California, and New York law for classifying plaintiffs as unpaid interns instead of paid employees. Glatt worked as an unpaid intern on production of the film *Black Swan*. The court found that internships on Fox movies did not include formal training or education and that Searchlight received benefits from the unpaid work for which otherwise would have required paid employees. "The Defendants were the 'primary beneficiaries' of the relationship, not [the interns]." Disheartened by his brief stint in the movie industry, Glatt went to law school.

b. EXEMPT EMPLOYEES

Page 408. Please delete *In re Novartis Wage & Hour Litigation* and replace with the following case.

Christopher v. Smithkline Beecham Corp.
132 S.Ct. 2156 (2012).

■ JUSTICE ALITO delivered the opinion of the Court.

The Fair Labor Standards Act (FLSA) imposes minimum wage and maximum hours requirements on employers, but those requirements do not apply to workers employed "in the capacity of outside salesman." This case requires us to decide whether the term "outside sales man," as defined by Department of Labor (DOL or Department) regulations, encompasses pharmaceutical sales representatives whose primary duty is to obtain nonbinding commitments from physicians to prescribe their employer's prescription drugs in appropriate cases. We conclude that these employees qualify as "outside salesm[e]n."

* * *

Congress did not define the term "outside salesman," but it delegated authority to the DOL to issue regulations "from time to time" to "defin[e] and delimi[t]" the term. The DOL promulgated such regulations in 1938, 1940, and 1949. In 2004, following notice-and-comment procedures, the DOL reissued the regulations with minor amendments. The current regulations are nearly identical in substance to the regulations issued in the years immediately following the FLSA's enactment.

* * *

The general regulation sets out the definition of the statutory term "employee employed in the capacity of outside salesman." It defines the term to mean "any employee . . . [w]hose primary duty is . . . making sales within the meaning of [29 U.S.C. § 203(k)]" and "[w]ho is customarily and regularly engaged away from the employer's place or places of business in performing such primary duty." The referenced statutory provision states that " '[s]ale' or 'sell' includes any sale, exchange, contract to sell, consignment for sale, shipment for sale, or other disposition." Thus, under the general regulation, an outside salesman is any employee whose primary duty is making any sale, exchange, contract to sell, consignment for sale, shipment for sale, or other disposition.

The sales regulation restates the statutory definition of sale discussed above and clarifies that "[s]ales within the meaning of [29 U.S.C. § 203(k)] include the transfer of title to tangible property, and in certain cases, of tangible and valuable evidences of intangible property."

Finally, the promotion-work regulation identifies "[p]romotion-work" as "one type of activity often performed by persons who make sales, which may or may not be exempt outside sales work, depending upon the circumstances under which it is performed." Promotion work that is "performed incidental to and in conjunction with an employee's own outside sales or solicitations is exempt work," whereas promotion work that is "incidental to sales made, or to be made, by someone else is not exempt outside sales work."

* * *

Respondent SmithKline Beecham Corporation is in the business of developing, manufacturing, and selling prescription drugs. The prescription drug industry is subject to extensive federal regulation, including the now-familiar requirement that prescription drugs be dispensed only upon a physician's prescription. In light of this requirement, pharmaceutical companies have long focused their direct marketing efforts, not on the retail pharmacies that dispense prescription drugs, but rather on the medical practitioners who possess the authority to prescribe the drugs in the first place. Pharmaceutical companies promote their prescription drugs to physicians through a process called "detailing," whereby employees known as "detailers" or "pharmaceutical sales representatives" provide information to physicians about the company's products in hopes of persuading them to write prescriptions for the products in appropriate cases. The position of "detailer" has existed in the pharmaceutical industry in substantially its current form since at least the 1950's, and in recent years the industry has employed more than 90,000 detailers nationwide.

Respondent hired petitioners Michael Christopher and Frank Buchanan as pharmaceutical sales representatives in 2003. During the roughly four years when petitioners were employed in that capacity, they were responsible for calling on physicians in an assigned sales territory to discuss the features, benefits, and risks of an assigned portfolio of respondent's prescription drugs. Petitioners' primary objective was to obtain a nonbinding commitment from the physician to prescribe those drugs in appropriate cases, and the training that petitioners received underscored the importance of that objective.

Petitioners spent about 40 hours each week in the field calling on physicians. These visits occurred during normal business hours, from about 8:30 a.m. to 5 p.m. Outside of normal business hours, petitioners spent an additional 10 to 20 hours each week attending events, reviewing product information, returning phone calls, responding to e-mails, and performing other miscellaneous tasks. Petitioners were not required to punch a clock or report their hours, and they were subject to only minimal supervision.

Petitioners were well compensated for their efforts. On average, Christopher's annual gross pay was just over $72,000, and Buchanan's was just over $76,000.[7] Petitioners' gross pay included both a base salary and incentive pay. The amount of petitioners' incentive pay was based on the sales volume or market share of their assigned drugs in their assigned sales territories, and this amount was uncapped. Christopher's incentive pay exceeded 30 percent of his gross pay during

---

[7]   The median pay for pharmaceutical detailers nationwide exceeds $90,000 per year.

each of his years of employment; Buchanan's exceeded 25 percent. It is undisputed that respondent did not pay petitioners time-and-a half wages when they worked in excess of 40 hours per week.

* * *

The DOL first announced its view that pharmaceutical detailers are not exempt outside salesmen in an amicus brief filed in the Second Circuit in 2009, and the Department has subsequently filed similar amicus briefs in other cases, including the case now before us. While the DOL's ultimate conclusion that detailers are not exempt has remained unchanged since 2009, the same cannot be said of its reasoning. In both the Second Circuit and the Ninth Circuit, the DOL took the view that "a 'sale' for the purposes of the outside sales exemption requires a consummated transaction directly involving the employee for whom the exemption is sought." Perhaps because of the nebulous nature of this "consummated transaction" test, the Department changed course after we granted certiorari in this case. The Department now takes the position that "[a]n employee does not make a 'sale' for purposes of the 'outside salesman' exemption unless he actually transfers title to the property at issue." Petitioners and the DOL assert that this new interpretation of the regulations is entitled to controlling deference.

* * *

In this case, there are strong reasons for withholding the deference that Auer v. Robbins, 519 U.S. 452 (1997), generally requires. Petitioners invoke the DOL's interpretation of ambiguous regulations to impose potentially massive liability on respondent for conduct that occurred well before that interpretation was announced. To defer to the agency's interpretation in this circumstance would seriously undermine the principle that agencies should provide regulated parties "fair warning of the conduct [a regulation] prohibits or requires."

This case well illustrates the point. Until 2009, the pharmaceutical industry had little reason to suspect that its longstanding practice of treating detailers as exempt outside salesmen transgressed the FLSA. The statute and regulations certainly do not provide clear notice of this. The general regulation adopts the broad statutory definition of "sale," and that definition, in turn, employs the broad catchall phrase "other disposition." This catchall phrase could reasonably be construed to encompass a nonbinding commitment from a physician to prescribe a particular drug, and nothing in the statutory or regulatory text or the DOL's prior guidance plainly requires a contrary reading. Even more important, despite the industry's decades long practice of classifying pharmaceutical detailers as exempt employees, the DOL never initiated any enforcement actions with respect to detailers or otherwise suggested that it thought the industry was acting unlawfully. We acknowledge that an agency's enforcement decisions are informed by a host of factors, some bearing no relation to the agency's views regarding whether a violation has occurred. But where, as here, an agency's announcement of its interpretation is preceded by a very lengthy period of conspicuous inaction, the potential for unfair surprise is acute.

* * *

Accordingly, whatever the general merits of Auer deference, it is unwarranted here. We instead accord the Department's interpretation a measure of deference proportional to the " 'thoroughness evident in its consideration, the validity of its reasoning, its consistency with earlier and later pronouncements, and all those factors which give it power to persuade.' "

* * *

We begin with the text of the FLSA. Although the provision that establishes the overtime salesman exemption does not furnish a clear answer to the question before us, it provides at least one interpretive clue: It exempts anyone "employed . . . in the capacity of [an] outside salesman." "Capacity," used in this sense, means "[o]utward condition or circumstances; relation; character; position." The statute's emphasis on the "capacity" of the employee counsels in favor of a functional, rather than a formal, inquiry, one that views an employee's responsibilities in the context of the particular industry in which the employee works.

* * *

Petitioners made sales for purposes of the FLSA and therefore are exempt outside salesmen within the meaning of the DOL's regulations. Obtaining a nonbinding commitment from a physician to prescribe one of respondent's drugs is the most that petitioners were able to do to ensure the eventual disposition of the products that respondent sells. This kind of arrangement, in the unique regulatory environment within which pharmaceutical companies must operate, comfortably falls within the catch-all category of "other disposition."

That petitioners bear all of the external indicia of salesmen provides further support for our conclusion. Petitioners were hired for their sales experience. They were trained to close each sales call by obtaining the maximum commitment possible from the physician. They worked away from the office, with minimal supervision, and they were rewarded for their efforts with incentive compensation. It would be anomalous to require respondent to compensate petitioners for overtime, while at the same time exempting employees who function identically to petitioners in every respect except that they sell physician administered drugs, such as vaccines and other inject able pharmaceuticals, that are ordered by the physician directly rather than purchased by the end user at a pharmacy with a prescription from the physician.

Our holding also comports with the apparent purpose of the FLSA's exemption for outside salesmen. The exemption is premised on the belief that exempt employees "typically earned salaries well above the minimum wage" and enjoyed other benefits that "se[t] them apart from the nonexempt workers entitled to overtime pay." It was also thought that exempt employees performed a kind of work that "was difficult to standardize to any time frame and could not be easily spread to other workers after 40 hours in a week, making compliance with the overtime provisions difficult and generally precluding the potential job expansion intended by the FLSA's time and-a-half overtime premium." Petitioners—each of whom earned an average of more than $70,000 per year and spent between 10 and 20 hours outside normal business hours each week performing work related to his assigned portfolio of drugs in his assigned sales territory—are hardly the kind of employees that the FLSA was intended to protect. And it would be challenging, to say the least, for pharmaceutical companies to compensate detailers for overtime going forward without significantly changing the nature of that position.

* * *

For these reasons, we conclude that petitioners qualify as outside salesmen under the most reasonable interpretation of the DOL's regulations. The judgment of the Court of Appeals is *Affirmed*.

JUSTICE BREYER, with whom JUSTICE GINSBURG, JUSTICE SOTOMAYOR, and JUSTICE KAGAN join, dissenting.

* * *

Unless we give the words of the statute and regulations some special meaning, a detailer's primary duty is not that of "making sales" or the equivalent. A detailer might convince a doctor to prescribe a drug for a particular kind of patient. If the doctor encounters such a patient, he might prescribe the drug. The doctor's client, the patient, might take the prescription to a pharmacist and ask the pharmacist to fill the prescription. If so, the pharmacist might sell the manufacturer's drug to the patient, or might substitute a generic version. But it is the pharmacist, not the detailer, who will have sold the drug.

To put the same fairly obvious point in the language of the regulations and of § 3(k) of the FLSA, the detailer does not "sell" anything to the doctor. Nor does he, during the course of that visit or immediately thereafter, "exchange" the manufacturer's product for money or for anything else. He enters into no "contract to sell" on behalf of anyone. He "consigns" nothing "for sale." He "ships" nothing for sale. He does not "dispose" of any product at all.

What the detailer does is inform the doctor about the nature of the manufacturer's drugs and explain their uses, their virtues, their drawbacks, and their limitations. The detailer may well try to convince the doctor to prescribe the manufacturer's drugs for patients. And if the detailer is successful, the doctor will make a "nonbinding commitment" to write prescriptions using one or more of those drugs where appropriate. If followed, that "nonbinding commitment" is, at most, a nonbinding promise to consider advising a patient to use a drug where medical indications so indicate (if the doctor encounters such a patient), and to write a prescription that will likely (but may not) lead that person to order that drug under its brand name from the pharmacy. (I say "may not" because 30% of patients in a 2–year period have not filled a prescription given to them by a doctor. And when patients do fill prescriptions, 75% are filled with generic drugs.)

Where in this process does the detailer *sell* the product? At most he obtains from the doctor a "nonbinding commitment" to advise his patient to take the drug (or perhaps a generic equivalent) as well as to write any necessary prescription. I put to the side the fact that neither the Court nor the record explains exactly what a "nonbinding commitment" is. Like a "definite maybe," an "impossible solution," or a "theoretical experience," a "nonbinding commitment" seems to claim more than it can deliver. Regardless, other than in colloquial speech, to obtain a commitment to *advise* a client to buy a product is not to obtain a commitment to *sell* that product, no matter how often the client takes the advice (or the patient does what the doctor recommends).

* * *

Taken together, the statute, regulations, ethical codes, and Labor Department Reports indicate that the drug detailers do not promote their "own sales," but rather "sales made, or to be made, by someone else." Therefore, detailers are not "outside salesmen." And the detailers do not fall within that category. For these reasons, with respect, I dissent.

Page 415.   Please replace note 1 with the following note.

The Seventh Circuit considered overtime eligibility for another group of pharmaceutical sales representatives and avoided the issue of the "outside sales exemption" by holding that the representatives meet the requirements for the "administrator exemption." This means that the sales reps' "primary duty includes the exercise of discretion and independent judgment with respect to matters of significance." Schaefer-LaRose v. Eli Lilly & Co., 679 F.3d 560 (7th Cir. 2012).

Page 420.   Please add the following at the end of note 6.

The Obama administration has proposed amending the FLSA's companionship services exemption to grant minimum wage and overtime wage protection to homecare workers employed by third parties such as staffing agencies. The proposed amendments would limit the definition of "companionship services" to duties directly related to the provision of fellowship and protection rather than personal care services such as grooming, dressing, and driving to appointments. The Department of Labor acknowledges that most home care workers already earn above the minimum wage but, beginning January 1, 2015, employers must also begin paying such employees overtime at one-and-a-half times their regular rate of pay for hours worked over 40. Fact Sheet #25: Home Health Care and the Companionship Services Exemption Under the Fair Labor Standards Act (FLSA), U.S. Dep't of Labor. http://www.dol.gov/whd/regs/compliance/whdfs25.pdf.

d.   WAGES

Page 423.   Please add the following notes.

8.   Restaurant servers alleged that their employers showed service charges on customers' bills but did not give the servers the money. Their salaries were above minimum wage. New York law forbids an employer from retaining "any charge purported to be a gratuity." The state's highest court held that this provision applies not only to tips presented by the customer, but also to a service charge shown on the bill that the customer is likely to think is a tip. Samiento v. World Yacht Inc., 883 N.E.2d 990 (N.Y. 2008).

See also Matamoros v Starbucks Corp., 699 F.3d 129 (1st Cir. 2012), holding that Massachusetts' "Tips Act" does not permit Starbucks to share customer gratuities with "shift supervisors" as well as with baristas because the shift supervisors perform a small degree of supervisory work.

9. fision meant that the workers need not be paid for changing clothes. Justice Scalia discussed in detail the possible meanings of the word "clothes," because at least some of these workers had to wear protective gear: "a flame-retardant jacket, pair of pants, and hood; a hardhat; a 'snood'; 'wristlets'; work gloves . . . safety glasses, earplugs; and a respirator." Judge Richard Posner's decision in the court of appeals, reaching the result that the Supreme Court affirmed, had included a photograph of a male model wearing these items. Justice Scalia also discussed the meaning of "changing," saying that "layer[ing] garments" is covered as is taking off one item of clothing and replacing it with another. He said that glasses, earplug, and a respirator are not "clothes," but that adding those items takes little time so the additional seconds or minutes need not be compensated. Sandifer v. United States Steel Corp., 134 S.Ct. 870 (2014).

e.   HOURS

Page 431.   Please add the following notes.

10. U.S. Steel workers sued the company for violating the FLSA by not paying for the time spent changing clothes at the plant and for walking to and from their work stations. The company's and union's collective bargaining agreement did not provide compensation for that time. 29 U.S.C. § 203(o) of the statute excludes from entitled time "any time spent in changing clothes or washing . . . which was excluded . . . by the express terms of . . . a bona-fide collective bargaining agreement." The court of appeals held that the statutory provision meant that the workers need not be paid for changing clothes nor for their walks to and from the workplace. Sandifer v. United States Steel Corp., 678 F.3d 590 (7th Cir. 2012) (Posner, J.), cert granted, 133 S.Ct. 1240 (2013).

11. West Yellowstone, Montana, employed a police force of four. They worked 12-hour shifts but had to be on-call for the 12 hours preceding a shift. When on call they had to stay within cell phone access and keep the ringer loud enough to wake them if they were asleep. If called, the officer would get a minimum of 2.5 hours of overtime pay. A jury, influenced by evidence that Sergeant Stubblefield was in fact called out only 18 times in 609 on-call shifts (with similar numbers for two other officers), ruled for the town and the Montana Supreme Court refused to overturn the jury verdict. Stubblefield v. Town of West Yellowstone, 298 P.3d 419 (Mont. 2013).

g.   ENFORCEMENT OF THE FLSA

Page 441.   Please add the following notes.

5. The FLSA's anti-retaliation provision forbids employers from discharging or discriminating against any employee because, *inter alia*, the employee "filed any complaint" against such employer. Fair Labor Standards Act, 29 U.S.C. § 215(a)(3). In Kasten v. Saint-Gobain Performance Plastics Corp., 131 S.Ct. 1325 (2011), the Supreme Court considered whether the statutory phrase "filed any complaint" applies to oral as well as written complaints. On several occasions Kevin Kasten complained to his employers that the position of the timeclocks between the area where workers donned and doffed work-related protective gear violated the FLSA. Kasten argued that the oral complaints led the company to discipline him and eventually dismiss him. The Supreme Court held that the FLSA's anti-retaliation provision protects both oral and written complaints. Although the statutory text alone was inconclusive on the subject, Justice Breyer reasoned that both congressional intent to protect oral complaints and deference to an EEOC interpretation finding that oral complaints were covered weighed in favor of the holding. The Court limited protection to oral complaints which a reasonable, objective person would have understood as putting the employer on notice that the employee was asserting statutory rights under the Act. In a dissenting opinion, Justice Scalia, joined by Justice Thomas, argued that the plain meaning of the statutory phrase "filed any complaint" applied only to complaints filed with a government body and not complaints delivered from an employee to an employer. The majority declined to reach the issue addressed by the dissent, since the issue was not raised in the certiorari petitions.

6. Plaintiff, formerly a registered nurse at Pennypack Center in Philadelphia, sued on behalf of herself and "all other persons similarly situated." She said that petitioners violated the FLSA by deducting 30 minutes per shift for meal breaks even when the employees worked during those breaks. Defendant offered to settle the case for $7,500 in unpaid wages plus attorneys' fees and other costs. Plaintiff did not respond to defendant's offer. The Supreme Court, in an opinion by Justice Thomas, decided that because plaintiff had been offered full compensation and no other individuals had joined her suit, she no longer possessed a personal stake and her lawsuit was therefore moot. Justice Kagan, dissenting, wrote: "[A]n unaccepted offer of judgment cannot moot a case. When a plaintiff rejects such an offer . . . her interest in the lawsuit remains just what it was before. And so too does the court's ability to grant her relief." Genesis Healthcare Corp. v. Symczyk, 133 S.Ct. 1523 (2013) (5–4).

B. WHAT IS A JOB WORTH?

2. WAGE COMPARABILITY FOR INDIVIDUALS: THE QUEST FOR PAY EQUITY

b. TITLE VII OF THE CIVIL RIGHTS ACT OF 1964

Page 486.   Please add the following note before the Sullivan reading.

NOTE

The Texas Supreme Court held that since the Texas Legislature has enacted nothing comparable to the Lily Ledbetter Act, a plaintiff suing pursuant to the Texas Commission on Human Rights Act, modeled after Title VII, must file a claim within 180 days of the date the employee learns what his or her pay will be. Prairie View A&M University v. Chatha, 381 S.W.3d 500 (Tex. 2012). Chief Justice Jefferson, dissenting, said: "This [decision] creates innumerable problems, not the least of which are the elimination of equitable defenses and a divergence between the Act and the statute it was enacted to promote. . . . I would hold that the 180-day period . . . is not a statutory prerequisite to suit."

CHAPTER 6

HEALTH BENEFITS

A. INTRODUCTION

Page 494.   Please add the following at the end of the first paragraph of Large Employer Penalty.

The employer mandate, scheduled to begin on January 1, 2014 was postponed until January 1, 2015. http://www.treasury.gov/connect/blog/ Pages/Continuing-to-Implement-the-ACA-in-a-Careful-Thoughtful-Manner-.aspx

Page 495.   Please add the following before the first full paragraph.

The Department of Health and Human Services (HHS) issued regulations in 2012 holding that the ACA provision requiring health plans to cover "preventive health services without cost sharing," 42 U.S.C. 300gg–13(a)(4), included all FDA-approved contraceptive methods and sterilization procedures, including the "morning-after pill." 77 Fed. Reg. 8725 (2012). There is a "religious employers" exemption, 45 C.F.R. § 147.130(a)(1)(iv)(A)–(B), but the exemption does not apply to for-profit businesses. In Burwell v. Hobby Lobby, 134 S. Ct. ___, 2014 WL 2921709 (2014), the Supreme Court, five-to-four, held that "closely held," for-profit companies run on religious principles can challenge government actions pursuant to the Religious Freedom Restoration Act and that such companies can seek an exemption from the birth control mandate of the ACA. The Obama Administration previously had provided an accommodation to permit employees of religious-affiliated nonprofits to obtain insurance coverage without direct employer involvement, by authorizing insurers to provide the coverage directly. It is likely that this provision will be extended to religiously oriented, for-profit companies. Notwithstanding the decision in *Hobby Lobby* laws in 28 states provide that health insurance policies covering prescription drugs are required to cover all FDA-approved contraceptive drugs and devices.

Page 496.   Please note the following in the first paragraph.

The Free Choice Voucher provision was repealed in 2011.

Page 499.   Please add the following before the Note on Employer-Sponsored Wellness Programs.

JUDICIAL CHALLENGE

The controversial Affordable Care Act (ACA) was subject to several judicial challenges alleging the statute is unconstitutional. The cases were consolidated in a much-anticipated Supreme Court decision in June 2012. In National Federation of Independent Business v. Sebelius, 132 S.Ct. 2566 (2012), the Supreme Court, five-to-four, in an opinion by Chief Justice Roberts, rejected challenges to the constitutionality of the ACA. There were two main issues. First, the challengers asserted that the individual mandate is not a valid exercise of congressional power under the Commerce Clause. Although a majority of the Court agreed that the Commerce Clause did not permit regulation of individuals who were doing nothing (i.e., not buying health insurance), a majority held that the individual mandate was a legitimate exercise of Congress' taxing power. Second, a majority of the Court held that the Medicaid expansion violates the Spending Clause of the Constitution by threatening states with the loss of their existing Medicaid funding if they decline to participate in the expansion. Nevertheless, the Court held that the constitutional violation is fully remedied by precluding the Secretary of Health and Human Services from withdrawing current Medicaid funding from any state electing not to participate in the expansion. Under the ACA states are eligible for 100 percent federal funding for three years to increase Medicaid eligibility to individuals with incomes below 133 percent of the federal poverty level ($30,657 for a family of four). After three years the federal payment drops to 90 percent.

Although the specific provisions applicable to employers were not the basis of the challenges to the ACA, employers certainly were interested in the outcome of the case. The effect of the Court's decision is to confirm the obligations of employers, including reporting of the value of health coverage on employees' Form W–2 (beginning 2013), limiting to $2,500 the amount of employer contributions to employees' flexible health care spending accounts (beginning 2013), and the employer mandate. The mandate for all employers, originally scheduled to take effect on January 1, 2014, was delayed until January 1, 2015. The mandate for mid-size employers (51–100 employees) was delayed until January 1, 2016.

Page 500.   Please add the following before B.

The Departments of Treasury, Health and Human Services, and Labor proposed new wellness regulations to implement the Affordable Care Act. The proposals would increase the maximum permissible reward for an individual by an employer-sponsored group health plan from 20 percent to 30 percent. In addition, wellness programs to prevent or reduce tobacco use would have a maximum permissible reward of 50 percent. Incentives for Nondiscriminatory Wellness Programs in Group Health Plans; Proposed Rule, 77 Fed. Reg. 60620 (2012).

Employers are displaying a keen interest in offering these programs. According to a 2012 report by the Society for Human Resource Management, the percentage of companies offering health insurance premium discounts for (1) participating in a weight loss program increased from 4% in 2009 to 9% in 2012; (2) not using tobacco products increased from 8% in 2009 to 20% in 2012; and (3) getting an annual health risk assessment increased from 10% in 2009 to 21% in 2012.

The issue of incentives for employees to participate in employer-sponsored wellness programs continues to generate substantial scholarly interest. See Jennifer S. Bard, When Public Health and Genetic Privacy Collide: Positive and Normative Theories Explaining How ACA's Expansion of Corporate Wellness Programs Conflicts with GINA's Privacy Rules, 39 J.L. Med. & Ethics 469 (2011); Kristin M. Madison, Kevin G. Volpp, & Scott D. Halpern, The Law, Policy, and Ethics of Employers' Use of Financial

Incentives to Improve Health, 39 J.L. Med. & Ethics 450 (2011); Harald Schmidt, Wellness Incentives, Equity, and the 5 Groups Problem, 102 Am. J. Pub. Health 49 (2012).

B. ERISA—SUBSTANTIVE PROVISIONS

1. DENIAL OF BENEFITS

Page 507.   Please add the following note.

6A. An employee was seriously injured in a car accident and the administrator of his ERISA-qualified health plan paid $66,866 for his medical expenses. In a subsequent lawsuit the employee recovered $110,000 from third parties. The plan administrator then brought an action to recover full payment from the employee, even though it was more than his net recovery (less attorney fees and costs). The Supreme Court held that general equitable principles, such as unjust enrichment, are inapplicable to an action under section 502(a)(3) of ERISA based on equitable lien by agreement. Although the ERISA plan's terms govern, equitable principles may be used in construing the contract terms. Because the plan is silent about allocating the costs of recovery, it is reasonable to apply the "common fund rule" as the default position. The effect of the rule is to allocate a portion of the attorney fees to US Airways. US Airways, Inc. v. McCutchen, 133 S.Ct. 1537 (2013).

D. FAMILY AND MEDICAL LEAVE

Page 540.   Please delete *Ragsdale* and replace with the following:

Balllard v. Chicago Park District

741 F.3d 838 (7th Cir. 2014).

■ FLAUM, Circuit Judge.

The Family and Medical Leave Act gives eligible employees a right to twelve workweeks of leave "[i]n order to care for the spouse, or a son, daughter, or parent, of the employee, if such spouse, son, daughter, or parent has a serious health condition." 29 U.S.C. § 2612(a)(1)(C). This case is about what qualifies as "caring for" a family member under the Act. In particular, it is about whether the FMLA applies when an employee requests leave so that she can provide physical and psychological care to a terminally ill parent while that parent is traveling away from home. For the reasons set forth below, we conclude that such an employee is seeking leave "to care for" a family member within the meaning of the FMLA.

I. Background

Beverly Ballard is a former Chicago Park District employee. In April 2006, Beverly's mother, Sarah, was diagnosed with end-stage congestive heart failure and began receiving hospice support through Horizon Hospice & Palliative Care. Beverly lived with Sarah and acted as her primary caregiver; among other things, she cooked her mother's meals, administered insulin and other medication, drained fluids from her heart, bathed and dressed her, and prepared her for bed. In 2007,

Sarah and a Horizon Hospice social worker met to discuss Sarah's end-of-life goals. Sarah said that she had always wanted to take a family trip to Las Vegas. The social worker was able to secure funding from the Fairygodmother Foundation, a nonprofit that facilitated these sorts of opportunities for terminally ill adults. The six-day trip was scheduled for January 2008.

Ballard requested unpaid leave from the Chicago Park District so that she could accompany her mother to Las Vegas. (The parties dispute many particulars of Ballard's request, including whether Ballard gave the Park District sufficient notice, but these issues are not germane to this appeal and we will ignore them.) The Park District ultimately denied the request, although Ballard maintains that she was not informed of the denial prior to her trip.

Ballard and her mother traveled to Las Vegas as planned, where they spent time together and participated in typical tourist activities. Beverly continued to serve as her mother's caretaker during the trip. In addition to performing her usual responsibilities, Beverly drove her mother to a hospital when a fire unexpectedly prevented them from reaching their hotel room, where Sarah's medicine was stored.

Several months later, the Chicago Park District terminated Ballard for unauthorized absences accumulated during her trip. Ballard filed suit under the FMLA. The Park District moved for summary judgment, arguing in part that Ballard did not "care for" her mother in Las Vegas because she was already providing Sarah with care at home and because the trip was not related to a continuing course of medical treatment. The district court denied the motion, explaining that "[s]o long as the employee provides 'care' to the family member, where the care takes place has no bearing on whether the employee receives FMLA protections." The Park District moved for an interlocutory appeal.

II. Discussion

We begin with the text of the statute: an eligible employee is entitled to leave "[i]n order to care for" a family member with a "serious health condition." 29 U.S.C. § 2612(a)(1)(C). The Park District does not dispute that Sarah Ballard suffered from a serious health condition. Instead, it claims that Beverly did not "care for" Sarah in Las Vegas. It would have us read the FMLA as limiting "care," at least in the context of an away-from-home trip, only to services provided in connection with ongoing medical treatment.

One problem with the Park District's argument is that § 2612(a)(1)(C) speaks in terms of "care," not "treatment." The latter term does appear in other subsections of § 2612, but Ballard does not rely on those provisions for her leave, and the Park District does not argue that they are implicated in this case. Furthermore, the Park District does not explain why participation in ongoing treatment is required when the employee provides away-from-home care, but not when she provides at-home care. Certainly we see no textual basis for that distinction in the statute.

Another problem is that the FMLA's text does not restrict care to a particular place or geographic location. For instance, it does not say that an employee is entitled to time off "to care *at home* for" a family member. The only limitation it places on care is that the family member must have a serious health condition. We are reluctant, without good reason, to read in another limitation that Congress has not provided.

Still, the FMLA does not define "care," so perhaps there is room to disagree about whether Ballard can be said to have cared for her mother in Las Vegas. We therefore turn to the Department of Labor's regulations to clear away any lurking ambiguity. There are no regulations specifically interpreting 29 U.S.C. § 2612(a)(1)(C). There are, however, regulations interpreting a closely related provision concerning health-care provider certification. Those regulations state:

What does it mean that an employee is "needed to care for" a family member?

(a) The medical certification provision that an employee is "needed to care for" a family member encompasses both physical and psychological care. It includes situations where, for example, because of a serious health condition, the family member is unable to care for his or her own basic medical, hygienic, or nutritional needs or safety, or is unable to transport himself or herself to the doctor, etc. The term also includes providing psychological comfort and reassurance which would be beneficial to a child, spouse or parent with a serious health condition who is receiving inpatient or home care.

* * *

29 C.F.R. § 825.116 (2008).

We see nothing in these regulations to support the Park District's argument, either. The first sentence defines "care" expansively to include "physical and psychological care"—again without any geographic limitation. The only part of the regulations suggesting that the location of care might make a difference is the statement that psychological care "includes providing psychological comfort and reassurance to [a family member] . . . who is *receiving inpatient or home care*." Even so, as the district court correctly observed, this example of what constitutes psychological care does not purport to be exclusive. Moreover, this example only concerns psychological care. The examples of what constitutes physical care use no location-specific language whatsoever.

Sarah's basic medical, hygienic, and nutritional needs did not change while she was in Las Vegas, and Beverly continued to assist her with those needs during the trip. In fact, as the district court observed, Beverly's presence proved quite important indeed when a fire at the hotel made it impossible to reach their room, requiring Beverly to find another source of insulin and pain medicine. Thus, at the very least, Ballard requested leave in order to provide physical care. That, in turn, is enough to satisfy 29 U.S.C. § 2612(a)(1)(C).

The Park District nevertheless argues that any care Ballard provided in Las Vegas needed to be connected to ongoing medical treatment in order for her leave to be protected by the FMLA. But, like the statute itself, the regulations never use the term "treatment" in their definition of care. Rather, they speak in terms of basic medical, hygienic, and nutritional needs—needs that, as in this case, do not change merely because a person is not undergoing active medical treatment. And it would be odd to read an ongoing-treatment requirement into the definition of "care" when the definition of "serious health condition" explicitly states that active treatment is *not* a prerequisite.

In support of its ongoing-treatment argument, the Park District principally relies on out-of-circuit case law construing 29 U.S.C. § 2612(a)(1)(C). First, it cites a pair of Ninth Circuit cases holding that "caring for a family member with a serious health condition 'involves some level of participation in ongoing treatment of that condition.'" *Tellis v. Alaska Airlines, Inc.*, 414 F.3d 1045, 1047 (9th Cir.2005) (quoting *Marchisheck v. San Mateo Cnty.*, 199 F.3d 1068, 1076 (9th Cir.1999)). Tellis involved an employee who flew cross-country to pick up a car and drive it back to his pregnant wife; Marchisheck involved an employee who brought her son to the Philippines because she worried that his social environment in Los Angeles was unhealthy. Next, the Park District cites a First Circuit case about an employee who took leave to accompany her seriously ill husband on a "healing pilgrimage" to the Philippines. *Tayag v. Lahey Clinic Hosp., Inc.*, 632 F.3d 788 (1st Cir.2011). Before considering whether the pilgrimage qualified as medical care under the FMLA, the *Tayag* court noted that the employee "properly does not claim that caring for her husband would itself be protected leave" if the pair traveled "for reasons unrelated to medical treatment of [her husband's] illnesses."

We respectfully part ways with the First and Ninth Circuits on this point. The only one of these cases that purports to ground its conclusion in the text of the statute or regulations is *Marchisheck*. However, as explained above, we do not see how that conclusion follows. The relevant rule says that, so long as the employee attends to a family member's basic medical, hygienic, or nutritional needs, that employee is caring for the family member, even if that care is not part of ongoing treatment of the condition. Furthermore, none of the cases explain why certain services provided to a family member at home should be considered "care," but those same services provided away from home should not be. Again, we see no basis for that distinction in either the statute or the regulations.

At points in its briefing, the Park District describes Ballard's travel as a "recreational trip" or a "non-medically related pleasure trip." It also raises the specter that employees will help themselves to (unpaid) FMLA leave in order to take personal vacations, simply by bringing seriously ill family members along. So perhaps what the Park District means to argue is that the real reason Beverly requested leave was in order to take a free pleasure trip, and not in order to care for her mother. Whether that sort of argument is borne out by the record—which suggests that Sarah arranged the trip with her social worker as part of her end-of-life hospice planning, that Beverly consulted with Sarah's doctor about what would be required on the trip, and that Beverly did in fact provide care in Las Vegas—is not for us to decide at this stage. However, we note that an employer concerned about the risk that employees will abuse the FMLA's leave provisions may of course require that requests be certified by the family member's health care provider. And any worries about opportunistic leave-taking in this case should be tempered by the fact that this dispute arises out of the hospice and palliative care context.

If Beverly had sought leave to care for her mother in Chicago, her request would have fallen within the scope of the FMLA. So too if Sarah had lived in Las Vegas instead of with her daughter, and Beverly had requested leave to care for her mother there. Ultimately, other than a concern that our straightforward reading will "open the door to increased FMLA requests," the Park District gives us no reason to treat the current scenario any differently. Yet even if we credit the Park District's policy concern, "[d]esire for what we may consider a more sensible result cannot justify a judicial rewrite" of the FMLA.

III. Conclusion

We AFFIRM the judgment of the district court.

QUESTIONS

The court notes that the Park District's main objection was that Ballard was seeking to take a recreational trip that was not medically necessary. Do you think part of the Park District's concern was about avoiding the "slippery slope" of FMLA leave takers? If so, is it realistic to assume there will be other requests for "recreational" leave?

Page 548.   Please add the following notes.

7A. Employees may bring FMLA actions for "interference" with their statutory rights or "retaliation" for exercising those rights. In either type of case the employer may defend by proving it had an independent reason for taking the adverse action, such as discharging the employee. If the employer has an "honest belief" in its legitimate reason for the adverse action there will be no liability under the FMLA, even if the employer's reason is ultimately found to be mistaken. See Jaszczyszyn v. Advantage Health Physician Network, 504 Fed. Appx. 440 (6th Cir. 2012).

8A. Alan McFarland, a maintenance director at a nursing home, suffered a stroke and was placed on FMLA leave by his employer. When McFarland sought to return to work, his employer refused to reinstate him because his doctor imposed a 20–pound lifting restriction. McFarland alleged an FMLA violation. The employer introduced evidence that while McFarland was off work he collected short-term disability benefits because "he was unable to perform the material duties of his regular occupation." The Third Circuit, in upholding the district court's dismissal and summary judgment on all claims, applied judicial estoppel to prevent the plaintiff from asserting he was able to work. The court also noted that employers have no duty of reasonable accommodation under the FMLA. Macfarlan v. Ivy Hall SNF, LLC, 675 F.3d 266 (3d Cir. 2012).

8B. In Seeger v. Cincinnati Bell Tel. Co., 681 F.3d 274 (6th Cir. 2012), an employee on FMLA leave for a herniated disc and sciatica was observed by coworkers walking at the Oktoberfest in downtown Cincinnati. When this was reported to management, the employee was discharged for filing a fraudulent FMLA (and paid disability leave) claim. In upholding the employer, the Sixth Circuit applied the "honest belief" test, under which the employer merely needs to act in good faith, as opposed to an objective test, under which the employer needs to be correct in its factual conclusions. What are the advantages and disadvantages of each approach?

Page 549.   Please add the following to the end of note 11.

In Coleman v. Court of Appeals of Maryland, 132 S.Ct. 1327 (2012), an employee of the court brought an action under the FMLA alleging his employer denied him leave necessitated by his own serious health condition. The Supreme Court distinguished *Hibbs* and held that, unlike the FMLA's "family-care" provisions designed to redress a history of sex discrimination in leave policies, the "self-care" provision did not validly abrogate the state's immunity from suit. Therefore, subjecting states to FMLA suits for damages violates § 5 of the Fourteenth Amendment.

12. In June 2013, the New York City Council overrode Mayor Bloomberg's veto and approved a bill (effective April 1, 2014) requiring businesses with 20 or more employees (15 or more as of October 1, 2015) to provide employees with five days of paid sick leave per year. Paid sick leave laws also have been enacted in Portland, San Francisco, Seattle, and Washington, D.C. In 2011, Connecticut was the first state to enact a paid sick leave law.

A related issue is paid family leave. According to the Bureau of Labor Statistics, 11% of private sector employees and 16% of state and local government employees have access to some paid family leave. Legislation in California, New Jersey, and New York provides some family leave benefits. California also requires 30 days of paid leave for an employee who is an organ donor. Cal. Lab. Code §§ 1508–1513.

E. NONDISCRIMINATION IN BENEFITS

3. SEXUAL ORIENTATION

Page 571.   Please add the following to the end of note 9.

In Golinski v. U.S. Office of Personnel Mgmt., 824 F.Supp.2d 968 (N.D. Cal. 2012), a lesbian staff attorney for the Ninth Circuit, who was legally married in California, was prevented from enrolling her wife on her family insurance plan by the federal Office of Personnel Management, which asserted it was prevented from doing so by the Defense of Marriage Act (DOMA). The district court held "that DOMA, as applied to Ms. Golinski, violates her right to equal protection of the law under the Fifth Amendment to the United States Constitution by, without substantial justification or rational basis, refusing to recognize her lawful marriage to prevent provision of health insurance coverage to her spouse."

CHAPTER 7

FREEDOM IN THE WORKPLACE

A. GROOMING AND DRESS

Page 579.   Please add the following to the end of note 6.

See also EEOC v. Abercrombie & Fitch Stores, Inc., 731 F.3d 1106 (10th Cir. 2013) (clothing retailer did not have notice that an applicant, who was Muslim, wore a head scarf based on her religious beliefs, and therefore the employer had no duty to accommodate the applicant's religion).

Page 579.   Please add the following note.

8A. On the issue of racial discrimination in employer hair policies, see D. Wendy Greene, Black Women Can't Have Blonde Hair ... in the Workplace, 14 J. Gender, Race & Justice 405 (2011).

B. HARASSMENT

Page 596.   Please add the following note.

3A. According to a 2014 survey released by the Workplace Bullying Institute, 27 percent of U.S. workers have experienced abusive conduct in the past, and another 21 percent witnessed it. The survey, reported that 40.1 percent of respondents said bosses were the main bullies; 69 percent said the bullies were men, who mostly (57 percent) bullied women. Employer reactions to bullying complaints varied, but only 6 percent of respondents said their employers had a zero tolerance for bullying.

Page 599.   Please add the following note.

13. Melissa Nelson worked as a dental assistant for Dr. James Knight for ten-and-a half years. Dr. Knight occasionally remarked that Nelson's clothing was too tight or revealing and that she was "distracting." Dr. Knight's wife (who also worked at the dental practice) demanded that Nelson be fired because her presence was a threat to their marriage. After Knight fired her, Dr. Knight explained to Nelson's husband that even though nothing was going on between them, he feared that he would try to have an affair with her. Has Dr. Knight committed actionable sex discrimination or sexual harassment? See Nelson v. Knight, 834 N.W.2d 64 (Iowa 2013) (held: no).

Page 604.   Please add the following note.

6A. Under *Ellerth and Faragher* employers are liable for harassment committed by a co-worker only if it was negligent in controlling the working conditions. If the harassment is committed by a supervisor, however, the employer is vicariously liable. In Vance v. Ball State University, 133 S.Ct. 2434 (2013), the Supreme Court, 5–4, in an opinion by Justice Alito, held that an employee is a supervisor for purposes of vicarious liability under Title VII only if he or she is empowered by the employer to take tangible employment actions against the victim, such as firing, demoting, or disciplining the employee. In dissent, Justice Ginsburg would have adopted the EEOC's definition of a supervisor, which included an individual authorized to direct the employee's daily work activities. The power to assign an individual's work duties, typically associated with being a supervisor, gives the harasser leverage over the individual, thereby diminishing the likelihood an internal complaint will be filed to alert the employer of the need to investigate and, where necessary, correct the situation or face liability under Title VII.

C. PRIVACY

Page 628.   Please add the following notes.

5A. When Stanton, the president and CEO of a commercial printing company, "caught wind" that one of its "exclusive outside sales persons," Sitton, was competing with the company, he entered Sitton's office and viewed e-mails on Sitton's laptop computer that Sitton used at work. When Sitton was terminated from employment, he sued for statutory and common law computer theft and invasion of privacy. The employer counterclaimed for breach of duty of loyalty. In affirming the trial court's judgment for the defendant and an award of $39,000 in damages, the court held that Stanton did not intend to convert Sitton's property, damage the computer, or examine personal data. Furthermore, Stanton had the authority to inspect the computer, regardless of ownership, pursuant to the employer's computer usage policy. Sitton v. Print Direction, Inc., 718 S.E.2d 532 (Ga. Ct. App. 2011).

5B. The Computer Fraud and Abuse Act of 1986, Pub. L. No. 99–474, provides for the liability of a person who "intentionally accesses a computer without authorization or exceeds authorized access, and thereby obtains . . . information from any protected computer." Does this make it unlawful where an authorized employee user violates the use policies of an employer? In International Airport Centers, LLC v. Citrin, 440 F.3d 418 (7th Cir. 2006), the Seventh Circuit held that when an employee accesses a computer or information on a computer to further interests that are adverse to his employer, he violates his duty of loyalty, thereby terminating his agency relationship and losing any authority he has to access the computer or any information on it. By contrast, in WEC Carolina Energy Solutions, LLC v. Miller, 687 F.3d 199 (4th Cir. 2012), cert. dismissed, 133 S.Ct. 831 (2013), the Fourth Circuit agreed with the Ninth Circuit that "without authorization" and "exceeds authorized access" should be read narrowly as applying only to situations where an individual accesses a computer or information on a computer without permission. See generally Pauline T. Kim, Electronic Privacy and Employee Speech, 87 Chi-Kent L. Rev. 901 (2012).

Page 628.   Please add the following to note 6.

See also Cate v. City of Burlington, 79 A.3d 854 (Vt. 2013) (upholding city's discipline of employee for secretly accessing and viewing coworkers' e-mail accounts).

D. FREEDOM OF EXPRESSION

1. PUBLIC SECTOR

Page 647.　Please add the following notes.

2A. After the Borough of Duryea, Pennsylvania, fired Guarnieri as its police chief, he filed a union grievance that led to his reinstatement. When the borough council later issued directives instructing Guarnieri how to perform his duties, he filed a second grievance, and an arbitrator ordered that some of the directives be modified or withdrawn. Guarnieri then brought an action under 42 U.S.C. § 1983 alleging that the directives were issued in retaliation for the filing of his first grievance, thereby violating his First Amendment right to petition the government for redress of grievances. The Supreme Court held, based on *Garcetti,* there is no liability under the petition clause unless the employee's petition relates to a matter of public concern. Borough of Duryea v. Guarnieri, 131 S.Ct. 2488 (2011).

3A. In Jackler v. Byrne, 658 F.3d 225 (2d Cir. 2011), the Second Circuit clarified its analysis of *Garcetti* as expressed in *Weintraub.* According to the court, *Garcetti* requires that the subject of the employee's speech was a matter of public concern and that the employee was speaking "as a citizen" and not "solely" as an employee. It was on this latter point that the plaintiff in *Weintraub* failed, because his protest was as an employee and not as a citizen. By contrast, in *Jackler*, a probationary police officer alleged he was discharged for failing to file a false report about an incident involving police misconduct in an arrest. Even though his action arose in the line of duty it was protected because a civilian would be similarly protected. "We conclude that Jackler's refusal to comply with orders to retract his truthful Report and file one that was false has a clear civilian analogue and that Jackler was not simply doing his job in refusing to obey those orders from the department's top administrative officers and the chief of police." See also Gschwind v. Heiden, 692 F.3d 844 (7th Cir. 2012) (teacher's filing of criminal complaint against student who threatened him involved a matter of public concern, thereby making school's alleged retaliation actionable).

Page 648.　Please add the following notes.

4A. David Kristofek, a police officer, arrested a driver for traffic violations. When the arrested driver turned out to be the son of a former mayor of a nearby town, the police chief ordered Kristofek to let him go. Concerned about what he believed to be political corruption, Kristofek complained to fellow officers, his supervisors, and eventually the FBI. When the police chief learned of this conduct, he fired Kristofek. The district court granted the defendant's motion to dismiss on the ground that Kristofek's speech did not involve a matter of public concern because his speech was self-interested. On appeal, what result? See Kristofek v. Village of Orland Hills, 712 F.3d 979 (7th Cir. 2013) (held: public concern need not be the *sole* reason for speech; plaintiff stated a claim for relief even if the speech had a mixed motive).

5A. For a discussion of the various state laws protecting certain types of speech by private sector employees, see Eugene Volokh, Private Employees' Speech and Political Activity: Statutory Protection against Employer Retaliation, 16 Tex. Rev. L. & Politics 295 (2012).

2. PRIVATE SECTOR

Page 652.   Please add the following note.

1A. In Schumann v. Dianon Systems, Inc., 43 A.3d 111 (Conn. 2012), an experienced cytopathologist for a medical testing laboratory complained to his supervisor that new diagnostic procedures were a safety risk and he refused to perform them. After he was subsequently discharged, the plaintiff brought suit under a Connecticut law prohibiting any employer in the state from discharging an employee because of the exercise of rights guaranteed by the First Amendment. The court held that the plaintiff was not entitled to protection under *Garcetti* because his speech was in the course of his employment duties.

Page 654.   Please add the following before E.

A NOTE ON EMPLOYER ACCESS TO EMPLOYEE SOCIAL NETWORKS

It is well known that many individuals place personal information on Facebook and other social media sites. Some employers in the public and private sectors have demanded that employees and applicants provide their user names and passwords so that the employer can monitor their employees' personal postings. As of 2014, 11 states enacted laws prohibiting employers from making social network access a condition of employment. Proposed federal legislation was narrowly defeated in the House of Representatives in 2013.

Is clicking the "like" button on the Facebook page of a candidate for office political speech protected by the First Amendment? See Bland v. Roberts, 730 F.3d 368, 386 (4th Cir. 2013) ("merely 'liking' a Facebook page is sufficient speech to merit constitutional protection").

If multiple employees use Facebook to discuss work-related concerns, it may be considered protected concerted activity under the National Labor Relations Act. See Hispanics United of Buffalo, Inc., 359 NLRB No. 37 (2012).

CHAPTER 8

OCCUPATIONAL SAFETY AND HEALTH

Page 683.   Please add these updated figures to the first paragraph.

According to the latest compilation of data by the Centers for Disease Control and Prevention, in 2012, a total of 4,383 U.S. workers died from work-related injuries. Although most deaths from occupational illness are not captured by the reporting system, for 2007, the estimate of total deaths from occupational illness was 53,445. In 2012, there were nearly 3 million nonfatal work-related injuries and illnesses in the private sector and 793,000 in state and local government. Also, in 2012, about 2.8 million work-related injuries were treated in emergency departments, with 140,000 hospitalizations. In 2007, the total economic cost for work-related deaths, injuries, and illnesses was $250 billion. Centers for Disease Control and Prevention, Workers' Memorial Day—April 28, 2014, 63(16) Morbidity & Mortality Weekly Rep. 346 (April 25, 2014).

A. INTRODUCTION

2. JURISDICTION

Page 703.   Please add the following notes.

6A. The Board of Registration in Dentistry of Massachusetts suspended the license of a dentist in large part because he failed to comply with OSHA's infection control standards, including the handling of medical waste, the disposal of sharp instruments, and the maintaining of accurate records of hepatitis B inoculations by employees. In appealing his suspension the dentist argued that, based on *Gade*, the OSH Act preempts the state from applying OSHA standards in a disciplinary proceeding. What result? See Chadwick v. Board of Registration in Dentistry, 958 N.E.2d 500 (Mass. 2011) (held: OSH Act preempts state from regulating working conditions through its licensure process; case remanded based on separate violation of CDC guidelines not the subject of any OSHA standard).

6B. In Steel Institute of New York v. City of New York, 716 F.3d 31 (2d Cir. 2013), industry plaintiffs challenged the validity of municipal regulations governing construction cranes on the ground that they were preempted by OSHA's crane standards. In rejecting the preemption argument, the court held that the municipal regulations were laws of general applicability—not just at construction sites—and were designed to protect the public from falling cranes. Therefore, they did not conflict with the OSHA crane standards.

C. EMPLOYER DUTIES

2. GENERAL DUTY CLAUSE

Page 721.   Please replace *Pepperidge Farm* with the following case.

SeaWorld of Florida, LLC v. Perez

748 F.3d 1202 (D.C. Cir.2014).

ROGERS, Circuit Judge: SeaWorld of Florida, LLC, operates a theme park in Orlando, Florida, that is designed to entertain and educate paying customers by displaying and studying marine animals. Following the death of one of SeaWorld's trainers while working in close contact with a killer whale during a performance, the Occupational Safety and Health Review Commission found that SeaWorld had violated the general duty clause, § 5(a)(1) of the Occupational Safety and Health Act of 1970, 29 U.S.C. § 654(a)(1), by exposing the trainers to recognized hazards when working in close contact with killer whales during performances, and that the abatement procedures recommended by the Secretary of Labor were feasible. SeaWorld challenges the order with respect to one citation. Concluding its challenges are unpersuasive, we deny the petition for review.

I.

On February 24, 2010, SeaWorld trainer Dawn Brancheau was interacting with Tilikum, a killer whale, during a performance before a live audience in a pool at Shamu Stadium in Orlando. Ms. Brancheau was reclined on her back on a platform a few inches below the water surface. Tilikum was supposed to mimic her behavior by rolling over. Instead, the killer whale grabbed her and pulled her off the platform into the pool, refusing to release her. She suffered traumatic injuries and drowned as a result of Tilikum's actions.

The Secretary of Labor issued three citations to SeaWorld after an investigation by an Occupational Safety and Health Administration ("OSHA") compliance officer. Only the second citation is at issue. It alleged two instances of a "willful" violation of the general duty clause for exposing animal trainers to the recognized hazards of drowning or injury when working with killer whales during performances. The first instance related to animal trainers working with Tilikum being exposed to "struck-by and drowning hazards" by being "allowed unprotected contact with Tilikum" while conducting " 'drywork' performances on pool ledges, slideouts and platforms." In SeaWorld's terms, when trainers are out of the pool or on submerged ledges called "slideouts" in water no deeper than their knees, their interactions with killer whales are called "drywork." Any interaction in deeper water is "waterwork." According to the Secretary, "[a]mong other methods, one feasible and acceptable means of abatement would be to not allow animal trainers to have any contact with Tilikum unless they are protected by a physical barrier. . . ." The second instance concerned animal trainers working with killer whales other than Tilikum who were exposed to struck-by and drowning hazards when they were "allowed to engage in 'waterwork' and 'drywork' performances with the killer whales without adequate protection." The Secretary listed as possible abatement methods "prohibit[ing] animal trainers from working with killer whales, including 'waterwork' or 'dry work,' unless the trainers are protected through the use of physical barriers or through the use of decking systems, oxygen supply systems or other engineering or administrative controls that provide the same or greater level of protection for the trainers." The Secretary proposed a penalty of $70,000.

* * *

II.

The general duty clause, § 5(a)(1) of the Occupational Safety and Health Act, provides: "Each employer [ ] shall furnish to each of his employees employment and a place of employment which are free from recognized hazards that are causing or are likely to cause death or serious physical harm to his employees."

* * *

"To establish a violation of the General Duty Clause, the Secretary must establish that: (1) an activity or condition in the employer's workplace presented a hazard to an employee, (2) either the employer or the industry recognized the condition or activity as a hazard, (3) the hazard was likely to or actually caused death or serious physical harm, and (4) a feasible means to eliminate or materially reduce the hazard existed." Fabi Constr. Co. v. Sec'y of Labor, 508 F.3d 1077, 1081 (D.C.Cir.2007) Tempering the range of potential remedies that might be imposed upon finding a violation of the clause, the court explained: "In other words, 'the *Secretary* must prove that a reasonably prudent employer familiar with the circumstances of the industry would have protected against the hazard in the manner specified by the Secretary's citation." '

SeaWorld contests only the second and fourth elements regarding recognized hazard and feasibility. In challenging the general duty citation, SeaWorld does not perforce contend that the Secretary of Labor or the Occupational Safety and Health Review Commission lack legal authority to require employers to provide a reasonably safe working environment for employees. Rather, SeaWorld takes issue with the interpretation by these officials of what constitutes a recognized hazard that would subject an employer to citation under the Occupational Safety and Health Act. First, SeaWorld contends that the finding that it exposed its employees to a "recognized hazard" is unsupported by substantial evidence. Second, it contends that "when some risk is inherent in a business activity, that risk cannot constitute a 'recognized hazard.' " Third, it contends that the ALJ's decision was based on unreliable expert testimony about the extent of killer whale predictability after SeaWorld's training and precautions. As regards the feasibility of physical barriers and minimum distances SeaWorld contends that the Secretary failed to prove feasible abatement methods (or that SeaWorld had already implemented these measures), and that the ALJ failed to consider evidence these abatement measures present additional hazards and erred because eliminating close contact changes the nature of a trainer's job.

* * *

A.

Whether a work condition poses a recognized hazard is a question of fact. Substantial evidence supports the finding that "drywork" and "waterwork" with killer whales were recognized hazards. Tilikum is a 32-year-old male killer whale with known aggressive tendencies who in 1991 killed a whale trainer at a marine park in Vancouver, British Columbia. SeaWorld had established special protocols for Tilikum, which prohibited "waterwork" and, among other things, required non-killer whale personnel and guests to stay five feet behind pool walls or three feet from Tilikum's head, indicating that SeaWorld recognized the possibility of harm to people standing outside of the pool on land. Although "drywork" with Tilikum continued, SeaWorld limited it to a team of experienced trainers who used extra caution. The caution with which SeaWorld treated Tilikum even when trainers were poolside or on "slideouts" in the pool indicates that it recognized the hazard the killer whale posed, not that it considered its protocols rendered Tilikum safe.

As to other killer whales, SeaWorld suggests that close contact with these whales was not a recognized hazard because all whales behave differently and its incident reports help SeaWorld improve training. But SeaWorld's incident reports demonstrate that it recognized the danger its killer whales posed to trainers notwithstanding its protocols. At the time of Ms. Brancheau's death, seven killer whales were at the Orlando park. Even though SeaWorld had not recorded incident reports on all of its killer whales, a substantial portion of SeaWorld's killer whale population had at least one reported incident. The ALJ also relied on the many comments by SeaWorld management personnel, including corporate curators of animal training, who described the need for caution around killer whales generally, not only around certain killer whales. Killer whales bit trainers' body parts on several occasions (although not generally puncturing skin) and in 2006 a killer whale pulled a trainer underwater by the foot and submerged him repeatedly for approximately 10 minutes. Although this incident occurred during "waterwork," substantial evidence supports the finding with regard to "drywork" as well. On numerous occasions, trainers fell or were pulled into the water, as later happened with Tilikum and Ms. Brancheau, or killer whales lunged out of the water toward trainers. These incidents constitute substantial evidence to support the ALJ's finding that "drywork" was also a recognized hazard.

* * *

SeaWorld's suggestion that because trainers "formally accepted and controlled their own exposure to . . . risks," the hazard of close contact with killer whales cannot be recognized, contravenes Congress's decision to place the duty to ensure a safe and healthy workplace on the employer, not the employee. This court has long held "this duty is not qualified by such common law doctrines as assumption of risk, contributory negligence, or comparative negligence."

* * *

The Secretary and the Commission could also reasonably determine that the remedy does not go to the essence of SeaWorld's productions. SeaWorld has had no "waterwork" performances since Ms. Brancheau's death in 2010, and it temporarily suspended "waterwork" after other incidents, such as the killing of a trainer by a killer whale in 2009 at a non SeaWorld park in Spain. With distance and physical barriers between Tilikum and trainers during drywork, Tilikum can still perform almost the same behaviors performed when no barriers were present. The nature of SeaWorld's workplace and the unusual nature of the hazard to its employees performing in close physical contact with killer whales do not remove SeaWorld from its obligation under the General Duty Clause to protect its employees from recognized hazards.

* * *

C.

Substantial evidence supports the ALJ's findings that it was feasible for SeaWorld to abate the hazard to its employees by using barriers or minimum distance between trainers and killer whales, most notably because SeaWorld has implemented many of these measures on its own. When an employer has existing safety procedures, the burden is on the Secretary to show that those procedures are inadequate. The record evidence showed that SeaWorld's training and protocols did not prevent continued incidents, including the submerging and biting of one trainer in 2006, the killing of a trainer by a SeaWorld-trained and—owned killer whale in 2009 at an amusement park in Spain, and Ms. Brancheau's death in 2010. SeaWorld employees repeatedly acknowledged the unpredictability of its killer whales. This record evidence supports the ALJ's finding that existing protocols were inadequate to eliminate or materially reduce the hazard to SeaWorld's trainer employees performing with killer whales.

Abatement is "feasible" when it is "economically and technologically capable of being done." After Ms. Brancheau's death, SeaWorld required that all trainers work with Tilikum from a minimum distance or behind a barrier, and "waterwork" ceased with all of its killer whales. As the ALJ noted, SeaWorld had not argued the Secretary's proposed abatement was not economically or technologically feasible and had already implemented abatement for at least one of its killer whales and needed only to apply the same or similar protective contact measures it used with Tilikum to other killer whales. Consequently, the Secretary was not required to specify the precise manner in which abatement should be implemented.

* * *

Accordingly, we deny the petition for review.

KAVANAUGH, Circuit Judge, dissenting: Many sports events and entertainment shows can be extremely dangerous for the participants. Football. Ice hockey. Downhill skiing. Air shows. The circus. Horse racing. Tiger taming. Standing in the batter's box against a 95 mile per hour fastball. Bull riding at the rodeo. Skydiving into the stadium before a football game. Daredevil motorcycle jumps. Stock car racing.

Cheerleading vaults. Boxing. The balance beam. The ironman triathlon. Animal trainer shows. Movie stunts. The list goes on.

* * *

The broad question implicated by this case is this: When should we as a society paternalistically decide that the participants in these sports and entertainment activities must be protected from themselves—that the risk of significant physical injury is simply too great even for eager and willing participants? And most importantly for this case, *who decides* that the risk to participants is too high?

* * *

In my view, the Department of Labor either has authority to regulate sports and entertainment so as to prevent injuries to participants, or it does not. The fact that the Department expressly disclaims its authority over the NFL and NASCAR, and that the Department goes to such lengths to draw head-scratching distinctions between sports events on the one hand and entertainment shows on the other, shows that something is up. What's up is that the Department is treating similar cases dissimilarly, the paradigmatic arbitrary and capricious agency action.

* * *

To the extent sports or entertainment activities raise concern about the risk of injury to the participants, several extant legal bodies possess significant authority to clamp down on unreasonable dangers: Congress, state legislatures, state regulators, courts applying state tort law. I take no position here on whether SeaWorld—or for that matter the NFL or NASCAR—should be subject to more stringent government regulation or liability, or otherwise should voluntarily make its activities safer. That *policy* question is not before us. My *legal* disagreement with the majority opinion boils down to one basic question: Who decides? Under current law, it is not the Department of Labor. I respectfully dissent.

NOTES AND QUESTIONS

1. Tilikum is not just any killer whale; he is the largest killer whale in captivity. Despite a series of behavioral problems, Tilikum was reportedly very valuable to Sea World's breeding program. In 2013, a controversial documentary, *Blackfish*, chronicled the 2010 incident and other killer whale attacks. It is not clear why Tilikum attacked Dawn Brancheau, but one theory is that she had run out of the food used to reward him for performing certain tricks.

2. In some respects, *Sea World* parallels *Frank Diehl* (p. 692 of main volume). Both cases raise the issue of the appropriateness of OSHA regulation beyond "traditional" workplace hazards. Unlike *Frank Diehl*, which involved interpretation of an OSHA standard, *Sea World* involved section 5(a)(1) of the OSH Act, a section specifically designed to use when no standard applies.

3. The majority argued that there is a difference between the sports and entertainment industries, and that OSHA has been used to regulate entertainment. The dissent merged sports and entertainment to argue that Congress did not intend to regulate such sports as NASCAR or the NFL and, in any event, the employees in those fields assumed the risk of injury.

4. OSHA enforcement actions brought against entertainment employers are not uncommon. For example, on June 29, 2013, in the final scene of Cirque du Soleil's Las Vegas show, *Ka*, a wire rope broke, causing Sarah Guillot-Guyard to fall more than 90 feet to her death. Nevada OSHA (a state plan) cited both Cirque du Soleil and the MGM Grand, where the accident took place.

5. Suppose the NFL Players' Association filed a complaint with OSHA alleging that certain types of artificial turf are extremely dangerous and cause a much higher rate of severe knee injuries, and that the defective design of helmets cause a high incidence of concussions. Would OSHA have the authority to cite the NFL under section 5(a)(1)? As mentioned in the case, OSHA has "disclaimed" any authority over the NFL. Can you explain this?

E. ENFORCEMENT AND ADJUDICATION

2. ADJUDICATORY PROCESS

Page 745.   **Please add the following before F.**

In 1994, Dayton Tire was issued a citation alleging over 100 willful violations. Dayton contested the citations and, after a 31–day hearing in 1997, a Commission ALJ affirmed the violations and assessed a total penalty of $518,000. The Commission granted petitions for discretionary review in March 1997, but it did not issue a decision in the matter until September 2010, which affirmed all but one violation and increased the total penalties to $1.975 million. On judicial review, Dayton Tire argued that the Commission's delay violated the Administrative Procedure Act. The D.C. Circuit, while critical of the Commission, held that the delay did not render the penalty inequitable or inconsistent with the goals of the OSH Act. Dayton Tire v. Secretary of Labor, 671 F.3d 1249 (D.C. Cir. 2012).

Delay in adjudication not only harms employers, but employees as well, because there is no abatement order until a final decision of the Commission. There are numerous reasons for delays, such as gaps in the nomination and confirmation of new Commission members. Is there any way to speed up the process? Could the Commission adopt a rule that in any case pending on review for two years without a decision, the ALJ's decision would be affirmed by operation of law, thereby allowing the aggrieved party to seek judicial review?

CHAPTER 9

DISABLING INJURY AND ILLNESS

B. WORKERS' COMPENSATION COVERAGE

2. "COURSE OF EMPLOYMENT"

Page 771.   Please add the following at the end of note 2.

Troy Mitchell, a lead lineman for a utility company with nine years of experience, was replacing a 40 foot power pole with a 45 foot pole. While in a bucket lift near the top of the new pole, a copper ground wire that he held in his bare hands came into contact with a transformer on the older, charged pole, five feet below. He received an electrical shock of approximately 7,200 volts, and suffered serious injuries to his hands and side. His employer contested workers' compensation benefits because, while in the bucket lift, Mitchell had removed his protective gloves, a violation of company safety policy. What result? See Mitchell v. Fayetteville Public Utilities, 368 S.W.3d 442 (Tenn. 2012) (held: because the employee knew and understood the rationale for a clearly stated and strictly enforced safety rule, his conduct amounted to "willful misconduct" and disqualified him from receiving benefits). Do you agree with the result?

Page 773.   Please add the following to the end of note 8.

Michael Bernard worked as a host and waiter at TGI Friday's restaurant. When new food selections were added to the menu, he and other employees often sampled the food so they could make recommendations to customers. One day, while sampling a quesadilla, he choked on a partially chewed bite of food and dislodging it damaged his esophagus. In affirming the denial of his workers' compensation claim, the court held that even though the injury occurred in the "course of employment," it did not "arise out of employment," because swallowing a quesadilla was not a unique hazard of the job and was a risk he faced equally on and off the job. Bernard v. Carlson Cos.-TGIF, 728 S.E.2d 508 (Va. Ct. App. 2012).

C. OCCUPATIONAL DISEASE

2. BURDEN OF PROOF

Page 780.   Please add the following to the end of note 1.

In Runstrom v. Alaska Native Medical Center, 280 P.3d 567 (Alaska 2012), a patient services assistant who was helping a nurse in the critical care unit was splashed in the eye with fluids from an HIV-positive patient. Despite receiving antiviral medication and repeatedly testing negative for HIV, she was emotionally unable to return to work and applied for temporary total disability benefits. The Supreme Court of Alaska held that the employee failed to prove that her HIV exposure was the substantial cause of her inability to return to work.

Page 781.   Please add the following to note 4.

See also Schuette v. City of Hutchinson, 843 N.W.2d 233 (Minn. 2014) (police officer who developed post-traumatic stress disorder after responding to accident did not suffer a compensable mental injury).

D. DETERMINING BENEFIT LEVELS

1. IMPAIRMENT AND DISABILITY

Page 786.   Please add the following to the end of note 4.

See McMasters v. State, 271 P.3d 422 (Wyo. 2012) (once claimant established prima facie case of entitlement to total permanent disability under the odd lot doctrine the burden shifted to the workers' compensation division to prove that the claimant could perform work that was available).

3. A NOTE ON DISPUTED CLAIMS

Page 797.   Please add the following before 4.

Hopkins v. Uninsured Employers' Fund

251 P.3d 118 (Mont. 2011).

■ CHIEF JUSTICE MIKE MCGRATH delivered the Opinion of the Court.

Russell Kilpatrick appeals the decision of the Workers' Compensation Court (WCC), concluding that Brock Hopkins was employed by Kilpatrick, and Hopkins was acting in the course and scope of employment at the time of his injuries. We affirm.

BACKGROUND

Great Bear Adventures (the Park), is located near West Glacier, Montana. Visitors to the Park enjoy a drive-thru experience of bears in their natural habitat, surrounded by multiple layers of electrified fence. Kilpatrick owns the Park and lives on adjacent property. Hopkins began working there in 2002, doing various tasks, including maintenance and feeding the bears. In the past, some workers have been known to smoke marijuana on the premises. Although Kilpatrick professed to not condone marijuana use by workers, testimony established that he had smoked marijuana at the Park in the past, and on occasion had done so with Hopkins.

On November 2, 2007, Hopkins traveled to work at the Park at Kilpatrick's request. On the way, Hopkins smoked marijuana. Kilpatrick instructed Hopkins to raise the boards on the Park's front gates so they would not freeze to the ground. Before proceeding, Hopkins asked Kilpatrick if he should feed the bears as well. Testimony regarding Kilpatrick's answer conflicted. However, the WCC ultimately found that Kilpatrick never told Hopkins not to feed the bears.

After completing work on the gates, Hopkins returned to Kilpatrick's house. Kilpatrick was asleep inside. Hopkins mixed food for the bears and used Kilpatrick's truck to drive into the Park. He entered the bears' pen and began to place food out. Once inside, nothing separated him from the bears. At some point while Hopkins was working, the largest bear, Red, attacked him. The bear knocked Hopkins to the ground, sat on him, and bit his leg, knee and rear-end. While this was occurring, another bear, Brodie, came up from behind, and bit Red. In response, Red moved off of Hopkins momentarily, and Hopkins escaped by crawling under one of the electrified wires surrounding the pen. Kilpatrick eventually found Hopkins, and he was transported to the hospital by helicopter. He suffered severe injuries.

Kilpatrick did not carry workers' compensation insurance. Hopkins petitioned the WCC for workers' compensation benefits from the Uninsured Employers' Fund. Both the Uninsured Employers' Fund and Kilpatrick opposed Hopkins' petition. The WCC found for Hopkins, concluding that (1) Hopkins was employed by Kilpatrick at the time of Hopkins' injuries, (2) Hopkins was in the course and scope of his employment at the time of his injuries, (3) marijuana use was not the major contributing cause of Hopkins' injuries, and (4) Hopkins was not performing services in return for aid or sustenance only. Kilpatrick appealed to this Court.

DISCUSSION

Whether Hopkins was employed by Kilpatrick.

The WCC correctly concluded that Kilpatrick, "unquestionably controlled the details of Hopkins' work at the bear park." Hopkins had worked at the Park since 2002, received regular payments from Kilpatrick, and engaged in tasks at Kilpatrick's command. Furthermore, Kilpatrick's assertion that Hopkins was a volunteer is without support. As the WCC succinctly stated, "[t]here is a term of art used to describe the regular exchange of money for favors—it is called 'employment.'"

Whether Hopkins was in the course and scope of his employment.

Factors considered in a "course and scope" analysis include (1) whether the activity was undertaken at the employer's request, (2) whether the employer, directly or indirectly, compelled the employee's attendance at the activity, (3) whether the employer controlled or participated in the activity, and (4) whether the employer and the employee mutually benefited from the activity. The presence or absence of any given factor is not dispositive, as the determination is dependent on a totality of the circumstances.

On November 2, 2007, Kilpatrick compelled Hopkins to work at the Park. Even though there was conflicting testimony as to whether Kilpatrick agreed that Hopkins should feed the bears on that day, an employee's injuries are compensable unless the employee is not "attending to employment-related matters" and has abandoned the course and scope of his employment. Feeding the bears was one of Hopkins' regular employment duties. Hopkins testified he was engaged in the "same routine" he had done for two or three years and would not have fed the bears had Kilpatrick expressly so instructed him. Feeding the bears was not a personal activity "severed" from the continuity of Hopkins' employment-related duties at the Park. Additionally, the WCC found that "Kilpatrick benefitted from the care and feeding of the bears that Hopkins provided since presumably customers are unwilling to pay cash to see dead and emaciated bears." The WCC did not err when it concluded that Hopkins was acting in the course and scope of his employment at the time of his injuries.

Whether marijuana was the major contributing cause of Hopkins' injuries.

Non-prescription drug consumption will preclude an injured employee's benefits if consumption was the leading cause contributing to the result, when compared to all others. No evidence was presented regarding Hopkins' level of impairment. The WCC aptly noted, "Hopkins' use of marijuana to kick off a day of working around grizzly bears was ill-advised to say the least and mind-bogglingly stupid to say the most." However, the WCC further noted that grizzlies are "equal opportunity maulers," without regard to marijuana consumption. Without evidence of Hopkins' level of impairment, the WCC correctly concluded that marijuana was not the major contributing cause of Hopkins' injuries.

* * *

Affirmed.

NOTES

1. The courts are reluctant to disqualify workers from compensation for misconduct because the system is "no fault," and only serious acts of misconduct will disqualify a claimant. See Appeal of Phillips, 75 A.3d 1083 (N.H. 2013) (fact that claimant was intoxicated at the time of the accident does not prove that intoxication was the cause of the accident).

2. In Bassinger v. Nebraska Heart Hosp., 806 N.W.2d 395 (Neb 2011), the Nebraska Supreme Court declined to hold that a claimant should be disqualified because she had misrepresented her history of work-related injuries on a preemployment questionnaire. Although noting that the jurisdictions are divided on the applicability of a common law misrepresentation defense in workers' compensation, the court rejected the applicability of the defense. "[J]udicially engrafting an affirmative defense onto their workers' compensation law to deny benefits months or years after the employee was hired is inconsistent with liberally construing these statutes in favor of providing benefits."

F. TORT ACTIONS AND "EXCLUSIVITY"

1. ACTIONS AGAINST THE EMPLOYER

a. DUAL CAPACITY

Page 811. Please add the following note.

4A. Employees who are not covered by workers' compensation, often including agricultural employees, are not barred from bringing negligence claims for work-related injuries. Adam Martensen was a farmhand who used an all-terrain vehicle (ATV) as he was repairing fences on a 400–acre pasture on his employer's ranch. One day, when the ATV overturned it pinned Martensen's right leg. He was unable to move or summon help. When he did not return from his work at the end of the day Martensen's employer considered searching for him, but decided it was unnecessary. A search party organized by Martensen's father the next day found him in 10 minutes. Martensen's leg was amputated above the right knee. According to the court, the existence of an employer-employee relationship can give rise to a duty to act. Martensen v. Rejda Bros., Inc., 808 N.W.2d 855 (Neb. 2012).

PART IV

TERMINATING THE RELATIONSHIP

CHAPTER 10

DISCHARGE

A. STATUTORY AND CONSTITUTIONAL PROTECTIONS OF EMPLOYEES

1. WHISTLEBLOWER LAWS

Page 843.   Please add the following note.

2A. Wiest sued Tyco pursuant to Sarbanes-Oxley's whistleblower protection provision, section 806.   Held: the district court erred in requiring that Wiest's communications to his superiors "definitively and specifically relate to" a violation of an anti-fraud law as opposed to expressing "a reasonable belief the actions of managers could run afoul" of a law. One issue was whether a "Mermaid Greeters" and "Costumed Pirates/Wenching" party at a resort in the Bahamas held by Tyco (after Tyco and its then-CEO Dennis Kozlowski had been in trouble for various corporate scandals) was an appropriate advertising event. Wiest alleged that his dismissal was unlawful retaliation for this and other disagreements with Tyco management about corporate expenditures. Wiest v. Lynch, 710 F.3d 121 (3d Cir. 2013).   On remand, the U.S. District Court held that Wiest had "adequately pleaded [an] alternative, agency based relationship so as to bring the company and [a] fourth individual within the rule extending SOX Act protection to employees of agents of public held companies." Wiest v. Lynch, 2014 WL 1490250 (E.D. Pa. 2014).

C. TORT EXCEPTIONS TO AT-WILL EMPLOYMENT

2. PUBLIC POLICY

a. LEGAL DUTIES

Page 919.   Please add the following note.

4. In 2006, Debra Parks was fired by Alpharma, Inc. after having complained about Alpharma's policy of failing to inform doctors and the FDA that its drug Kadian could be harmful if taken in conjunction with other pain medications or with alcohol. Parks argued that a public policy exception should apply because the public has an interest in not being unknowingly poisoned. The Court of Appeals of Maryland declined to apply a public policy exception, noting that "Maryland has adopted a more conservative view of what is actionable, not wishing to involve the courts in borderline claims where the violation of public policy is not so clear." Parks v. Alpharma, Inc., 25 A.3d 200 (Md. 2011).   The Fourth Circuit essentially affirmed, holding that Parks failed to satisfy the notice prong of her retaliation claim.   The court emphasized that the employer must be aware of an employee's conduct to be held to have unlawfully retaliated.   U.S. ex rel. Parks v. Alpharma, Inc., 493 F. App'x 380 (4th Cir. 2012) (unpublished).

b.   STATUTORY AND CONSTITUTIONAL RIGHTS

Page 925.   Please add the following notes.

11. Nathan Berry, employed by Liberty Holdings, was involved in an auto accident with Premier Concrete Pumping. Both Premier and Liberty were partially owned by the same person, Brent Voss. Berry successfully filed a personal injury lawsuit and nine months later was fired. Berry asserted that public policy protected him from being terminated for exercising his right to file lawsuits. The Iowa Supreme Court said that much like the right to consult with an attorney, the right to file lawsuits against an employer is not supported by public policy. The court said that the existence of a legal framework permitting an activity is insufficient to prove a state public policy in favor of the activity. More broadly, "legislative pronouncements that are limited in scope may not support a public policy beyond the specific scope of the statute." Berry v. Liberty Holdings, Inc., 803 N.W.2d 106 (Iowa 2011).

12. Joyce Martin had been working at Clinical Pathology Laboratories (CPL) for three years when she requested permission to leave work early to vote in the general election. CPL refused permission, but Martin nonetheless left work 15 minutes early to vote. Two days later, CPL terminated Martin's employment. Martin claimed public policy protection for her right to vote, citing the Texas Election Code, which prohibits employers from refusing to permit employees to be absent from work on election day for the purpose of attending the polls to vote. The Texas Court of Appeals, however, concluded that the criminal penalties of the Texas Election Code were sufficient and that the legislature did not intend to create a common-law exception to at-will employment: "Our general rule is that we, as an intermediate appellate court, will not adopt new common-law exceptions to the employment-at-will doctrine." Martin v. Clinical Pathology Laboratories, Inc., 343 S.W.3d 885 (Tex. Ct. Civ. App. 2011).

c.   PUBLIC HEALTH AND SAFETY

Page 929.   Please add the following note.

5. Phyllis Delaney said she was dismissed for seeking four weeks off from work to donate a kidney to her brother. The Missouri court of appeals held that the state's public policy encourages organ donation and reversed a trial court decision dismissing Ms. Delaney's lawsuit. Delaney v. Signature Health Care Foundation, 376 S.W.3d 55 (Mo. Ct. App. 2012).

CHAPTER 11

EMPLOYEES' DUTIES TO THE EMPLOYER

A. BREACH OF CONTRACT BY AN EMPLOYEE

2. BREACH OF IMPLIED TERMS

Page 980.   **Please add the following note.**

2.   Rehab Solutions alleged that its in-house accountant, Mignon Willis, failed to fulfill many duties of her employment which eventually resulted in tax liens levied against Rehab's building. The Supreme Court of Mississippi held that theories of unjust enrichment and negligence do not support lawsuits by Rehab against Willis for nonfeasance of Willis's duties. Willis v. Rehab Solutions, PLLC, 82 So.3d 583 (Miss. 2012). The court cited the facts that Willis did not engage in illegal activity and that Rehab failed to properly oversee Willis.

Page 990.   **Please add to the end of Note 3.**

This is also the position of the Restatement (Third) of Employment Law, approved by the American Law Institute in 2014. Section 8.01 provides that only employees "in a position of trust and confidence" owe a fiduciary duty to their employers. The Comments explain that "Employees occupy such a position when they exercise managerial responsibilities for the employer or have substantial discretion and little direct oversight in carrying out their tasks, and especially when they have been entrusted with the employer's trade secrets."

Page 991.   **Please add the following note.**

6.   Should it make a difference if the former employee sets out on her own or if she joins a different company? In Fox v. Millman, 45 A.3d 332 (N.J. 2012), the defendant had worked for Target Industries, a plastic bag manufacturer, as a sales representative. When her employment was terminated, she took her former employer's customer list with her, despite the confidentiality agreement that she had signed. When she was hired by a new employer, Polymer Plastics, shortly thereafter, she gave them the customer list, which she presented as her own. When questioned by Polymer, she denied that she was under any confidentiality agreement with Target. Polymer made no further inquiries into the matter, such as contacting Target, and subsequently used the list to generate substantial profits. Polymer Plastics admitted that they knew that Millman had previously worked at Target, and at no other plastic manufacturing company, and that Polymer themselves required all of their employees to sign confidentiality agreements. Nonetheless, the New Jersey Supreme Court held that an employer does not have a duty to inquire as to whether materials received from a new employee are bound by a prior confidentiality agreement.

B. POST-EMPLOYMENT RESTRICTIONS

1. FUTURE EMPLOYMENT

Page 997.   Please add to the end of Note 3.

Florida court decisions on this subject were overturned by the Florida Legislature. According to the current Florida statute, Fla. Stat. § 542.335(1)(c), the party seeking enforcement has to show that the covenant was necessary to protect its legitimate interests.

Page 998.   Please add to the end of Note 6.

In New York, both considerations—the risk that employers will be overly broad or overly cautious—are taken into account. Courts will allow for partial enforcement of overly broad restrictive covenants, but only if the employer demonstrates "an absence of overreaching, coercive use of dominant bargaining power, or other anti-competitive misconduct." BDO Seidman v. Hirshberg, 712 N.E. 2d 1220 (N.Y. 1999). This is essentially the position of the Restatement as well, see § 8.08 of the Restatement (Third) of Employment Law, approved by the American Law Institute in 2014.

Page 1001.   Please add the following note.

18. A recent article in the New York Times discussed the trend towards a proliferation of non-compete agreements, even amongst hair stylists and summer camp counselors. *Noncompete Clauses Increasingly Pop Up in Array of Jobs,* http://www.nytimes.com/2014/06/09/business/noncompete-clauses-increasingly-pop-up-in-array-of-jobs.html?_r=0. Although there may not be hard data regarding exactly how much the use of non-compete clauses has increased, a study conducted for The Wall Street Journal found that the number of published U.S. court decisions involving non-compete agreements rose 61% between 2002 and 2013. The study attributed this increase in large part to the increased enforcement of non-compete agreements against lower-level employees. *Litigation Over Noncompete Clauses Is Rising,* http://online.wsj.com/news/articles/SB1000142412788732 3446404579011501388418552.

2. TRADE SECRETS

Page 1010.   Please add the following notes.

9. In order to promote the utilization of inventions arising from federally supported research, the Bayh-Dole Act sets forth a three-tier system for patent rights ownership of "subject inventions." 35 U.S.C. §§ 200, 202–203 (2012). For "subject inventions," which include "any invention of the contractor conceived or first actually reduced to practice in the performance of work under a funding agreement," the Act awards patent rights first to the federal contractor, second to the federal government, and third to the inventor.

The National Institutes of Health provided Stanford with funding for research related to HIV measurement techniques. As part of his employment with Stanford, Dr. Mark Holodniy signed an agreement stating that he agreed to assign his interest in any invention to the university. Holodniy then began conducting research at Cetus, a California-based company, as part of his employment with Stanford. Holodniy signed an agreement stating that he was assigning his interest in any invention to Cetus. Later, Roche Molecular Systems, Inc. acquired Cetus and commercialized the HIV measurement technique developed by Holodniy and patented by Stanford.

Stanford sued Roche for patent infringement. The Supreme Court held that Roche had acquired an ownership interest in the patents from Holodniy's assignment of rights to Cetus and that this interest was not extinguished by the Bayh-Dole Act. The Court reasoned that when Congress had previously divested inventors of their rights in inventions, it had done so unambiguously. Here, the Act applied only to an "invention of the contractor"—for example, an invention which had been properly assigned to the contractor—and did not automatically divest an inventor of rights in an invention. Board of Trustees of the Leland Stanford Junior University v. Roche Molecular Systems, 131 S.Ct. 2188 (2011).

Note that the Court did not say that patent rights cannot be automatically assigned to the employer, only that the BDA should not be construed to have done so. In Alzheimer's Institute of America, Inc. v. Avid Radiopharmaceuticals, 952 F.Supp.2d 740 (E.D. Pa. 2011), a federal district court made note of this, holding that a University of South Florida employee automatically assigned the patent rights to his discovery of the Swedish Mutation, linked to Alzheimer's disease, to the university. That court noted that the Florida statute—as opposed to the BDA—unambiguously assigned ownership of patents earned by Florida universities' employees' to the universities.

10. Many states have blacklisting statutes aimed at preventing employers from exchanging information about past employees with the intent of preventing those employees from obtaining future employment within the industry. Do employer suits to enforce non-compete agreements and to protect trade secrets fall within the scope of a state's blacklisting statute? Indiana's blacklisting statute prohibits any company from permitting its agents to blacklist a discharged employee or "attempt[ing] by . . . any means whatever, to prevent such discharged employee, or any employee who may have voluntarily left said company's service, from obtaining employment with any other person, or company . . . " Ind. Code § 22–5–3–2 (2012). The Supreme Court of Indiana ruled that a suit to protect alleged trade secrets does not fall within the scope of the state's blacklisting statute because the language of the statute did not support such a construction and an employee's interests in being free from frivolous litigation were better served by other remedies and defenses including the common law torts of malicious prosecution and abuse of process, motions to dismiss under federal and state rules of civil procedure, and anti-trust laws. Loparex, LLC v. MPI Release Technologies, LLC, 964 N.E.2d 806 (Ind. 2012).

CHAPTER 12

UNEMPLOYMENT

B. PLANT CLOSINGS

Page 1048. Please add the following notes.

12. The Ninth Circuit held in Collins v. Gee West Seattle LLC that an employee who leaves his or her job because the business was closing has not "voluntarily departed" and may be eligible for WARN Act relief just like an employee who suffers an "employment loss": departure because of a business closing, therefore, is "generally not voluntary, but a consequence of the shutdown and must be considered a loss of employment . . ." Collins v. Gee West Seattle LLC, 631 F.3d 1001, 1006 (9th Cir. 2011). The court added that employees who would have retired, would have been discharged for cause, or voluntarily departed independently of a business closure are not considered to have suffered an employment loss.

13. Kohler Company hired temporary workers in the middle of a strike and then dismissed them at the strike's conclusion without providing WARN Act notice. The court of appeals held that only workers fired and not replaced count for determining whether there was a mass layoff. Here 123 temporary workers were laid off and 103 striking workers were rehired to their jobs so the layoff was of only twenty, not enough to satisfy the WARN Act numerosity requirement. Sanders v. Kohler Co., 641 F.3d 290 (8th Cir. 2011).

14. United Steel Workers sued U.S. Steel for failing to provide WARN Act notice prior to a mass layoff in a Keewatin, Minnesota plant in December 2008, at the height of the financial crisis. Held: the statute's exception for unforeseeable business circumstances prevents this from being a statutory violation. (Nearly all the workers were rehired by December 2009.) The court wrote: "U.S. Steel thought it could survive the economic downturn until the unprecedented effects on the steel industry manifested themselves in late November 2008, thus requiring immediate action . . ." United Steel Workers of America Local 2670 v. United States Steel Corp., 683 F.3d 882 (8th Cir. 2012).

C. DISPLACED WORKERS

Page 1050. Please add at the end of the note:

In 2014, New York's City Council amended the city's Human Rights Law to ban employment discrimination based on a job applicant's status as unemployed. A number of states have a similar law, but New York City's is the first to create a private right of action for employer violations.

D. UNEMPLOYMENT INSURANCE

3. LEGAL ISSUES IN UNEMPLOYMENT INSURANCE

b. SEPARATIONS

(ii) Discharge for Misconduct

Page 1090.   Please add the following note.

13. AnMed Health fired Pamela Crowe because she refused to comply with its policy requiring her to get a flu shot. Crowe's daughter had died at age 25, possibly from a disease triggered by a flu shot. Held: Crowe was not discharged for cause so is eligible for unemployment benefits. AnMed Health v. South Carolina Dep't of Employment & Workforce, 404 S.C. 224 (Ct. of App. 2013).

CHAPTER 13

RETIREMENT

B. THE PRIVATE PENSION SYSTEM

2. ERISA

c. FIDUCIARY DUTIES UNDER ERISA

Page 1155.   Please add the following note.

13. Concerning the equitable relief available when the fiduciary duty is violated, see Great-West Life & Annuity Ins. Co. v. Knudson, page 506 of casebook. See also CIGNA Corp. v. Amara, 131 S.Ct. 1866 (2011), holding that the Summary Plan Description is not an enforceable part of the ERISA plan; that ERISA does not give a federal court the authority to reform the terms of the plan as remedy; but that a court can grant "other appropriate equitable relief," including the benefits to which the plan says employees and prior employees are entitled.

14. Plaintiffs failed to establish that Morgan Stanley Investment Management knew or should have known that certain mortgage-backed securities were pension investments that failed to meet their fiduciary responsibilities. A decline in market price (stemming from the real-estate bubble and subsequent financial crisis) of a type of security does not, by itself, give rise to a reasonable inference that it was imprudent to purchase or hold that type of security." The court applied "the duty of prudence . . . 'measured according to the objective prudent person standard developed in the common law of trusts.' " Pension Benefit Guaranty Corp. on behalf of Saint Vincent Catholic Medical Centers Retirement Plan v. Morgan Stanley Investment Management Inc., 712 F.3d 705 (2d Cir. 2013) (2–1).

15. Plaintiffs stated a claim for violation of the ERISA duty of care when they alleged that Amgen violated its fiduciary duties to provide Amgen stock as an investment alternative for employees when Amgen officials knew that the stock's price was artificially inflated due to material omissions and misrepresentations concerning the safety of cancer drugs Amgen was selling. Harris v. Amgen, Inc., 738 F.3d 1026 (9th Cir. 2013).

d. ARBITRARY AND CAPRICIOUS DECISIONS BY PENSION FUND TRUSTEES

Page 1159.   Please add the following note.

8. If an ERISA plan grants interpretive discretion to the plan administrator, is that discretion revoked if the administrator makes a wrong decision? The Supreme Court said no, rejecting the "one strike and you're out" approach that some lower federal courts had applied. Chief Justice Roberts wrote: "People make mistakes. Even administrators of ERISA plans. That should come as no surprise, given that [ERISA] is an 'enormously complex and detailed statute' . . . " Justice Breyer, dissenting, said the administrator had made three mistakes, but he did not make the point that "three strikes and you're out." Conkright v. Frommert, 559 U.S. 506 (2010) (5–3).

e.   FEDERAL PREEMPTION OF STATE LAW

Page 1160. Please add the following note.

2.   A U.S. statute applying to federal employees allows an employee to name a beneficiary for life insurance proceeds. A Virginia statute revokes a beneficiary designation from a former spouse where there was a change in the decedent's marital status. Virginia, home of many federal employees, established a cause of action rendering the former spouse liable to give an insurance benefit back to the party (often presumably a latter spouse or offspring) who would have received the money had not the federal law preempted Virginia's attempt to regulate the payments. The Supreme Court held that Virginia cannot interfere in this way with rules laid down by the national government. Hillman v. Maretta, 133 S.Ct. 1943 (2013).

C. SOCIAL SECURITY RETIREMENT BENEFITS

3. GENDER DISCRIMINATION IN SOCIAL SECURITY

Page 1192.   Please add the following at the end of note 3.

In 2012, the Supreme Court decided that whether or not posthumously conceived children qualify for Social Security survivor benefits depends on state intestacy law. Although one court of appeals had held that children conceived in vitro after the father's death are "children" within the definition of Social Security Act, Gillett-Netting v. Barnhart, 371 F.3d 593 (9th Cir. 2004), the Supreme Court held that "it was nonetheless Congress' prerogative to legislate for the generality of cases. It did so here by employing eligibility to inherit under state intestacy law as a workable substitute for burdensome case-by-case determinations whether the child was, in fact, dependent on her father's earnings." The Court then applied Florida law and found that a posthumously conceived offspring was not eligible for survivor benefits. Astrue v. Capato ex rel. B.N.C., 132 S.Ct. 2021 (2012).

4. SOCIAL SECURITY POLICY

Page 1195.   Please add the following note.

3.   In their 2013 report, the trustees of Social Security reported that the system can pay full benefits until 2035, when it will be able to pay about three-fourths of promised benefits. The average current monthly benefit is about $1,250, thus about $15,000 per annum. Most people age 65 and older get two-thirds or more of their income from Social Security. As of 2004, Social Security replaced about 42 percent of the typical retiree's pre-retirement earnings. Planned changes now in the law will reduce that number to about 31 percent by 2030.

D. RETIREE HEALTH CARE

Page 1203.   Please add the following at the end of note 2.

But even though plans can be terminated unless they clearly say the contrary, when human resources personnel were not truthful with employees deciding whether to take a retirement deal, the company was obligated to reinstate those employees' retirement health benefits. In re Unisys Corp. Retiree Medical Benefits ERISA Litigation, 579 F.3d 220 (3d Cir. 2009).

Page 1204.   Please add the following note.

5. Constitutional issues have recently arisen as state and local governments have sought to reduce the budget consequences of generous retiree health benefits. The Michigan Court of Appeals found unconstitutional a 2010 statute requiring public school districts to withhold three percent of each employee's wages and remit the money as an "employer contribution" to the trust that funds retiree health care benefits. AFT Michigan v. State of Michigan, 825 N.W.2d 595 (Mich. Ct. App. 2012), review denied, 822 N.W.2d 226 (Mich. 2012).

Cincinnati reduced retiree healthcare benefits in 2009, adding a deductible of $200 and an out-of-pocket cap of $2,000. Held: these changes were not unconstitutional. Gamel v. City of Cincinnati, 983 N.E.2d 375 (Ohio Ct. App. 2012).

But see Savela v. City of Duluth, Minnesota, 806 N.W.2d 793 (Minn. 2011), holding that the collective bargaining agreements between Duluth and its employees guarantees to retirees the same health insurance benefits that the city provides to current employees.

Page 1208.   Please add this new case at the bottom of the page.

Reese v. CNH America LLC

694 F.3d 681 (6th Cir. 2012).

■ SUTTON, Circuit Judge.

In litigation, as in film, sequels rarely satisfy. This case is no exception. Three years ago, we remanded this dispute to the district court for factfinding necessary to determine whether CNH America's proposed modifications to its retiree healthcare benefits are reasonable. The district court did not reach the reasonableness question and did not create a factual record that would permit us to answer the question on our own. As a result, we reverse and remand for further proceedings.

Our previous opinion makes it unnecessary to recount the protracted history of this litigation. There, we considered two questions: "Did [CNH] in the 1998 CBA agree to provide health-care benefits to retirees and their spouses for life? And, if so, does the scope of this promise permit CNH to alter these benefits in the future?" In answering the first question, we rejected CNH's claim that the CBA permitted the company to terminate the benefits, holding that eligibility for lifetime healthcare benefits had "vested."

In answering the second question ("What does vesting mean in this setting?"), we rejected the suggestion that the *scope* of this commitment in the context of healthcare benefits, as opposed to pension benefits, meant that CNH could make no changes to the healthcare benefits provided to retirees. Unlike pension obligations, we explained, healthcare benefits cannot readily be monetized at retirement or for that matter practically fixed. Doctors and medical-insurance providers come and go. Medical plans change from year to year. And fixed, unalterable medical benefits at all events are not what retirees want. Nothing, indeed, would make employers happier than to know that vesting in the healthcare-benefits context meant the *same thing* as vesting in the pension context. For then, a company faced with the obligation could account for what it had spent on each employee for healthcare benefits on the day of retirement, then commit to spend no less through the end of the retiree's (and spouse's) life. Nor would most employers be troubled if this commitment, like most defined-benefit pension plans, increased based on inflation as measured by the consumer-price index. The reality is that, even though we have relied on language tying healthcare benefits to pension benefits as a basis for determining that healthcare benefits have vested, vesting in the context of healthcare benefits provides an evolving, not a fixed, benefit.

The rub for retirees and employers alike is that healthcare benefits—what is provided and what it costs—have not been remotely static in modern memory. The reason has little to do with traditional causes of inflation and more to do with the expansion of the benefit: the remarkable growth in modern life-saving and comfort-improving medical procedures, devices and drugs. New and better medical procedures arise while others become obsolete. And it is the rare medical innovation that costs *less* than the one it replaces. Retirees, quite understandably, do not want lifetime eligibility for the medical-insurance plan in place on the day of retirement, even if that means they would pay no premiums for it. They want eligibility for up-to-date medical-insurance plans, all with access to up-to-date medical procedures and drugs. Whatever else vesting in the healthcare context means, all appear to agree that it does not mean that beneficiaries receive a bundle of services fixed once and for all. Companies want the freedom to change health-insurance plans. And beneficiaries want something more than a fixed, unalterable bundle of services; they want coverage to account for new and better, yet likely more expensive, procedures and medications than the ones in existence at retirement.

All of this was borne out by the parties' implementation of the relevant collective bargaining agreements—in at least two respects. As explained in our prior opinion, the 1998 CBA "created a Managed Health Care Network Plan for past and future retirees. In other words, it imposed managed care on all of them, which represented a reduction in the effective choices of coverage available for all retirees and the coverage actually provided to many, if not most, of them." "Pre-1998 retirees thus saw their coverage downgraded in at least one respect: Unlike the prior plan, under which they could choose any doctor without suffering a financial penalty, they generally had to pay more for choosing an out-of-plan doctor." Other cases reach the same conclusion.

Also confirming that the parties did not perceive the relevant CBAs as establishing fixed, unalterable benefits was the passage of the

Medicare Prescription Drug, Improvement, and Modernization Act of 2003. No one batted an eye when the healthcare plans for which retirees were eligible were modified to account for the creation of Medicare Part D, the prescription-drug benefit for seniors.

In view of the distinction between the vesting of eligibility for a benefit and the scope of that commitment and in view of the parties' practice under the 1998 CBA of altering healthcare benefits under CBAs with materially identical language, we concluded that CNH could make "reasonable" changes to the healthcare plan covering eligible retirees. We listed three considerations: Does the modified plan provide benefits "reasonably commensurate" with the old plan? Are the proposed changes "reasonable in light of changes in health care"? And are the benefits "roughly consistent with the kinds of benefits provided to current employees"? * * *

The plaintiffs and the district court misread the panel opinion. In holding that "CNH . . . may reasonably alter" the plaintiffs' benefits, we recognized that CNH could alter them *on its own,* not as part of a new collective-bargaining process. * * *

To gauge whether CNH has proposed reasonable modifications to its healthcare benefits for retirees, the district court should consider whether the new plan provides benefits "reasonably commensurate" with the old plan, whether the changes are "reasonable in light of changes in health care" (including access to new medical procedures and prescriptions) and whether the benefits are "roughly consistent with the kinds of benefits provided to current employees." In doing so, the district court should take evidence on the following questions (and others it considers relevant to the reasonableness question):

- What is the average annual total out-of-pocket cost to retirees for their healthcare under the old plan (the 1998 Group Benefit Plan)? What is the equivalent figure for the new plan (the 2005 Group Benefit Plan)?

- What is the average per-beneficiary cost to CNH under the old plan? What is the equivalent figure for the new plan?

- What premiums, deductibles and copayments must retirees pay under the old plan? What about under the new plan?

- How fast are the retirees' out-of-pocket costs likely to grow under the old plan? What about under the new plan? How fast are CNH's per-beneficiary costs likely to grow under each?

- What difference (if any) is there between the quality of care available under the old and new plans?

- What difference (if any) is there between the new plan and the plans CNH makes available to current employees and people retiring today?

- How does the new plan compare to plans available to retirees and workers at companies similar to CNH and with demographically similar employees?

It is not lost on us that the reasonableness inquiry is a vexing one. But the difficulty of the inquiry flows at least in part from the vagueness of the commitment underlying this litigation. It is well to remember the language of the relevant commitment: "Employees who retire under the Case Corporation Pension Plan for Hourly Paid Employees after 7/1/94, or their surviving spouses eligible to receive a spouse's pension under the provisions of that Plan, shall be eligible for the Group benefits as described in the following paragraphs." What that means in the context of ever-changing medical-care developments, and ever-changing healthcare plans, is not easy. But if the parties cannot resolve the point on their own, we (and the district court) will do our best to resolve it for them. * * *

For these reasons, we reverse and remand for proceedings consistent with this opinion.

BERNICE B. DONALD, Circuit Judge, dissenting.

My review of the issues presented here leads me to the conclusion that the majority's approach to modifying the scope of the retirees' vested health care benefits, both past and present, involves a misapprehension of the relevant law. While reasonableness is a common standard in the law, I cannot agree that resorting to what is reasonable provides the proper analytical framework in the instant case. When faced with contract terms that result in unanticipated consequences for the parties, courts are naturally tempted to play the role of arbiter and seek to resolve the case equitably. This Court, however, is one of law and not equity. Because the resolution of this case, as well as the prior appeal, represents a departure from current law, I respectfully dissent.

When affirming in part the district court's first grant of summary judgment to Plaintiffs in the instant dispute, this Court held that the retirees "have a vested right to receive health care benefits for life." On this issue, *Reese I* was consistent with prior decisions of this Court holding that when an employer ties eligibility for welfare benefits to eligibility for pension benefits those welfare benefits vest for life.

At the same time, the Court reversed the district court's holding that "these [vested health care] benefits must be maintained precisely at the level provided for in the 1998 CBA." The Court remanded to the district court to determine "how and in what circumstances CNH may alter such benefits." Upon close reexamination, I have determined that our holding that CNH may *unilaterally* alter Appellees' vested health care benefits was in error, and the majority's resolution of the case fails to correct this error. * * *

Several decisions of this Court, as well as Supreme Court precedent, express the principle that, once a retiree's health care benefits have vested for life, an employer's unilateral modification of the scope of those benefits is a violation of the Labor Management Relations Act....The retiree, moreover, would have a federal remedy under § 301 of the Labor Management Relations Act for breach of contract if his benefits were unilaterally changed." * * *

Thus, clearly established precedent in this Circuit leads to the conclusion that, because retirees' health care benefits vested for life, the level of those benefits must be deemed vested in scope and *not* subject to unilateral modification by CNH. Accordingly, the district court correctly applied the law of this Circuit when it held on remand that "even if changes can be made to retiree vested health care benefits, those changes must be reached through negotiation and agreement between the union and the employer." * * *

I recognize that the terms of the 1998 CBA, as interpreted according to Sixth Circuit precedent, pose a fundamental problem for the employer: how to fulfill its open-ended obligation to provide the health care benefits described in the CBA in spite of the rapid change and growth in the health care and health insurance industries. While this case presents a difficult choice between diametrically opposed interpretations of the 1998 CBA, it is the parties to the contract—not the court—who bear the burden of solving this dilemma. Presumably the parties have a shared interest in reaching an accommodation which ensures the retirees the continuity of health care coverage to which they are contractually entitled without bankrupting the employer or obligating it to provide services which are no longer appropriate. The Court's role in this context is to underscore that such an accommodation cannot be imposed by one party on the other, or by the court.

* * *

QUESTIONS

Should non-union retirees have a voice when their health benefits are being changed? And can unions be fair to retirees when the interests of the retirees and of the current workers are so different? Is the judiciary the right decision-maker when the goal is "reasonable" decisions, the tradeoffs are difficult, and the circumstances and context are changing rapidly? Indeed, should companies stop offering retiree health benefits and put those former employees in Medicare with most Americans over age 65?

PART I

BACKGROUND

CHAPTER 1

WORK AND LAW

A. WORK AND SOCIETY

Page 6. Please delete the Greenhouse reading and replace with the following:

Nicholas Kristof, It's Now the Canadian Dream[*]

New York Times, May 15, 2014, A25.

It was in 1931 that the historian James Truslow Adams coined the phrase "the American dream."

The American dream is not just a yearning for affluence, Adams said, but also for the chance to overcome barriers and social class, to become the best that we can be. Adams acknowledged that the United States didn't fully live up to that ideal, but he argued that America came closer than anywhere else.

Adams was right at the time, and for decades. When my father, an eastern European refugee, reached France after World War II, he was determined to continue to the United States because it was less class bound, more meritocratic and offered more opportunity.

Yet today the American dream has derailed, partly because of growing inequality. Or maybe the American dream has just swapped citizenship, for now it is more likely to be found in Canada or Europe— and a central issue in this year's political campaigns should be how to repatriate it.

A report last month in The Times by David Leonhardt and Kevin Quealy noted that the American middle class is no longer the richest in the world, with Canada apparently pulling ahead in median after-tax income. Other countries in Europe are poised to overtake us as well.

In fact, the discrepancy is arguably even greater. Canadians receive essentially free health care, while Americans pay for part of their health care costs with after-tax dollars. Meanwhile, the American worker toils, on average, 4.6 percent more hours than a Canadian worker, 21 percent more hours than a French worker and an astonishing 28 percent more hours than a German worker, according to data from the Organization for Economic Cooperation and Development.

Canadians and Europeans also live longer, on average, than Americans do. Their children are less likely to die than ours. American women are twice as likely to die as a result of pregnancy or childbirth as Canadian women. And, while our universities are still the best in the world, children in other industrialized countries, on average, get a better education than ours. Most sobering of all: A recent O.E.C.D.

---

report found that for people aged 16 to 24, Americans ranked last among rich countries in numeracy and technological proficiency.

Economic mobility is tricky to measure, but several studies show that a child born in the bottom 20 percent economically is less likely to rise to the top in America than in Europe. A Danish child is twice as likely to rise as an American child.

When our futures are determined to a significant extent at birth, we've reverted to the feudalism that our ancestors fled.

"Equality of opportunity—the 'American dream'—has always been a cherished American ideal," Joseph Stiglitz, the Nobel-winning economist at Columbia University, noted in a recent speech. "But data now show that this is a myth: America has become the advanced country not only with the highest level of inequality, but one of those with the least equality of opportunity."

Consider that the American economy has, over all, grown more quickly than France's. But so much of the growth has gone to the top 1 percent that the bottom 99 percent of French people have done better than the bottom 99 percent of Americans.

Three data points:

- The top 1 percent in America now own assets worth more than those held by the entire bottom 90 percent.

- The six Walmart heirs are worth as much as the bottom 41 percent of American households put together.

- The top six hedge fund managers and traders averaged more than $2 billion each in earnings last year, partly because of the egregious "carried interest" tax break. President Obama has been unable to get financing for universal prekindergarten; this year's proposed federal budget for pre-K for all, so important to our nation's future, would be a bit more than a single month's earnings for those six tycoons.

* * *

It's time to bring the American dream home from exile.

NOTES AND QUESTIONS

1.   The current level of income and wealth inequality in the United States is comparable to the period at the beginning of the twentieth century, before enactment of the federal income tax, the Fair Labor Standards Act and state minimum wage laws, Social Security and income support for the elderly, unionization and collective bargaining, the G.I. Bill and widespread access to higher education, and other laws and policies that fostered development of the middle class. One of the rationalizations for American laissez-faire capitalism and its "rugged individualism" social policy has been that, even though there are wide gaps between the "haves" and "have nots," there is vertical social mobility. In other words, through talent and hard work, in a few years or a few generations (especially for immigrants), an individual or his or her children can go from the bottom to the top of the

income ladder. What effect does the new "locked in" nature of socioeconomic position have on America's social narrative?

2. Among the recent scholarship on the issue of economic inequality are Thomas Piketty, Capital in the Twenty-first Century (2014) and Joseph E. Stigletz, The Price of Inequality: How Today's Divided Society Endangers Our Future (2013).

3. For the purposes of this course, there are two related questions. First, how, if at all, have labor and employment laws contributed to the rising inequality? Second, how, if at all, have labor and employment laws been affected by the rising inequality?

PART II

ESTABLISHING THE EMPLOYMENT RELATIONSHIP

CHAPTER 3

THE HIRING PROCESS

B. THE LABOR POOL

1. UNDOCUMENTED ALIENS

Page 73. **Please add the following case before Residency Requirements.**

Chamber of Commerce v. Whiting

131 S.Ct. 1968 (2011).

■ CHIEF JUSTICE ROBERTS delivered the opinion of the Court, except as to Parts II–B and III–B.

Federal immigration law expressly preempts "any State or local law imposing civil or criminal sanctions (other than through licensing and similar laws) upon those who employ . . . unauthorized aliens." 8 U.S.C. § 1324a(h)(2). A recently enacted Arizona statute—the Legal Arizona Workers Act—provides that the licenses of state employers that knowingly or intentionally employ unauthorized aliens may be, and in certain circumstances must be, suspended or revoked. The law also requires that all Arizona employers use a federal electronic verification system to confirm that the workers they employ are legally authorized workers. The question presented is whether federal immigration law preempts those provisions of Arizona law. Because we conclude that the State's licensing provisions fall squarely within the federal statute's savings clause and that the Arizona regulation does not otherwise conflict with federal law, we hold that the Arizona law is not preempted.

In 1952, Congress enacted the Immigration and Nationality Act (INA). That statute established a "comprehensive federal statutory scheme for regulation of immigration and naturalization" and set "the terms and conditions of admission to the country and the subsequent treatment of aliens lawfully in the country." De Canas v. Bica, 424 U.S. 351, 353, 359 (1976).

In the years following the enactment of the INA, several States took action to prohibit the employment of individuals living within state borders who were not lawful residents of the United States.

* * *

We first addressed the interaction of federal immigration law and state laws dealing with the employment of unauthorized aliens in *De Canas*. In that case, we recognized that the "[p]ower to regulate immigration is unquestionably . . . a federal power." At the same time, however, we noted that the "States possess broad authority under their police powers to regulate the employment relationship to protect workers within the State," that "prohibit[ing] the knowing employment

. . . of persons not entitled to lawful residence in the United States, let alone to work here, is certainly within the mainstream of [the State's] police power," and that the Federal Government had "at best" expressed "a peripheral concern with [the] employment of illegal entrants" at that point in time. As a result, we declined to hold that a state law assessing civil fines for the employment of unauthorized aliens was preempted by federal immigration law.

Ten years after *De Canas*, Congress enacted the Immigration Reform and Control Act (IRCA). IRCA makes it "unlawful for a person or other entity . . . to hire, or to recruit or refer for a fee, for employment in the United States an alien knowing the alien is an unauthorized alien." 8 U.S.C. § 1324a(a)(1)(A). IRCA defines an "unauthorized alien" as an alien who is not "lawfully admitted for permanent residence" or not otherwise authorized by the Attorney General to be employed in the United States.

* * *

IRCA also restricts the ability of States to combat employment of unauthorized workers. The Act expressly preempts "any State or local law imposing civil or criminal sanctions (other than through licensing and similar laws) upon those who employ, or recruit or refer for a fee for employment, unauthorized aliens." Under that provision, state laws imposing civil fines for the employment of unauthorized workers like the one we upheld in *De Canas* are now expressly preempted.

* * *

Acting against this statutory and historical background, several States have recently enacted laws attempting to impose sanctions for the employment of unauthorized aliens through, among other things, "licensing and similar laws." Arizona is one of them. The Legal Arizona Workers Act of 2007 allows Arizona courts to suspend or revoke the licenses necessary to do business in the State if an employer knowingly or intentionally employs an unauthorized alien.

Under the Arizona law, if an individual files a complaint alleging that an employer has hired an unauthorized alien, the attorney general or the county attorney first verifies the employee's work authorization with the Federal Government pursuant to 8 U.S.C. § 1373(c). Section 1373(c) provides that the Federal Government "shall respond to an inquiry by a" State "seeking to verify or ascertain the citizenship or immigration status of any individual . . . by providing the requested verification or status information." The Arizona law expressly prohibits state, county, or local officials from attempting "to independently make a final determination on whether an alien is authorized to work in the United States." If the § 1373(c) inquiry reveals that a worker is an unauthorized alien, the attorney general or the county attorney must notify United States Immigration and Customs Enforcement officials, notify local law enforcement, and bring an action against the employer.

When a complaint is brought against an employer under Arizona law, "the court shall consider only the federal government's determination pursuant to" 8 U.S.C. § 1373(c) in "determining whether an employee is an unauthorized alien." Good-faith compliance with the federal I–9 process provides employers prosecuted by the State with an affirmative defense.

A first instance of "knowingly employ[ing] an unauthorized alien" requires that the court order the employer to terminate the employment of all unauthorized aliens and file quarterly reports on all new hires for a probationary period of three years. The court may also "order the appropriate agencies to suspend all licenses . . . that are held by the employer for [a period] not to exceed ten business days." A second knowing violation requires that the adjudicating court "permanently revoke all licenses that are held by the employer specific to the business location where the unauthorized alien performed work."

For a first intentional violation, the court must order the employer to terminate the employment of all unauthorized aliens and file quarterly reports on all new hires for a probationary period of five years. The court must also suspend all the employer's licenses for a minimum of 10 days. A second intentional violation requires the permanent revocation of all business licenses.

With respect to both knowing and intentional violations, a violation qualifies as a "second violation" only if it occurs at the same business location as the first violation, during the time that the employer is already on probation for a violation at that location.

The Arizona law also requires that "every employer, after hiring an employee, shall verify the employment eligibility of the employee" by using E-Verify. "[P]roof of verifying the employment authorization of an employee through the e-verify program creates a rebuttable presumption that an employer did not knowingly employ an unauthorized alien."

* * *

The Court of Appeals affirmed the District Court in all respects, holding that Arizona's law was a " 'licensing and similar law[ ]' " falling within IRCA's savings clause and that none of the state law's challenged provisions was "expressly or impliedly preempted by federal policy."

II.

The Chamber of Commerce argues that Arizona's law is expressly preempted by IRCA's text and impliedly preempted because it conflicts with federal law. We address each of the Chamber's arguments in turn.

A.

* * *

IRCA expressly preempts States from imposing "civil or criminal sanctions" on those who employ unauthorized aliens, "other than through licensing and similar laws." The Arizona law, on its face, purports to impose sanctions through licensing laws. The state law authorizes state courts to suspend or revoke an employer's business licenses if that employer knowingly or intentionally employs an unauthorized alien. The Arizona law defines "license" as "any agency permit, certificate, approval, registration, charter or similar form of authorization that is required by law and that is issued by any agency for the purposes of operating a business in" the State. That definition largely parrots the definition of "license" that Congress codified in the Administrative Procedure Act.

Apart from that general definition, the Arizona law specifically includes within its definition of "license" documents such as articles of incorporation, certificates of partnership, and grants of authority to foreign companies to transact business in the State. These examples have clear counterparts in the APA definition just quoted.

A license is "a right or permission granted in accordance with law . . . to engage in some business or occupation, to do some act, or to engage in some transaction which but for such license would be unlawful." Webster's Third New International Dictionary 1304 (2002). Articles of incorporation and certificates of partnership allow the formation of legal entities and permit them as such to engage in business and transactions "which but for such" authorization "would be unlawful." As for state-issued authorizations for foreign businesses to operate within a State, we have repeatedly referred to those as "licenses." Moreover, even if a law regulating articles of incorporation, partnership certificates, and the like is not itself a "licensing law," it is at the very least "similar" to a licensing law, and therefore comfortably within the savings clause.

The Chamber and the United States as amicus argue that the Arizona law is not a "licensing" law because it operates only to suspend and revoke licenses rather than to grant them. Again, this construction of the term runs contrary to the definition that Congress itself has codified. It is also contrary to common sense. There is no basis in law, fact, or logic for deeming a law that grants licenses a licensing law, but a law that suspends or revokes those very licenses something else altogether.

* * *

B.

As an alternative to its express preemption argument, the Chamber contends that Arizona's law is impliedly preempted because it conflicts with federal law. At its broadest level, the Chamber's argument is that Congress "intended the federal system to be exclusive," and that any state system therefore necessarily conflicts with federal law. But Arizona's procedures simply implement the sanctions that Congress expressly allowed Arizona to pursue through licensing laws. Given that Congress specifically preserved such authority for the States, it stands to reason that Congress did not intend to prevent the States from using appropriate tools to exercise that authority.

And here Arizona went the extra mile in ensuring that its law closely tracks IRCA's provisions in all material respects. The Arizona law begins by adopting the federal definition of who qualifies as an "unauthorized alien."

Not only that, the Arizona law expressly provides that state investigators must verify the work authorization of an allegedly unauthorized alien with the Federal Government, and "shall not attempt to independently make a final determination on whether an alien is authorized to work in the United States." What is more, a state court "shall consider only the federal government's determination" when deciding "whether an employee is an unauthorized alien." As a result, there can by definition be no conflict between state and federal law as to worker authorization, either at the investigatory or adjudicatory stage.

* * *

The Chamber and JUSTICE BREYER assert that employers will err on the side of discrimination rather than risk the " 'business death penalty' " by "hiring unauthorized workers." That is not the choice. License termination is not an available sanction simply for "hiring unauthorized workers." Only far more egregious violations of the law trigger that consequence. The Arizona law covers only knowing or intentional violations. The law's permanent licensing sanctions do not come into play until a second knowing or intentional violation at the same business location, and only if the second violation occurs while the employer is still on probation for the first. These limits ensure that licensing sanctions are imposed only when an employer's conduct fully justifies them. An employer acting in good faith need have no fear of the sanctions.

As the Chamber points out, IRCA has its own anti-discrimination provisions, Arizona law certainly does nothing to displace those. Other federal laws, and Arizona anti-discrimination laws, provide further protection against employment discrimination—and strong incentive for employers not to discriminate.

All that is required to avoid sanctions under the Legal Arizona Workers Act is to refrain from knowingly or intentionally violating the employment law. Employers enjoy safe harbors from liability when they use the I–9 system and E-Verify—as Arizona law requires them to do. The most rational path for employers is to obey the law—both the law barring the employment of unauthorized aliens and the law prohibiting discrimination—and there is no reason to suppose that Arizona employers will choose not to do so.

As with any piece of legislation, Congress did indeed seek to strike a balance among a variety of interests when it enacted IRCA. Part of that balance, however, involved allocating authority between the Federal Government and the States. The principle that Congress adopted in doing so was not that the Federal Government can impose large sanctions, and the States only small ones. IRCA instead preserved state authority over a particular category of sanctions—those imposed "through licensing and similar laws."

* * *

III.

* * *

Because Arizona's unauthorized alien employment law fits within the confines of IRCA's savings clause and does not conflict with federal immigration law, the judgment of the United States Court of Appeals for the Ninth Circuit is affirmed.

It is so ordered.

■ JUSTICE KAGAN took no part in the consideration or decision of this case.

■ JUSTICE BREYER, with whom JUSTICE GINSBURG joins, dissenting.

* * *

Arizona calls its state statute a "licensing law," and the statute uses the word "licensing." But the statute strays beyond the bounds of the federal licensing exception, for it defines "license" to include articles of incorporation and partnership certificates, indeed virtually every state-law authorization for any firm, corporation, or partnership to do business in the State. Congress did not intend its "licensing" language to create so broad an exemption, for doing so would permit States to eviscerate the federal Act's pre-emption provision, indeed to subvert the Act itself, by undermining Congress' efforts (1) to protect lawful workers from national-origin-based discrimination and (2) to protect lawful employers against erroneous prosecution or punishment.

* * *

First, the state statute seriously threatens the federal Act's antidiscriminatory objectives by radically skewing the relevant penalties. For example, in the absence of the Arizona statute, an Arizona employer who intentionally hires an unauthorized alien for the second time would risk a maximum penalty of $6,500. But the Arizona statute subjects that same employer (in respect to the same two incidents) to mandatory, permanent loss of the right to do business in Arizona—a penalty that Arizona's Governor has called the "business death penalty." At the same time, the state law leaves the other side of the punishment balance—the antidiscrimination side—unchanged.

This is no idle concern. Despite the federal Act's efforts to prevent discriminatory practices, there is evidence that four years after it had become law, discrimination was a serious problem. In 1990, the General Accounting Office identified "widespread discrimination . . . as a result of" the Act. Sixteen percent of employers in Los Angeles admitted that they applied the I–9 requirement "only to foreign-looking or foreign-sounding persons," and 22 percent of Texas employers reported that they "began a practice to (1) hire only persons born in the United States or (2) not hire persons with temporary work eligibility documents" because of the Act. If even the federal Act (with its carefully balanced penalties) can result in some employers discriminating, how will employers behave when erring on the side of discrimination leads only to relatively small fines, while erring on the side of hiring unauthorized workers leads to the "business death penalty"?

Second, Arizona's law subjects lawful employers to increased burdens and risks of erroneous prosecution. In addition to the Arizona law's severely burdensome sanctions, the law's procedures create enforcement risks not present in the federal system. The federal Act creates one centralized enforcement scheme, run by officials versed in immigration law and with access to the relevant federal documents. The upshot is an increased likelihood that federal officials (or the employer) will discover whether adverse information flows from an error-prone source and that they will proceed accordingly, thereby diminishing the likelihood that burdensome proceedings and liability reflect documentary mistakes.

Contrast the enforcement system that Arizona's statute creates. Any citizen of the State can complain (anonymously or otherwise) to the state attorney general (or any county attorney), who then "shall investigate," and, upon a determination that that the "complaint is not false and frivolous . . . shall notify the appropriate county attorney to bring an action." This mandatory language, the lower standard ("not frivolous" instead of "substantial"), and the removal of immigration officials from the state screening process (substituting numerous, elected county attorneys) increase the likelihood that suspicious circumstances will lead to prosecutions and liability of employers—even where more careful investigation would have revealed that there was no violation.

Why would Congress, after deliberately limiting ordinary penalties to the range of a few thousand dollars per illegal worker, want to permit far more drastic state penalties that would directly and mandatorily destroy entire businesses? Why would Congress, after carefully balancing sanctions to avoid encouraging discrimination, want to allow States to destroy that balance? Why would Congress, after creating detailed procedural protections for employers, want to allow States to undermine them? Why would Congress want to write into an express pre-emption provision—a provision designed to prevent States from undercutting federal statutory objectives—an exception that could so easily destabilize its efforts? The answer to these questions is that Congress would not have wanted to do any of these things. And that fact indicates that the majority's reading of the licensing exception—a reading that would allow what Congress sought to forbid—is wrong.

■ JUSTICE SOTOMAYOR, dissenting.

* * *

Congress made explicit its intent that IRCA be enforced uniformly. IRCA declares that "[i]t is the sense of the Congress that . . . the immigration laws of the United States should be enforced vigorously and uniformly." Congress structured IRCA's provisions in a number of ways to accomplish this goal of uniform enforcement.

First, and most obviously, Congress expressly displaced the myriad state laws that imposed civil and criminal sanctions on employers who hired unauthorized aliens. Congress could not have made its intent to preempt state and local laws imposing civil or criminal sanctions any more " 'clear [or] manifest.' "

Second, Congress centralized in the Federal Government enforcement of IRCA's prohibition on the knowing employment of unauthorized aliens. IRCA instructs the Attorney General to designate a specialized federal agency unit whose "primary duty" will be to prosecute violations of IRCA. IRCA also instructs the Attorney General to establish procedures for receiving complaints, investigating complaints having "a substantial probability of validity," and investigating other violations.

* * *

Third, Congress provided persons "adversely affected" by an agency order with a right of review in the federal courts of appeals. In this way, Congress ensured that administrative orders finding violations of IRCA would be reviewed by federal judges with experience adjudicating immigration-related matters.

Fourth, Congress created a uniquely federal system by which employers must verify the work authorization status of new hires. Under this system, an employer must attest under penalty of perjury on a form designated by the Attorney General (the I–9 form) that it has examined enumerated identification documents to verify that a new hire is not an unauthorized alien. Good-faith compliance with this verification requirement entitles an employer to an affirmative defense if charged with violating IRCA. Notably, however, IRCA prohibits use of the I–9 form for any purpose other than enforcement of IRCA and various provisions of federal criminal law. Use of the I–9 form is thus limited to federal proceedings, as the majority acknowledges.

Finally, Congress created no mechanism for States to access information regarding an alien's work authorization status for purposes of enforcing state prohibitions on the employment of unauthorized aliens. The relevant sections of IRCA make no provision for the sharing of work authorization information between federal and state authorities even though access to that information would be critical to a State's ability to determine whether an employer has employed an unauthorized alien. In stark contrast, a separate provision in the same title of IRCA creates a verification system by which States can ascertain the immigration status of aliens applying for benefits under programs such as Medicaid and the food stamp program.

* * *

NOTE

1.   In a related case, Arizona v. United States, 132 S.Ct. 2492 (2012), the Supreme Court declared unconstitutional three provisions of another Arizona immigration law, the Support Our Law Enforcement and Safe Neighborhoods Act. The Court held that federal law preempted the following provisions: (1) making it a state misdemeanor to fail to comply with federal alien-registration requirements; (2) making it a state misdemeanor for an unauthorized alien to seek or engage in work in the state; and (3) authorizing state and local officers to arrest without a warrant a person the officer has probable cause to believe has committed an act that makes the person "removable" from the United States. The Court, however, reversed an injunction prohibiting enforcement of a provision requiring officers making a stop, detention, or arrest to verify the person's immigration status.

4. HIRING THE UNEMPLOYED

According to the Bureau of Labor Statistics, as of April 2012, the mean duration of unemployment in the United States was 39.1 weeks, and the percentage of individuals unemployed for 27 or more weeks was 41.3%. www.bls.gov/news.release/empsit.t12.htm. The figures vary according to several demographic factors, including gender, race, and age. For example, workers age 55–64 have a much higher duration of unemployment.

Long-term unemployed workers (those out of work 27 or more weeks) have a more difficult time obtaining interviews or job offers for various reasons. Individuals who have been out of the work force for an extended period of time may lose some of their skills, lose touch with their network of contacts, or may fail to interview well because of numerous prior rejections. There are also some employers that simply refuse to consider any long-term unemployed individuals. According to one review of job vacancy postings on Monster.com, CareerBuilder, and Craigslist, hundreds of employers said they would only consider or "strongly prefer" currently employed or recently unemployed individuals. Catherine Rampell, The Help-Wanted Sign Comes With a Frustrating Asterisk, N.Y. Times July 26, 2011, at B1. Apparently, these employers believe that individuals out of work for extended periods of time are less capable, productive, or desirable.

Under current law, the most likely legal challenges to such employer practices would be "disparate impact" claims for age or race discrimination, under the ADEA and Title VII, but these types of cases are difficult to prove. See Chapter 4. At the state level, New Jersey was the first state to prohibit employment notices that bar unemployed workers from applying. At the federal level, the Obama Administration's "jobs bill" would have prohibited employers with 15 or more employees from discriminating against job applicants because they are unemployed. No action was taken on the bill.

Legislation has been introduced at the federal, state, and local levels to address this issue. At the federal level, the Fair Employment Opportunity Act of 2011, S. 1471, H.R. 2501, would have prohibited employers with 15 or more employees from discriminating against job applicants because they are unemployed. At the state level, legislation has been enacted in New Jersey, Oregon, and the District of Columbia prohibiting employers from listing "current employment" as a requirement in a job advertisement. In California, Governor Brown vetoed similar legislation because he was unhappy with certain amendments to the bill. At the city level, the New York City Council enacted legislation in 2013, over the veto of Mayor Bloomberg, that permits unemployed individuals who believe they were subject to discrimination because they were out of work to sue prospective employers for compensatory and punitive damages, and to obtain attorney fees.

C. APPLICATIONS, INTERVIEWS, AND REFERENCES

1. APPLICATIONS

Page 82.   Please add the following case after note 2.

NASA v. Nelson
131 S.Ct. 746 (2011).

■ JUSTICE ALITO delivered the opinion of the Court.

In two cases decided more than 30 years ago, this Court referred broadly to a constitutional privacy "interest in avoiding disclosure of personal matters." Whalen v. Roe, 429 U.S. 589, 599–600 (1977); Nixon v. Administrator of General Services, 433 U.S. 425, 457 (1977). Respondents in this case, federal contract employees at a Government laboratory, claim that two parts of a standard employment background investigation violate their rights under *Whalen* and *Nixon*. Respondents challenge a section of a form questionnaire that asks employees about treatment or counseling for recent illegal-drug use. They also object to certain open-ended questions on a form sent to employees' designated references.

We assume, without deciding, that the Constitution protects a privacy right of the sort mentioned in *Whalen* and *Nixon*. We hold, however, that the challenged portions of the Government's background check do not violate this right in the present case. The Government's interests as employer and proprietor in managing its internal operations, combined with the protections against public dissemination provided by the Privacy Act of 1974, 5 U.S.C. § 552a, satisfy any "interest in avoiding disclosure" that may "arguably ha[ve] its roots in the Constitution."

The National Aeronautics and Space Administration (NASA) is an independent federal agency charged with planning and conducting the Government's "space activities." NASA's workforce numbers in the tens of thousands of employees. While many of these workers are federal civil servants, a substantial majority are employed directly by Government contractors. Contract employees play an important role in NASA's mission, and their duties are functionally equivalent to those performed by civil servants.

One NASA facility, the Jet Propulsion Laboratory (JPL) in Pasadena, California, is staffed exclusively by contract employees. NASA owns JPL, but the California Institute of Technology (Cal Tech) operates the facility under a Government contract. JPL is the lead NASA center for deep-space robotics and communications. Most of this country's unmanned space missions—from the Explorer 1 satellite in 1958 to the Mars Rovers of today—have been developed and run by JPL. JPL scientists contribute to NASA earth-observation and technology-development projects. Many JPL employees also engage in pure scientific research on topics like "the star formation history of the universe" and "the fundamental properties of quantum fluids."

Twenty-eight JPL employees are respondents here. Many of them have worked at the lab for decades, and none has ever been the subject of a Government background investigation. At the time when respondents were hired, background checks were standard only for federal civil servants. In some instances, individual contracts required background checks for the employees of federal contractors, but no blanket policy was in place.

The Government has recently taken steps to eliminate this two-track approach to background investigations. In 2004, a recommendation by the 9/11 Commission prompted the President to order new, uniform identification standards for "[f]ederal employees," including "contractor employees." The Department of Commerce implemented this directive by mandating that contract employees with long-term access to federal facilities complete a standard background check, typically the National Agency Check with Inquiries (NACI).

An October 2007 deadline was set for completion of these investigations. In January 2007, NASA modified its contract with Cal Tech to reflect the new background-check requirement. JPL management informed employees that anyone failing to complete the NACI process by October 2007 would be denied access to JPL and would face termination by Cal Tech.

The NACI process has long been the standard background investigation for prospective civil servants. The process begins when the applicant or employee fills out a form questionnaire. Employees who work in "non-sensitive" positions (as all respondents here do) complete Standard Form 85 (SF–85).

Most of the questions on SF–85 seek basic biographical information: name, address, prior residences, education, employment history, and personal and professional references. The form also asks about citizenship, selective-service registration, and military service. The last question asks whether the employee has "used, possessed, supplied, or manufactured illegal drugs" in the last year. If the answer is yes, the employee must provide details, including information about "any treatment or counseling received." A "truthful response," the form notes, cannot be used as evidence against the employee in a criminal proceeding. The employee must certify that all responses on the form are true and must sign a release authorizing the Government to obtain personal information from schools, employers, and others during its investigation.

Once a completed SF–85 is on file, the "agency check" and "inquiries" begin. The Government runs the information provided by the employee through FBI and other federal-agency databases. It also sends out form questionnaires to the former employers, schools, landlords, and references listed on SF–85. The particular form at issue in this case—the Investigative Request for Personal Information, Form 42—goes to the employee's former landlords and references.

Form 42 is a two-page document that takes about five minutes to complete. It explains to the reference that "[y]our name has been provided by" a particular employee or applicant to help the Government determine that person's "suitability for employment or a security clearance." After several preliminary questions about the extent of the reference's associations with the employee, the form asks if the reference has "any reason to question" the employee's "honesty or trustworthiness." It also asks if the reference knows of any "adverse information" concerning the employee's "violations of the law," "financial integrity," "abuse of alcohol and/or drugs," "mental or emotional stability," "general behavior or conduct," or "other matters." If "yes" is checked for any of these categories, the form calls for an explanation in the space below. That space is also available for providing "additional information" ("derogatory" or "favorable") that may bear on "suitability for government employment or a security clearance."

All responses to SF–85 and Form 42 are subject to the protections of the Privacy Act. The Act authorizes the Government to keep records pertaining to an individual only when they are "relevant and necessary" to an end "required to be accomplished" by law. Individuals are permitted to access their records and request amendments to them. Subject to certain exceptions, the Government may not disclose records pertaining to an individual without that individual's written consent.

About two months before the October 2007 deadline for completing the NACI, respondents brought this suit, claiming, as relevant here, that the background-check process violates a constitutional right to informational privacy. The District Court denied respondents' motion for a preliminary injunction, but the Ninth Circuit granted an injunction pending appeal, and later reversed the District Court's order. The court held that portions of both SF–85 and Form 42 are likely unconstitutional and should be preliminarily enjoined.

* * *

As noted, respondents contend that portions of SF–85 and Form 42 violate their "right to informational privacy." This Court considered a similar claim in *Whalen*, which concerned New York's practice of collecting "the names and addresses of all persons" prescribed dangerous drugs with both "legitimate and illegitimate uses." In discussing that claim, the Court said that "[t]he cases sometimes characterized as protecting 'privacy'" actually involved "at least two different kinds of interests": one, an "interest in avoiding disclosure of personal matters"; the other, an interest in "making certain kinds of important decisions" free from government interference. The patients who brought suit in *Whalen* argued that New York's statute "threaten[ed] to impair" both their "nondisclosure" interests and their interests in making healthcare decisions independently. The Court, however, upheld the statute as a "reasonable exercise of New York's broad police powers."

Whalen acknowledged that the disclosure of "private information" to the State was an "unpleasant invasion of privacy," but the Court pointed out that the New York statute contained "security provisions" that protected against "public disclosure" of patients' information. This sort of "statutory or regulatory duty to avoid unwarranted disclosures" of "accumulated private data" was sufficient, in the Court's view, to protect a privacy interest that "arguably ha[d] its roots in the Constitution." The Court thus concluded that the statute did not violate "any right or liberty protected by the Fourteenth Amendment."

Four months later, the Court referred again to a constitutional "interest in avoiding disclosure." Former President Nixon brought a challenge to the Presidential Recordings and Materials Preservation Act, a statute that required him to turn over his presidential papers and tape recordings for archival review and screening. In a section of the opinion entitled "Privacy," the Court addressed a combination of claims that the review required by this Act violated the former President's "Fourth and Fifth Amendmen[t]" rights. The Court rejected those challenges after concluding that the Act at issue, like the statute in *Whalen*, contained protections against "undue dissemination of private materials." Indeed, the Court observed that the former President's claim was "weaker" than the one "found wanting . . . in *Whalen*," as the Government was required to return immediately all "purely private papers and recordings" identified by the archivists. Citing Fourth Amendment precedent, the Court also stated that the public interest in preserving presidential papers outweighed any "legitimate expectation of privacy" that the former President may have enjoyed.

The Court announced the decision in *Nixon* in the waning days of October Term 1976. Since then, the Court has said little else on the subject of an "individual interest in avoiding disclosure of personal matters." A few opinions have mentioned the concept in passing and in other contexts. But no other decision has squarely addressed a constitutional right to informational privacy.

As was our approach in *Whalen*, we will assume for present purposes that the Government's challenged inquiries implicate a privacy interest of constitutional significance. We hold, however, that, whatever the scope of this interest, it does not prevent the Government from asking reasonable questions of the sort included on SF–85 and Form 42 in an employment background investigation that is subject to the Privacy Act's safeguards against public disclosure.

As an initial matter, judicial review of the Government's challenged inquiries must take into account the context in which they arise. When the Government asks respondents and their references to fill out SF–85 and Form 42, it does not exercise its sovereign power "to regulate or license." Rather, the Government conducts the challenged background checks in its capacity "as proprietor" and manager of its "internal operation." Time and again our cases have recognized that the Government has a much freer hand in dealing "with citizen employees than it does when it brings its sovereign power to bear on citizens at large." This distinction is grounded on the "common-sense realization" that if every "employment decision became a constitutional matter," the Government could not function.

* * *

Respondents argue that, because they are contract employees and not civil servants, the Government's broad authority in managing its affairs should apply with diminished force. But the Government's interest as "proprietor" in managing its operations, the fact that respondents' direct employment relationship is with Cal Tech—which operates JPL under a Government contract—says very little about the interests at stake in this case. The record shows that, as a "practical matter," there are no "[r]elevant distinctions" between the duties performed by NASA's civil-service workforce and its contractor workforce. The two classes of employees perform "functionally equivalent duties," and the extent of employees' "access to NASA ... facilities" turns not on formal status but on the nature of "the jobs they perform."

At JPL, in particular, the work that contract employees perform is critical to NASA's mission. Respondents in this case include "the lead trouble-shooter for ... th[e] $568 [million]" Kepler space observatory, the leader of the program that "tests ... all new technology that NASA will use in space," and one of the lead "trajectory designers for ... the Galileo Project and the Apollo Moon landings." This is important work, and all of it is funded with a multibillion dollar investment from the American taxpayer. The Government has a strong interest in conducting basic background checks into the contract employees minding the store at JPL.

With these interests in view, we conclude that the challenged portions of both SF–85 and Form 42 consist of reasonable, employment-related inquiries that further the Government's interests in managing its internal operations. As to SF–85, the only part of the form challenged here is its request for information about "any treatment or counseling received" for illegal-drug use within the previous year. The "treatment or counseling" question, however, must be considered in context. It is a follow-up to SF–85's inquiry into whether the employee has "used, possessed, supplied, or manufactured illegal drugs" during the past year. The Government has good reason to ask employees about their recent illegal-drug use. Like any employer, the Government is entitled to have its projects staffed by reliable, law-abiding persons who will " 'efficiently and effectively' " discharge their duties. Questions about illegal-drug use are a useful way of figuring out which persons have these characteristics.

In context, the follow-up question on "treatment or counseling" for recent illegal-drug use is also a reasonable, employment-related inquiry. The Government, recognizing that illegal-drug use is both a criminal and a medical issue, seeks to separate out those illegal-drug users who are taking steps to address and overcome their problems. The Government thus uses responses to the "treatment or counseling" question as a mitigating factor in determining whether to grant contract employees long-term access to federal facilities.

This is a reasonable, and indeed a humane, approach, and respondents do not dispute the legitimacy of the Government's decision to use drug treatment as a mitigating factor in its contractor credentialing decisions. Respondents' argument is that, if drug treatment is only used to mitigate, then the Government should change the mandatory phrasing of SF–85—"Include [in your answer] any treatment or counseling received"—so as to make a response optional. As it stands, the mandatory "treatment or counseling" question is unconstitutional, in respondents' view, because it is "more intrusive than necessary to satisfy the government's objective."

We reject the argument that the Government, when it requests job-related personal information in an employment background check, has a constitutional burden to demonstrate that its questions are "necessary" or the least restrictive means of furthering its interests. So exacting a standard runs directly contrary to *Whalen*. The patients in

Whalen, much like respondents here, argued that New York's statute was unconstitutional because the State could not "demonstrate the necessity" of its program. The Court quickly rejected that argument, concluding that New York's collection of patients' prescription information could "not be held unconstitutional simply because" a court viewed it as "unnecessary, in whole or in part."

That analysis applies with even greater force where the Government acts, not as a regulator, but as the manager of its internal affairs. SF–85's "treatment or counseling" question reasonably seeks to identify a subset of acknowledged drug users who are attempting to overcome their problems. The Government's considered position is that phrasing the question in more permissive terms would result in a lower response rate, and the question's effectiveness in identifying illegal-drug users who are suitable for employment would be "materially reduced." That is a reasonable position, falling within the " 'wide latitude' " granted the Government in its dealings with employees.

* * *

In light of the protection provided by the Privacy Act's nondisclosure requirement, and because the challenged portions of the forms consist of reasonable inquiries in an employment background check, we conclude that the Government's inquiries do not violate a constitutional right to informational privacy.

* * *

For these reasons, the judgment of the Court of Appeals is reversed, and the case is remanded for further proceedings consistent with this opinion.

It is so ordered.

■ JUSTICE KAGAN took no part in the consideration or decision of this case.

■ JUSTICE SCALIA, with whom JUSTICE THOMAS joins, concurring in the judgment.

* * *

In sum, I would simply hold that there is no constitutional right to "informational privacy." Besides being consistent with constitutional text and tradition, this view has the attractive benefit of resolving this case without resort to the Court's exegesis on the Government's legitimate interest in identifying contractor drug abusers and the comfortingly narrow scope of NASA's "routine use" regulations. I shall not fill the U.S. Reports with further explanation of the incoherence of the Court's "substantive due process" doctrine in its many manifestations, since the Court does not play the substantive-due-process card. Instead, it states that it will "assume, without deciding" that there exists a right to informational privacy.

The Court's sole justification for its decision to "assume, without deciding" is that the Court made the same mistake before—in two 33-year-old cases, Whalen v. Roe, 429 U.S. 589 (1977) and Nixon v. Administrator of General Services, 433 U.S. 425 (1977). But stare decisis is simply irrelevant when the pertinent precedent assumed, without deciding, the existence of a constitutional right.

NOTES AND QUESTIONS

1. Although the background investigation in this case involved current employees, most background investigations take place before hiring. For a discussion of other privacy issues involving current employees, see Chapter 7.

2. Should the same privacy standards apply to private employers, private employers at government facilities, government employers, and government in its non-employer role? What does Justice Alito say?

3. In the three Supreme Court cases that assumed without deciding there is a constitutional right to informational privacy, *Whalen, Nixon,* and *Nelson,* the Court upheld the challenged government action. Similarly, virtually all of the lower courts have upheld information disclosure requirements. Therefore, merely recognizing a constitutional right may be insufficient to provide meaningful protection. See Mark A. Rothstein, Constitutional Right to Informational Health Privacy in Critical Condition, 39 J.L. Med. & Ethics 280 (2011).

F. DRUG TESTING AND OTHER LABORATORY PROCEDURES

1. DRUG TESTING

Page 109.   Please add the following note.

8. There has been a resurgence of efforts to require drug screening of various federal and state employees. Broad drug testing policies lacking a governmental need or purpose are likely to be held unconstitutional. For example, in National Federation of Federal Employees-IAM v. Vilsack, 681 F.3d 483 (D.C. Cir. 2012), the D.C. Circuit held unconstitutional the random drug testing of all employees working at Job Corp Civilian Conservation Centers operated by the U.S. Forest Service. According to the court, the policy did not come within the narrow exception for constitutionally permissible, suspicionless searches.

In 2011, Florida Governor Rick Scott signed an executive order mandating the drug testing of all new state employees and random testing of the existing 85,000 state employees. A U.S. District struck down the executive order as being unconstitutional under the Fourth Amendment. AFSCME v. Scott, 857 F.Supp.2d 1322, 2012 WL 1449644 (S.D. Fla. 2012). Separately, however, the Florida legislature enacted a law requiring that state agencies randomly drug test up to 10 percent of their employees every three months. The law, which exempts the governor and members of the state legislature, is also being challenged.

There also have been efforts in several states to mandate the drug testing of state judges under the theory that judges who use illegal drugs cannot provide fair and impartial trials. None of the judiciary drug testing bills has passed yet. Mandatory drug testing of all elected officials also has been proposed.

G. NEGLIGENT HIRING

Page 116.   Please add the following notes.

6A. Whether an employer has a duty to conduct a preemployment background check depends on the nature of the job. For example, after the Deepwater Horizon drilling rig exploded in the Gulf of Mexico contractors were hired to help with the cleanup. A general laborer whose job it was to manually remove tar balls from the coast was raped by another employee after driving her home. Although the perpetrator had a long criminal record, the contractor and its subcontractor failed to perform any background check. In holding there was no cause of action for negligent hiring under Mississippi law, the Fifth Circuit noted, among other things, that the legislature mandated criminal background checks for certain employees, such as substitute teachers and health care facility employees. Thus, there was a "strong inference" that it did not intend to mandate them for all employees. See Keen v. Miller Environmental Group, Inc., 702 F.3d 239 (5th Cir. 2012).

6B. The plaintiff must prove a causal relationship between the employer's act of negligence and a subsequent injury. In one case, a customer brought an action for negligent hiring against a restaurant for injuries allegedly caused by a broil cook's intentional placement of a human hair in her steak. The broil cook had a prior criminal record and was fired by another restaurant for drinking on the job. The Wisconsin Court of Appeals held there was no causal connection between the employer's negligent failure to discover the cook's background and the injury sustained by the customer. Hansen v. Texas Roadhouse, Inc., 827 N.W.2d 99 (Wis. Ct. App. 2012), petition for review denied, 827 N.W.2d 376 (Wis. 2013). Do you agree with the court? How closely do the prior and subsequent acts of misconduct have to align?

CHAPTER 4

DISCRIMINATION

A. DISCRIMINATION ON THE BASIS OF RACE OR SEX

2. WHAT IS UNLAWFUL DISCRIMINATION?

a. DISPARATE TREATMENT

Page 129.   Please add after last sentence of note 1.

In Coleman v. Donohoe, 667 F.3d 835 (7th Cir. 2012), the Seventh Circuit made clear that evidence of a similarly situated comparator may serve not only as an element of the plaintiff's prima facie case under *McDonnell Douglas* but also as evidence that the employer's legitimate nondiscriminatory reason was pretextual.

Page 129.   Please delete note 6 and replace with the following.

Wal-Mart Stores, Inc. v. Dukes

131 S.Ct. 2541 (2011).

■ JUSTICE SCALIA delivered the opinion of the Court.

We are presented with one of the most expansive class actions ever. The District Court and the Court of Appeals approved the certification of a class comprising about one and a half million plaintiffs, current and former female employees of petitioner Wal-Mart who allege that the discretion exercised by their local supervisors over pay and promotion matters violates Title VII by discriminating against women. In addition to injunctive and declaratory relief, the plaintiffs seek an award of backpay. We consider whether the certification of the plaintiff class was consistent with Federal Rules of Civil Procedure 23(a) and (b)(2).

Petitioner Wal-Mart is the Nation's largest private employer. It operates four types of retail stores throughout the country: Discount Stores, Supercenters, Neighborhood Markets, and Sam's Clubs. Those stores are divided into seven nationwide divisions, which in turn comprise 41 regions of 80 to 85 stores apiece. Each store has between 40 and 53 separate departments and 80 to 500 staff positions. In all, Wal-Mart operates approximately 3,400 stores and employs more than one million people.

Pay and promotion decisions at Wal-Mart are generally committed to local managers' broad discretion, which is exercised "in a largely subjective manner." Local store managers may increase the wages of hourly employees (within limits) with only limited corporate oversight. As for salaried employees, such as store managers and their deputies, higher corporate authorities have discretion to set their pay within preestablished ranges.

Promotions work in a similar fashion. Wal-Mart permits store managers to apply their own subjective criteria when selecting candidates as "support managers," which is the first step on the path to management. Admission to Wal-Mart's management training program, however, does require that a candidate meet certain objective criteria, including an above-average performance rating, at least one year's tenure in the applicant's current position, and a willingness to relocate. But except for those requirements, regional and district managers have discretion to use their own judgment when selecting candidates for management training. Promotion to higher office—e.g., assistant manager, co-manager, or store manager—is similarly at the discretion of the employee's superiors after prescribed objective factors are satisfied.

The named plaintiffs in this lawsuit, representing the 1.5 million members of the certified class, are three current or former Wal-Mart employees who allege that the company discriminated against them on the basis of their sex by denying them equal pay or promotions, in violation of Title VII of the Civil Rights Act of 1964.

Betty Dukes began working at a Pittsburgh, California, Wal-Mart in 1994. She started as a cashier, but later sought and received a promotion to customer service manager. After a series of disciplinary violations, however, Dukes was demoted back to cashier and then to greeter. Dukes concedes she violated company policy, but contends that the disciplinary actions were in fact retaliation for invoking internal complaint procedures and that male employees have not been disciplined for similar infractions. Dukes also claims two male greeters in the Pittsburgh store are paid more than she is.

Christine Kwapnoski has worked at Sam's Club stores in Missouri and California for most of her adult life. She has held a number of positions, including a supervisory position. She claims that a male manager yelled at her frequently and screamed at female employees, but not at men. The manager in question "told her to 'doll up,' to wear some makeup, and to dress a little better."

The final named plaintiff, Edith Arana, worked at a Wal-Mart store in Duarte, California, from 1995 to 2001. In 2000, she approached the store manager on more than one occasion about management training, but was brushed off. Arana concluded she was being denied opportunity for advancement because of her sex. She initiated internal complaint procedures, whereupon she was told to apply directly to the district manager if she thought her store manager was being unfair. Arana, however, decided against that and never applied for management training again. In 2001, she was fired for failure to comply with Wal-Mart's timekeeping policy.

These plaintiffs, respondents here, do not allege that Wal-Mart has any express corporate policy against the advancement of women. Rather, they claim that their local managers' discretion over pay and promotions is exercised disproportionately in favor of men, leading to an unlawful disparate impact on female employees. And, respondents say, because Wal-Mart is aware of this effect, its refusal to cabin its managers' authority amounts to disparate treatment. Their complaint seeks injunctive and declaratory relief, punitive damages, and backpay. It does not ask for compensatory damages.

Importantly for our purposes, respondents claim that the discrimination to which they have been subjected is common to all Wal-Mart's female employees. The basic theory of their case is that a strong and uniform "corporate culture" permits bias against women to infect, perhaps subconsciously, the discretionary decision making of each one of Wal-Mart's thousands of managers—thereby making every woman at the company the victim of one common discriminatory practice. Respondents therefore wish to litigate the Title VII claims of all female employees at Wal-Mart's stores in a nationwide class action.

* * *

The class action is "an exception to the usual rule that litigation is conducted by and on behalf of the individual named parties only." In order to justify a departure from that rule, "a class representative must be part of the class and 'possess the same interest and suffer the same injury' as the class members." Rule 23(a) ensures that the named plaintiffs are appropriate representatives of the class whose claims they wish to litigate. The Rule's four requirements—numerosity, commonality, typicality, and adequate representation—"effectively 'limit the class claims to those fairly encompassed by the named plaintiff's claims.'"

The crux of this case is commonality—the rule requiring a plaintiff to show that "there are questions of law or fact common to the class." That language is easy to misread, since "[a]ny competently crafted class complaint literally raises common 'questions.'" For example: Do all of us plaintiffs indeed work for Wal-Mart? Do our managers have discretion over pay? Is that an unlawful employment practice? What remedies should we get? Reciting these questions is not sufficient to obtain class certification. Commonality requires the plaintiff to demonstrate that the class members "have suffered the same injury," This does not mean merely that they have all suffered a violation of the same provision of law. Title VII, for example, can be violated in many ways—by intentional discrimination, or by hiring and promotion criteria that result in disparate impact, and by the use of these practices on the part of many different superiors in a single company. Quite obviously, the mere claim by employees of the same company that they have suffered a Title VII injury, or even a disparate-impact Title VII injury, gives no cause to believe that all their claims can productively be litigated at once. Their claims must depend upon a common contention—for example, the assertion of discriminatory bias on the part of the same supervisor. That common contention, moreover, must be of such a nature that it is capable of classwide resolution— which means that determination of its truth or falsity will resolve an issue that is central to the validity of each one of the claims in one stroke.

"What matters to class certification ... is not the raising of common 'questions'—even in droves—but, rather the capacity of a classwide proceeding to generate common answers apt to drive the resolution of the litigation. Dissimilarities within the proposed class are what have the potential to impede the generation of common answers."

* * *

In this case, proof of commonality necessarily overlaps with respondents' merits contention that Wal-Mart engages in a pattern or practice of discrimination. That is so because, in resolving an individual's Title VII claim, the crux of the inquiry is "the reason for a particular employment decision." Here respondents wish to sue about literally millions of employment decisions at once. Without some glue holding the alleged reasons for all those decisions together, it will be impossible to say that examination of all the class members' claims for relief will produce a common answer to the crucial question why *was I disfavored*.

* * *

Plaintiffs must produce "significant proof" that Wal-Mart "operated under a general policy of discrimination." That is entirely absent here. Wal-Mart's announced policy forbids sex discrimination, and as the District Court recognized the company imposes penalties for denials of equal employment opportunity. The only evidence of a "general policy of discrimination" respondents produced was the testimony of Dr. William Bielby, their sociological expert. Relying on "social framework" analysis, Bielby testified that Wal-Mart has a "strong corporate culture," that makes it " 'vulnerable' " to "gender bias." He could not, however, "determine with any specificity how regularly stereotypes play a meaningful role in employment decisions at Wal-Mart. At his deposition . . . Dr. Bielby conceded that he could not calculate whether 0.5 percent or 95 percent of the employment decisions at Wal-Mart might be determined by stereotyped thinking."

The only corporate policy that the plaintiffs' evidence convincingly establishes is Wal-Mart's "policy" of allowing discretion by local supervisors over employment matters. On its face, of course, that is just the opposite of a uniform employment practice that would provide the commonality needed for a class action; it is a policy against having uniform employment practices. It is also a very common and presumptively reasonable way of doing business—one that we have said "should itself raise no inference of discriminatory conduct."

To be sure, we have recognized that, "in appropriate cases," giving discretion to lower-level supervisors can be the basis of Title VII liability under a disparate-impact theory—since "an employer's undisciplined system of subjective decisionmaking [can have] precisely the same effects as a system pervaded by impermissible intentional discrimination." But the recognition that this type of Title VII claim "can" exist does not lead to the conclusion that every employee in a company using a system of discretion has such a claim in common. To the contrary, left to their own devices most managers in any corporation—and surely most managers in a corporation that forbids sex discrimination—would select sex-neutral, performance-based criteria for hiring and promotion that produce no actionable disparity at all. Others may choose to reward various attributes that produce disparate impact—such as scores on general aptitude tests or educational achievements. And still other managers may be guilty of intentional discrimination that produces a sex-based disparity. In such a company, demonstrating the invalidity of one manager's use of discretion will do nothing to demonstrate the invalidity of another's. A party seeking to certify a nationwide class will be unable to show that all the employees' Title VII claims will in fact depend on the answers to common questions.

Respondents have not identified a common mode of exercising discretion that pervades the entire company—aside from their reliance on Dr. Bielby's social frameworks analysis that we have rejected. In a company of Wal-Mart's size and geographical scope, it is quite unbelievable that all managers would exercise their discretion in a common way without some common direction. Respondents attempt to make that showing by means of statistical and anecdotal evidence, but their evidence falls well short.

The statistical evidence consists primarily of regression analyses performed by Dr. Richard Drogin, a statistician, and Dr. Marc Bendick, a labor economist. Drogin conducted his analysis region-by-region, comparing the number of women promoted into management positions with the percentage of women in the available pool of hourly workers. After considering regional and national data, Drogin concluded that "there are statistically significant disparities between men and women at Wal-Mart . . . [and] these disparities . . . can be explained only by gender discrimination." Bendick compared work-force data from Wal-Mart and competitive retailers and concluded that Wal-Mart "promotes a lower percentage of women than its competitors."

Even if they are taken at face value, these studies are insufficient to establish that respondents' theory can be proved on a classwide basis.

* * *

There is another, more fundamental, respect in which respondents' statistical proof fails. Even if it established (as it does not) a pay or promotion pattern that differs from the nationwide figures or the regional figures in all of Wal-Mart's 3,400 stores, that would still not demonstrate that commonality of issue exists. Some managers will claim that the availability of women, or qualified women, or interested women, in their stores' area does not mirror the national or regional statistics. And almost all of them will claim to have been applying some sex-neutral, performance-based criteria—whose nature and effects will differ from store to store. In the landmark case of ours which held that giving discretion to lower-level supervisors can be the basis of Title VII liability under a disparate-impact theory, the plurality opinion conditioned that holding on the corollary that merely proving that the discretionary system has produced a racial or sexual disparity is not enough. "[T]he plaintiff must begin by identifying the specific employment practice that is challenged." That is all the more necessary when a class of plaintiffs is sought to be certified. Other than the bare existence of delegated discretion, respondents have identified no "specific employment practice"—much less one that ties all their 1.5 million claims together. Merely showing that Wal-Mart's policy of discretion has produced an overall sex-based disparity does not suffice.

Respondents' anecdotal evidence suffers from the same defects, and in addition is too weak to raise any inference that all the individual, discretionary personnel decisions are discriminatory.

* * *

In sum, we agree with Chief Judge Kozinski that the members of the class:

> "held a multitude of different jobs, at different levels of Wal-Mart's hierarchy, for variable lengths of time, in 3,400 stores, sprinkled across 50 states, with a kaleidoscope of supervisors (male and female), subject to a variety of regional policies that all differed. . . . Some thrived while others did poorly. They have little in common but their sex and this lawsuit."

* * *

Wal-Mart is entitled to individualized determinations of each employee's eligibility for backpay. Title VII includes a detailed remedial scheme. If a plaintiff prevails in showing that an employer has discriminated against him in violation of the statute, the court "may enjoin the respondent from engaging in such unlawful employment practice, and order such affirmative action as may be appropriate, [including] reinstatement or hiring of employees, with or without backpay . . . or any other equitable relief as the court deems appropriate." But if the employer can show that it took an adverse employment action against an employee for any reason other than discrimination, the court cannot order the "hiring, reinstatement, or promotion of an individual as an employee, or the payment to him of any backpay."

We have established a procedure for trying pattern-or-practice cases that gives effect to these statutory requirements. When the plaintiff seeks individual relief such as reinstatement or backpay after establishing a pattern or practice of discrimination, "a district court must usually conduct additional proceedings . . . to determine the scope of individual relief." At this phase, the burden of proof will shift to the company, but it will have the right to raise any individual affirmative defenses it may have, and to "demonstrate that the individual applicant was denied an employment opportunity for lawful reasons."

The Court of Appeals believed that it was possible to replace such proceedings with Trial by Formula. A sample set of the class members would be selected, as to whom liability for sex discrimination and the backpay owing as a result would be determined in depositions supervised by a master. The percentage of claims determined to be valid would then be applied to the entire remaining class, and the number of (presumptively) valid claims thus derived would be multiplied by the average backpay award in the sample set to arrive at the entire class recovery—without further individualized proceedings. We disapprove that novel project. Because the Rules Enabling Act forbids interpreting Rule 23 to "abridge, enlarge or modify any substantive right," a class cannot be certified on the premise that Wal-Mart will not be entitled to litigate its statutory defenses to individual claims. And because the necessity of that litigation will prevent backpay from being "incidental" to the classwide injunction, respondents' class could not be certified even assuming, arguendo, that "incidental" monetary relief can be awarded to a 23(b)(2) class.

* * *

The judgment of the Court of Appeals is reversed.

■ JUSTICE GINSBURG, with whom JUSTICE BREYER, JUSTICE SOTOMAYOR, and JUSTICE KAGAN join, concurring in part and dissenting in part.

The class in this case, I agree with the Court, should not have been certified under Federal Rule of Civil Procedure 23(b)(2). The plaintiffs, alleging discrimination in violation of Title VII, seek monetary relief that is not merely incidental to any injunctive or declaratory relief that might be available. A putative class of this type may be certifiable under Rule 23(b)(3), if the plaintiffs show that common class questions "predominate" over issues affecting individuals—e.g., qualification for, and the amount of, backpay or compensatory damages—and that a class action is "superior" to other modes of adjudication.

Whether the class the plaintiffs describe meets the specific requirements of Rule 23(b)(3) is not before the Court, and I would reserve that matter for consideration and decision on remand. The Court, however, disqualifies the class at the starting gate, holding that the plaintiffs cannot cross the "commonality" line set by Rule 23(a)(2). In so ruling, the Court imports into the Rule 23(a) determination concerns properly addressed in a Rule 23(b)(3) assessment.

Rule 23(a)(2) establishes a preliminary requirement for maintaining a class action: "[T]here are questions of law or fact common to the class." The Rule "does not require that all questions of law or fact raised in the litigation be common," indeed, "[e]ven a single question of law or fact common to the members of the class will satisfy the commonality requirement."

* * *

The District Court certified a class of "[a]ll women employed at any Wal-Mart domestic retail store at any time since December 26, 1998." The named plaintiffs, led by Betty Dukes, propose to litigate, on behalf of the class, allegations that Wal-Mart discriminates on the basis of gender in pay and promotions. They allege that the company "[r]eli[es] on gender stereotypes in making employment decisions such as . . . promotion[s][and] pay." Wal-Mart permits those prejudices to infect personnel decisions, the plaintiffs contend, by leaving pay and promotions in the hands of "a nearly all male managerial workforce" using "arbitrary and subjective criteria." Further alleged barriers to the advancement of female employees include the company's requirement, "as a condition of promotion to management jobs, that employees be willing to relocate." Absent instruction otherwise, there is a risk that managers will act on the familiar assumption that women, because of their services to husband and children, are less mobile than men.

Women fill 70 percent of the hourly jobs in the retailer's stores but make up only "33 percent of management employees." "[T]he higher one looks in the organization the lower the percentage of women." The plaintiffs' "largely uncontested descriptive statistics" also show that women working in the company's stores "are paid less than men in every region" and "that the salary gap widens over time even for men and women hired into the same jobs at the same time."

The District Court identified "systems for . . . promoting in-store employees" that were "sufficiently similar across regions and stores" to conclude that "the manner in which these systems affect the class raises issues that are common to all class members." The selection of employees for promotion to in-store management "is fairly characterized as a 'tap on the shoulder' process," in which managers have discretion about whose shoulders to tap. Vacancies are not regularly posted; from among those employees satisfying minimum qualifications, managers choose whom to promote on the basis of their own subjective impressions.

Wal-Mart's compensation policies also operate uniformly across stores, the District Court found. The retailer leaves open a $2 band for every position's hourly pay rate. Wal-Mart provides no standards or criteria for setting wages within that band, and thus does nothing to counter unconscious bias on the part of supervisors.

Wal-Mart's supervisors do not make their discretionary decisions in a vacuum. The District Court reviewed means Wal-Mart used to maintain a "carefully constructed ... corporate culture," such as frequent meetings to reinforce the common way of thinking, regular transfers of managers between stores to ensure uniformity throughout the company, monitoring of stores "on a close and constant basis," and "Wal-Mart TV," "broadcas[t] ... into all stores."

The plaintiffs' evidence, including class members' tales of their own experiences, suggests that gender bias suffused Wal-Mart's company culture. Among illustrations, senior management often refer to female associates as "little Janie Qs."

* * *

The District Court's identification of a common question, whether Wal-Mart's pay and promotions policies gave rise to unlawful discrimination, was hardly infirm. The practice of delegating to supervisors large discretion to make personnel decisions, uncontrolled by formal standards, has long been known to have the potential to produce disparate effects. Managers, like all humankind, may be prey to biases of which they are unaware. The risk of discrimination is heightened when those managers are predominantly of one sex, and are steeped in a corporate culture that perpetuates gender stereotypes.

* * *

The plaintiffs' allegations state claims of gender discrimination in the form of biased decisionmaking in both pay and promotions. The evidence reviewed by the District Court adequately demonstrated that resolving those claims would necessitate examination of particular policies and practices alleged to affect, adversely and globally, women employed at Wal-Mart's stores. Rule 23(a)(2), setting a necessary but not a sufficient criterion for class-action certification, demands nothing further.

* * *

Wal-Mart's delegation of discretion over pay and promotions is a policy uniform throughout all stores. The very nature of discretion is that people will exercise it in various ways. A system of delegated discretion, is a practice actionable under Title VII when it produces discriminatory outcomes. A finding that Wal-Mart's pay and promotions practices in fact violate the law would be the first step in the usual order of proof for plaintiffs seeking individual remedies for company-wide discrimination. That each individual employee's unique circumstances will ultimately determine whether she is entitled to backpay or damages, should not factor into the Rule 23(a)(2) determination.

Page 140.   Please add before the last sentence of the first paragraph of note 7.

For a recent lucid account of the burdens and remedies under mixed motive law, see Harris v. City of Santa Monica, 56 Cal. 4th 203 (2013).

Page 140.   Please delete last paragraph of note 7 and replace with the following.

Direct evidence of discrimination is no longer required for a plaintiff to prevail in a mixed-motive Title VII case. The plaintiff can succeed by proving his or her case by a preponderance of the evidence using direct or circumstantial evidence. Desert Palace, Inc. v. Costa, 539 U.S. 90 (2003). After *Desert Palace*, courts have struggled to decide when a case should be analyzed at the pretrial stage using the *McDonnell Douglas* framework and when it should be analyzed using the mixed motives framework from *Price Waterhouse.* See Coleman v. Donohoe, 667 F.3d 835 (7th Cir. 2012) (Wood, J., concurring) (arguing that the two tests should be collapsed at the pretrial stage of a case, as they have been at the trial stage of a case, and the plaintiff should simply be required to present evidence showing that "the employer took . . . adverse action on account of her protected class"). In University of Texas Southwestern Medical Center v. Nassar, 133 S.Ct. 2517, 2530 (2013), the Supreme Court in dicta suggested that such a collapse of the two evidentiary frameworks was appropriate when it explained that the mixed-motive evidentiary framework "is not itself a substantive bar on discrimination. Rather, it is a rule that establishes the causation standard for proving a violation defined elsewhere in Title VII."

Page 145.   Please add at the end of note 2.

May a male employer terminate a female employee because the employer's wife finds the employee to be a threat to their marriage even in the absence of any inappropriate behavior on the part of the employee? See Nelson v. Knight, 2012 WL 6652747 (Iowa, Dec. 21, 2012) (finding no sex discrimination but noting that "[i]f an employer repeatedly took adverse employment actions against persons of a particular gender because of alleged personal relationship issues, it might well be possible to infer that gender and not the relationship was a motivating factor").

Page 146.   Please delete note 2 and replace with the following.

2. Courts have held that the PDA does not require employers to accommodate pregnant employees. "This is because the PDA does not require an employer to provide special accommodations to its pregnant employees; instead, the PDA only ensures that pregnant employees are given the same opportunities and benefits as *nonpregnant* employees who are similarly limited in their ability to work." Nelson v. Chattahoochee Valley Hosp. Soc., 731 F. Supp.2d 1217, 1230 (M.D. Ala. 2010). "If accommodations were offered to those "regarded as" disabled, employers would be compelled to offer accommodations to an ever-changing class of individuals based on the employer's individual conceptions." Young v. United Parcel Serv., Inc., 707 F.3d 437 (4th Cir. 2013), cert. granted 134 S.Ct. 2898 (2014) . State law may provide pregnant workers with greater protection. In 2014, New Jersey amended its Law Against Discrimination to not only explicitly prohibit discrimination against pregnant women but also to require employers to make reasonable accommodations available to pregnant workers. N.J. Stat. Ann. § 10:5–12. However, should an employer choose to provide special accommodations to pregnant employees, they may not necessarily be able to force the employees to accept the accommodations. This is particularly relevant when accommodations involve a reduction in hours or responsibilities resulting in a lower salary. In U.S. E.E.O.C. v. Catholic Healthcare W., 530 F. Supp. 2d 1096 (C.D. Cal. 2008), a federal district court applied the BFOQ test to Catholic Healthcare's unsolicited transfer of a pregnant radiology technologist to a different area of work. Catholic Healthcare's transfer was found to be discriminatory.

Page 147.   Please delete the final sentence of note 4 and replace with the following.

Recent decisions by courts have generally allowed a similar distinction between work-related disabilities and pregnancy. See Urbano v. Continental Airlines, Inc., 138 F.3d 204 (5th Cir. 1998), cert. denied, 525 U.S. 1000 (1998); Cunningham v. Dearborn Bd. of Educ., 246 Mich. App. 621, 633 N.W.2d 481 (2001); Young v. United Parcel Serv., Inc., 2011 WL 665321 (D. Md. Feb. 14, 2011); Brophy v. Day & Zimmerman Hawthorne Corp., 799 F. Supp. 2d 1185 (D. Nev. 2011); Serednyj v. Beverly Healthcare, LLC, 656 F.3d 540 (7th Cir. 2011).

Page 147.   Please delete note 6 and replace with the following.

6. In the case of religious institutions, pregnant women may be terminated not for the pregnancy itself but rather for premarital sex. In 1996, Leigh Cline's teaching contract with the Catholic Diocese of Toledo was not renewed due to the fact that Cline's due date was only five months after her wedding. The court of appeals reversed an award of summary judgment for the defendant. By engaging in premarital sex, Cline violated her duties to uphold the school's religious teachings; however, "a school cannot use the mere observation or knowledge of pregnancy as its sole method of detecting violations of its premarital sex policy." Cline v. Catholic Diocese of Toledo, 206 F.3d 651, 667 (6th Cir. 2000). In a similar case, Jarretta Hamilton was fired from Southland Christian School after informing the school administrator that she had engaged in premarital sex. In 2012, the court of appeals reversed an award of summary judgment for the school, finding "a genuine issue of material fact about the reason that Southland fired her." Hamilton v. Southland Christian Sch., Inc., 2012 WL 1694589 (11th Cir. May 16, 2012).

Page 148.   Please add the following note.

12. The PDA has generally not been interpreted to extend protection to women who seek to breastfeed at work. See, e.g., Wallace v. Pyro Mining Co., 951 F.2d 351 (6th Cir. 1991)(PDA did not give employee right to breastfeed at work because doing so was not a medical necessity); Barrash v. Bowen, 846 F.2d 927, 931 (4th Cir. 1988)(plaintiff could not establish disparate impact claim based on denial of breastfeeding leave because the PDA applied only to incapacitating illnesses). Recently, the Fifth Circuit held that lactation was a related medical condition of pregnancy for purposes of the PDA and that discrimination against a woman because she is lactating or expressing breast milk violates Title VII and the PDA. Importantly, however, the plaintiff in the case did not seek any accommodation to breastfeed and was allegedly fired simply for raising the issue of breastfeeding at work with her employer. See EEOC v. Houston Funding II, 2013 WL 2360114 (5th Cir., May 30, 2013). The Patient Protection and Affordable Care Act, H.R. 3590, which President Obama signed into law on March 23, 2010, does provide some limited protection to breastfeeding mothers. The Act amended the Fair Labor Standards Act of 1938 (29 U.S.C. § 207) to require an employer to provide reasonable break time for a non exempt employee to express breast milk for one year after a child's birth. As of 2014, twenty-five states also have laws providing some protection for breastfeeding in the workplace. See National Conference of State Legislatures, available at http://www.ncsl.org/issues-research/health/breastfeeding-state-laws.aspx (last visited July 30, 2014).

Page 154.   Please add the following note.

9.   Since a race-based disparate impact claim requires proof that those of a particular race are disproportionately excluded by a particular practice, plaintiffs must have some way of identifying or determining the race of those individuals who are and are not excluded by the challenged practice. In EEOC v. Kaplan Higher Education Corp., 748 F.3d 749 (6th Cir. 2014) , the Sixth Circuit dismissed the EEOC's disparate impact challenge to Kaplan's credit check policy for new employees on the grounds that the testimony presented by the EEOC's expert regarding racially disparate impact, which was based on a visual race rating of applicants, was inadmissible under Daubert v. Merrell Dow Pharmaceuticals, Inc., 509 U.S. 579 (1993). Without such expert testimony, the EEOC could not show race based impact. How could the EEOC have established the race of the relevant applicants so as to establish its disparate impact claim?

E. DISCRIMINATION BASED ON FACTORS OTHER THAN RACE OR SEX

1. RELIGION

Page 211.   Please add the following note.

12B.   What must an employee do to trigger an employer's duty to accommodate her religion? In EEOC v. Abercrombie & Fitch Stores, Inc., 731 F.3d 1106 (10th Cir. 2013), the Tenth Circuit placed the burden squarely on the applicant or employee to notify an employer that a particular practice was religiously motivated and would require accommodation. In the case, the EEOC presented evidence showing that the employer refused to hire the applicant because she wore a headscarf to the interview. The Tenth Circuit nonetheless reversed the district court's award of summary judgment for the EEOC and granted summary judgment for Abercrombie & Fitch on the ground that the applicant had not made clear during her interview that she wore the headscarf for religious reasons. As the court noted: "During the course of the interview, [the applicant] never informed [the employer] that she was Muslim, never brought up the subject of her headscarf, and never indicated that she wore the headscarf for religious reasons and that she felt obliged to do so, and thus would need an accommodation to address the conflict between her religious practice and Abercrombie's clothing policy."   731 F.3d at 1113. But see Adeyeye v. Heartland Sweeteners, LLC, 721 F.3d 444 (7th Cir. 2013), in which the Seventh Circuit held that an employee's request to take unpaid leave to attend the funeral ceremonies of his father in Nigeria was sufficient to put the employer on notice of the religious nature of request. The court explained that even though the plaintiff's religious beliefs and practices were unfamiliar to most Americans, his request for leave gave sufficient notice of the religious nature of the leave by referring to "a 'funeral ceremony,' a 'funeral rite,' and animal sacrifice." Id. at 450–51. Moreover, the court explained that "[i]f the managers who considered the request had questions about whether the request was religious, nothing would have prevented them from asking Adeyeye to explain a little more about the nature of his request. . . ." Id. at 451.

Page 211.   Please add the following after note 13.

Hosanna-Tabor Evangelical Lutheran Church & School v. EEOC

132 S.Ct. 694 (2012).

■ CHIEF JUSTICE ROBERTS delivered the opinion of the Court.

Certain employment discrimination laws authorize employees who have been wrongfully terminated to sue their employers for reinstatement and damages. The question presented is whether the Establishment and Free Exercise Clauses of the First Amendment bar such an action when the employer is a religious group and the employee is one of the group's ministers.

Petitioner Hosanna-Tabor Evangelical Lutheran Church and School is a member congregation of the Lutheran Church-Missouri Synod, the second largest Lutheran denomination in America. Hosanna-Tabor operated a small school in Redford, Michigan, offering a "Christ-centered education" to students in kindergarten through eighth grade.

The Synod classifies teachers into two categories: "called" and "lay." "Called" teachers are regarded as having been called to their vocation by God through a congregation. To be eligible to receive a call from a congregation, a teacher must satisfy certain academic requirements. One way of doing so is by completing a "colloquy" program at a Lutheran college or university. The program requires candidates to take eight courses of theological study, obtain the endorsement of their local Synod district, and pass an oral examination by a faculty committee. A teacher who meets these requirements may be called by a congregation. Once called, a teacher receives the formal title "Minister of Religion, Commissioned." A commissioned minister serves for an open-ended term; at Hosanna-Tabor, a call could be rescinded only for cause and by a supermajority vote of the congregation.

"Lay" or "contract" teachers, by contrast, are not required to be trained by the Synod or even to be Lutheran. At Hosanna-Tabor, they were appointed by the school board, without a vote of the congregation, to one-year renewable terms. Although teachers at the school generally performed the same duties regardless of whether they were lay or called, lay teachers were hired only when called teachers were unavailable.

Respondent Cheryl Perich was first employed by Hosanna-Tabor as a lay teacher in 1999. After Perich completed her colloquy later that school year, Hosanna-Tabor asked her to become a called teacher. Perich accepted the call and received a "diploma of vocation" designating her a commissioned minister.

Perich taught kindergarten during her first four years at Hosanna-Tabor and fourth grade during the 2003–2004 school year. She taught math, language arts, social studies, science, gym, art, and music. She also taught a religion class four days a week, led the students in prayer and devotional exercises each day, and attended a weekly school-wide chapel service. Perich led the chapel service herself about twice a year.

Perich became ill in June 2004 with what was eventually diagnosed as narcolepsy. Symptoms included sudden and deep sleeps from which she could not be roused. Because of her illness, Perich began the 2004–2005 school year on disability leave. On January 27, 2005, however, Perich notified the school principal, Stacey Hoeft, that she would be able to report to work the following month. Hoeft responded that the school had already contracted with a lay teacher to fill Perich's position for the remainder of the school year. Hoeft also expressed concern that Perich was not yet ready to return to the classroom.

On January 30, Hosanna-Tabor held a meeting of its congregation at which school administrators stated that Perich was unlikely to be physically capable of returning to work that school year or the next. The congregation voted to offer Perich a "peaceful release" from her call, whereby the congregation would pay a portion of her health insurance premiums in exchange for her resignation as a called teacher. Perich refused to resign and produced a note from her doctor stating that she would be able to return to work on February 22. The school board urged Perich to reconsider, informing her that the school no longer had a position for her, but Perich stood by her decision not to resign.

On the morning of February 22—the first day she was medically cleared to return to work—Perich presented herself at the school. Hoeft asked her to leave but she would not do so until she obtained written documentation that she had reported to work. Later that afternoon, Hoeft called Perich at home and told her that she would likely be fired. Perich responded that she had spoken with an attorney and intended to assert her legal rights.

Following a school board meeting that evening, board chairman Scott Salo sent Perich a letter stating that Hosanna-Tabor was reviewing the process for rescinding her call in light of her "regrettable" actions. Salo subsequently followed up with a letter advising Perich that the congregation would consider whether to rescind her call at its next meeting. As grounds for termination, the letter cited Perich's "insubordination and disruptive behavior" on February 22, as well as the damage she had done to her "working relationship" with the school by "threatening to take legal action." The congregation voted to rescind

Perich's call on April 10, and Hosanna-Tabor sent her a letter of termination the next day.

Perich filed a charge with the Equal Employment Opportunity Commission, alleging that her employment had been terminated in violation of the Americans with Disabilities Act. The ADA prohibits an employer from discriminating against a qualified individual on the basis of disability. It also prohibits an employer from retaliating "against any individual because such individual has opposed any act or practice made unlawful by [the ADA] or because such individual made a charge, testified, assisted, or participated in any manner in an investigation, proceeding, or hearing under [the ADA]."

The EEOC brought suit against Hosanna-Tabor, alleging that Perich had been fired in retaliation for threatening to file an ADA lawsuit. Perich intervened in the litigation, claiming unlawful retaliation under both the ADA and the Michigan Persons with Disabilities Civil Rights Act. The EEOC and Perich sought Perich's reinstatement to her former position (or frontpay in lieu thereof), along with backpay, compensatory and punitive damages, attorney's fees, and other injunctive relief.

Hosanna-Tabor moved for summary judgment. Invoking what is known as the "ministerial exception," the Church argued that the suit was barred by the First Amendment because the claims at issue concerned the employment relationship between a religious institution and one of its ministers. According to the Church, Perich was a minister, and she had been fired for a religious reason—namely, that her threat to sue the Church violated the Synod's belief that Christians should resolve their disputes internally.

The District Court agreed that the suit was barred by the ministerial exception and granted summary judgment in Hosanna-Tabor's favor.

* * *

The Court of Appeals for the Sixth Circuit vacated and remanded, directing the District Court to proceed to the merits of Perich's retaliation claims.

* * *

We granted certiorari.

The First Amendment provides, in part, that "Congress shall make no law respecting an establishment of religion, or prohibiting the free exercise thereof." We have said that these two Clauses "often exert conflicting pressures," and that there can be "internal tension ... between the Establishment Clause and the Free Exercise Clause." Not so here. Both Religion Clauses bar the government from interfering with the decision of a religious group to fire one of its ministers.

* * *

It was against this background that the First Amendment was adopted. Familiar with life under the established Church of England, the founding generation sought to foreclose the possibility of a national church. By forbidding the "establishment of religion" and guaranteeing the "free exercise thereof," the Religion Clauses ensured that the new Federal Government—unlike the English Crown—would have no role in filling ecclesiastical offices. The Establishment Clause prevents the Government from appointing ministers, and the Free Exercise Clause prevents it from interfering with the freedom of religious groups to select their own.

* * *

Until today, we have not had occasion to consider whether this freedom of a religious organization to select its ministers is implicated by a suit alleging discrimination in employment. The Courts of Appeals, in contrast, have had extensive experience with this issue. Since the passage of Title VII of the Civil Rights Act of 1964 and other employment discrimination laws, the Courts of Appeals have uniformly recognized the existence of a "ministerial exception," grounded in the First Amendment, that precludes application of such legislation to claims concerning the employment relationship between a religious institution and its ministers.

We agree that there is such a ministerial exception. The members of a religious group put their faith in the hands of their ministers. Requiring a church to accept or retain an unwanted minister, or punishing a church for failing to do so, intrudes upon more than a mere employment decision. Such action interferes with the internal governance of the church, depriving the church of control over the selection of those who will personify its beliefs. By imposing an unwanted minister, the state infringes the Free Exercise Clause, which protects a religious group's right to shape its own faith and mission through its appointments. According the state the power to determine which individuals will minister to the faithful also violates the Establishment Clause, which prohibits government involvement in such ecclesiastical decisions.

The EEOC and Perich acknowledge that employment discrimination laws would be unconstitutional as applied to religious groups in certain circumstances. They grant, for example, that it would violate the First Amendment for courts to apply such laws to compel the ordination of women by the Catholic Church or by an Orthodox Jewish seminary. According to the EEOC and Perich, religious organizations could successfully defend against employment discrimination claims in those circumstances by invoking the constitutional right to freedom of association—a right "implicit" in the First Amendment. The EEOC and Perich thus see no need—and no basis—for a special rule for ministers grounded in the Religion Clauses themselves.

We find this position untenable. The right to freedom of association is a right enjoyed by religious and secular groups alike. It follows under the EEOC's and Perich's view that the First Amendment analysis should be the same, whether the association in question is the Lutheran Church, a labor union, or a social club. That result is hard to square with the text of the First Amendment itself, which gives special solicitude to the rights of religious organizations. We cannot accept the remarkable view that the Religion Clauses have nothing to say about a religious organization's freedom to select its own ministers.

The EEOC and Perich also contend that our decision in Employment Div., Dept. of Human Resources of Ore. v. Smith, 494 U.S. 872 (1990), precludes recognition of a ministerial exception. In *Smith*, two members of the Native American Church were denied state unemployment benefits after it was determined that they had been fired from their jobs for ingesting peyote, a crime under Oregon law. We held that this did not violate the Free Exercise Clause, even though the peyote had been ingested for sacramental purposes, because the "right of free exercise does not relieve an individual of the obligation to comply with a valid and neutral law of general applicability on the ground that the law proscribes (or prescribes) conduct that his religion prescribes (or proscribes)."

It is true that the ADA's prohibition on retaliation, like Oregon's prohibition on peyote use, is a valid and neutral law of general applicability. But a church's selection of its ministers is unlike an individual's ingestion of peyote. Smith involved government regulation of only outward physical acts. The present case, in contrast, concerns government interference with an internal church decision that affects the faith and mission of the church itself. The contention that Smith forecloses recognition of a ministerial exception rooted in the Religion Clauses has no merit.

Having concluded that there is a ministerial exception grounded in the Religion Clauses of the First Amendment, we consider whether the exception applies in this case. We hold that it does.

Every Court of Appeals to have considered the question has concluded that the ministerial exception is not limited to the head of a religious congregation, and we agree. We are reluctant, however, to adopt a rigid formula for deciding when an employee qualifies as a minister. It is enough for us to conclude, in this our first case involving the ministerial exception, that the exception covers Perich, given all the circumstances of her employment.

To begin with, Hosanna-Tabor held Perich out as a minister, with a role distinct from that of most of its members. When Hosanna-Tabor extended her a call, it issued her a "diploma of vocation" according her the title "Minister of Religion, Commissioned." She was tasked with performing that office "according to the Word of God and the confessional standards of the Evangelical Lutheran Church as drawn from the Sacred Scriptures." The congregation prayed that God "bless [her] ministrations to the glory of His holy name, [and] the building of His church." In a supplement to the diploma, the congregation undertook to periodically review Perich's "skills of ministry" and "ministerial responsibilities," and to provide for her "continuing education as a professional person in the ministry of the Gospel."

* * *

Perich held herself out as a minister of the Church by accepting the formal call to religious service, according to its terms. She did so in other ways as well. For example, she claimed a special housing allowance on her taxes that was available only to employees earning their compensation " 'in the exercise of the ministry.' " In a form she submitted to the Synod following her termination, Perich again indicated that she regarded herself as a minister at Hosanna-Tabor, stating: "I feel that God is leading me to serve in the teaching ministry. . . . I am anxious to be in the teaching ministry again soon."

Perich's job duties reflected a role in conveying the Church's message and carrying out its mission. Hosanna-Tabor expressly charged her with "lead[ing] others toward Christian maturity" and "teach[ing] faithfully the Word of God, the Sacred Scriptures, in its truth and purity and as set forth in all the symbolical books of the Evangelical Lutheran Church." In fulfilling these responsibilities, Perich taught her students religion four days a week, and led them in prayer three times a day. Once a week, she took her students to a school-wide chapel service, and—about twice a year—she took her turn leading it, choosing the liturgy, selecting the hymns, and delivering a short message based on verses from the Bible. During her last year of teaching, Perich also led her fourth graders in a brief devotional exercise each morning. As a source of religious instruction, Perich performed an important role in transmitting the Lutheran faith to the next generation.

In light of these considerations—the formal title given Perich by the Church, the substance reflected in that title, her own use of that title, and the important religious functions she performed for the Church—we conclude that Perich was a minister covered by the ministerial exception.

* * *

Although the Sixth Circuit did not adopt the extreme position pressed here by the EEOC, it did regard the relative amount of time Perich spent performing religious functions as largely determinative. The issue before us, however, is not one that can be resolved by a stopwatch. The amount of time an employee spends on particular activities is relevant in assessing that employee's status, but that factor cannot be considered in isolation, without regard to the nature of the religious functions performed and the other considerations discussed above.

* * *

The EEOC and Perich foresee a parade of horribles that will follow our recognition of a ministerial exception to employment discrimination suits. According to the EEOC and Perich, such an exception could protect religious organizations from liability for retaliating against employees for reporting criminal misconduct or for testifying before a grand jury or in a criminal trial. What is more, the EEOC contends, the logic of the exception would confer on religious employers "unfettered discretion" to violate employment laws by, for example, hiring children or aliens not authorized to work in the United States.

Hosanna-Tabor responds that the ministerial exception would not in any way bar criminal prosecutions for interfering with law enforcement investigations or other proceedings. Nor, according to the Church, would the exception bar government enforcement of general laws restricting eligibility for employment, because the exception applies only to suits by or on behalf of ministers themselves. Hosanna-Tabor also notes that the ministerial exception has been around in the lower courts for 40 years.

The case before us is an employment discrimination suit brought on behalf of a minister, challenging her church's decision to fire her. Today we hold only that the ministerial exception bars such a suit. We express no view on whether the exception bars other types of suits, including actions by employees alleging breach of contract or tortious conduct by their religious employers. There will be time enough to address the applicability of the exception to other circumstances if and when they arise.

* * *

The interest of society in the enforcement of employment discrimination statutes is undoubtedly important. But so too is the interest of religious groups in choosing who will preach their beliefs, teach their faith, and carry out their mission. When a minister who has been fired sues her church alleging that her termination was discriminatory, the First Amendment has struck the balance for us. The church must be free to choose those who will guide it on its way.

The judgment of the Court of Appeals for the Sixth Circuit is reversed.

It is so ordered.

■ JUSTICE THOMAS, concurring.

I join the Court's opinion. I write separately to note that, in my view, the Religion Clauses require civil courts to apply the ministerial exception and to defer to a religious organization's good-faith understanding of who qualifies as its minister. As the Court explains, the Religion Clauses guarantee religious organizations autonomy in matters of internal governance, including the selection of those who will minister the faith. A religious organization's right to choose its ministers would be hollow, however, if secular courts could second-guess the organization's sincere determination that a given employee is a "minister" under the organization's theological tenets. Our country's religious landscape includes organizations with different leadership structures and doctrines that influence their conceptions of ministerial status. The question whether an employee is a minister is itself religious in nature, and the answer will vary widely. Judicial attempts to fashion a civil definition of "minister" through a bright-line test or multi-factor analysis risk disadvantaging those religious groups whose beliefs, practices, and membership are outside of the "mainstream" or unpalatable to some.

■ JUSTICE ALITO, with whom JUSTICE KAGAN joins, concurring.

I join the Court's opinion, but I write separately to clarify my understanding of the significance of formal ordination and designation as a "minister" in determining whether an "employee" of a religious group falls within the so-called "ministerial" exception. The term "minister" is commonly used by many Protestant denominations to refer to members of their clergy, but the term is rarely if ever used in this way by Catholics, Jews, Muslims, Hindus, or Buddhists. In addition, the concept of ordination as understood by most Christian churches and by Judaism has no clear counterpart in some Christian denominations and some other religions. Because virtually every religion in the world is represented in the population of the United States, it would be a mistake if the term "minister" or the concept of ordination were viewed as central to the important issue of religious autonomy that is presented in cases like this one. Instead, courts should focus on the function performed by persons who work for religious bodies.

NOTE

Relying on *Hosanna-Tabor*, the Fifth Circuit in Cannata v. Catholic Diocese of Austin, 700 F.3d 169 (5th Cir. 2012), held that the ministerial exception barred an ADEA claim by the church's music director because by playing the piano during services he "furthered the mission of the church and helped convey its message to the congregants." Id. at 177. The court emphasized that in determining when the ministerial exception applies "the *Hosanna-Tabor* Court engaged in a fact-intensive inquiry and explicitly rejected the adoption of a 'rigid formula' or bright-line test." Id. at 176.

3. AGE

Page 223.   Please add before last sentence of note 2.

However, an exception exists that allows state and local governments to set mandatory retirement ages for firefighters and law enforcement officers. See Sadi v. City of Cleveland, 2013 WL 2476729 (6th Cir., June 11, 2013) (finding no ADEA violation when police officers were forced to retire pursuant to mandatory retirement law).

4. DISABILITY

Page 230.   Please add the following at the end of *Minor and transitory impairments*.

Nonetheless, in Summers v. Altarum Institute, Corp., 740 F.3d 325 (4th Cir. 2014), the Fourth Circuit held that a temporary impairment, albeit one lasting more than six months, was not excluded from the definition of disability under the ADAAA.

Page 234.   Please add at the end of note 8.

As the Sixth Circuit explained in EEOC v. Ford Motor Co., 2014 WL 1584674 (6th Cir., Apr. 22, 2014): "When we first developed the principle that attendance is an essential requirement of most jobs, technology was such that the workplace and an employer's brick-and-mortar location were synonymous. However, as technology has advanced in the intervening decades, and an ever-greater number of employers and employees utilize remote work arrangements, attendance at the workplace can no longer be assumed to mean attendance at the employer's physical location." 2014 WL 1584674 at *6.

Page 235.   Please add after note 9.

10. Following the Supreme Court's ruling in Gross v. FBL Fin. Servs., Inc., 557 U.S. 167 (2009), in which the Supreme Court held that the mixed motives framework did not apply to ADEA claims, the Seventh Circuit has held that the mixed motives framework similarly does not apply to ADA claims. See Serwatka v. Rockwell Automation, Inc., 591 F.3d 957, 962 (7th Cir. 2010) (explaining that "in the absence of a cross-reference to Title VII's mixed-motive liability language or comparable stand-alone language in the ADA itself, a plaintiff complaining of discriminatory discharge under the ADA must show that his or her employer would not have fired him but for his actual or perceived disability; proof of mixed motives will not suffice").

5. SEXUAL ORIENTATION

Page 242.   Please delete note 7 and replace with the following:

7.   Traditionally, discrimination based on an individual's transsexualism was not prohibited under Title VII. The Seventh Circuit explained the reason for such exclusion in blunt terms in Ulane v. Eastern Airlines, 742 F.2d 1081 (7th Cir. 1984). According to the court, "The phrase in Title VII prohibiting discrimination based on sex, in its plain meaning, implies that it is unlawful to discriminate against women because they are women and against men because they are men. The words of Title VII do not outlaw discrimination against a person who has a sexual identity disorder." Id. at 1085.   In recent years, however, courts have increasingly held that discrimination against transsexual workers who are transitioning from one sex to the other violates the prohibition on sex stereotyping articulated by the Supreme Court in *Price Waterhouse*. The first circuit court to provide such protection was the Sixth Circuit in Smith v. City of Salem, 378 F.3d 566 (6th Cir. 2004). *Smith* involved a biologically male lieutenant in the Salem Fire Department who was disciplined after he began to express a more feminine appearance at work.   In reversing the district court's dismissal of Smith's claims, the Sixth Circuit explained that after *Price Waterhouse*, "employers who discriminate against men because they do wear dresses and makeup, or otherwise act femininely, are also engaging in sex discrimination because the discrimination would not occur but for the victim's sex." Id. at 574. See also Glenn v. Brumby, 663 F.3d 1312 (11th Cir. 2011) (holding that discriminating against someone on the basis of his or her gender non-conformity constitutes sex-based discrimination under the Equal Protection Clause).

Such protection has not, however, extended to transsexual workers' use of the bathroom of their choice. Transsexual workers continue to lose claims asserting a right to use the bathroom associated with their gender identity rather than their biological sex. For example, Etsitty v. Utah Transit Auth., 502 F.3d 1215 (10th Cir. 2007) involved a bus driver who informed her employer that she was transsexual and would begin to present as female at work and use female restrooms while on her route. Her employer terminated her because it was unable to accommodate her restroom needs. The Tenth Circuit held that Etsitty was not entitled to protection under Title VII because the employer's concern about potential liability stemming from her use of female restrooms, while still biologically male, was a legitimate business justification for burdening the plaintiff's gender expression. See also Kastle v. Maricopa County Community College District, 325 Fed. Appx. 492 (9th Cir. 2009) (explaining that "after *Hopkins* and *Schwenk*, it is unlawful to discriminate against a transgender (or any other person) because he or she does not behave in accordance with an employer's expectations for men or women," but holding that employer's ban on transsexual plaintiff's use of women's restroom for safety reasons did not constitute sex discrimination).   Transgendered individuals have also been held to be protected under at least one state sex discrimination law.   See, e.g., Enriquez v. West Jersey Health Sys., 777 A.2d 365

(N.J.App.Div.2001), cert. denied, 785 A.2d 439 (N.J.2001). See generally Ann C. McGinley, Erasing Boundaries: Masculinities, Sexual Minorities, and Employment Discrimination, 43 U. Mich. J. L Reform 713 (2010).

PART III

TERMS AND CONDITIONS OF EMPLOYMENT

CHAPTER 5

WAGES AND HOURS

A. FEDERAL AND STATE WAGE AND HOUR REGULATION

1. FEDERAL WAGE AND HOUR REGULATION: THE FAIR LABOR STANDARDS ACT

a. BASIC PROVISIONS OF THE FAIR LABOR STANDARDS ACT

(i) Minimum Wage

Page 247. Please delete the first paragraph under STATE MINIMUM WAGE LAWS and replace with the following note.

In all, 27 states have minimum wages higher than that required by federal law, and five of them are phasing in hourly minimums of $10 or more: California ($10); Connecticut, Hawaii and Maryland ($10.10); and Vermont ($10.50). This year, eight states and the District of Columbia have increased their minimums. In several more states and municipalities, voters will decide on minimum wage increases in November.

b. COVERAGE

(i) Who Is a Covered Employer?

Page 251. Please add the following note.

4. In Thompson v. Real Estate Mortgage Network, the Third Circuit Court of Appeals determined for the first time that a successor-employer may be held financially accountable for its predecessor's wage-and-hour violations under the Fair Labor Standards Act. Instead of applying the New Jersey state law test for determining whether successor liability applied, the court applied federal common law test, which allowed for a lower bar to relief. It requires consideration of the following factors in determining whether successor liability should be imposed: "(1) continuity in operations and work force of the successor and predecessor employers; (2) notice to the successor-employer of its predecessor's legal obligations; and (3) ability of the predecessor to provide adequate relief directly." By contrast, under New Jersey law, successor companies are considered legally distinct from their predecessors and do not assume any debts or obligations of the successor unless: (1) the successor agrees to assume such liabilities; (2) the transaction amounts to a consolidation or merger of the buyer and seller; (3) the purchasing company is merely a "continuation" of the selling company; or (4) the transaction was consummated to fraudulently escape its liabilities and debts. Thompson v. Real Estate Mortg. Network, 748 F.3d 142 (3d. Cir. 2014).

(ii) Who Is a Covered Employee?

a. WHO IS AN EMPLOYEE?

Page 260.   Please add the following to Note 4 after the sentence beginning "See Patel v. Quality Inn South..."

Congress's purposes in enacting the FLSA and the IRCA are in harmony. The IRCA unambiguously prohibits hiring unauthorized aliens, and the FLSA unambiguously requires that any unauthorized aliens—hired in violation of federal immigration law—be paid minimum and overtime wages. Holding employers who violate federal immigration law and federal employment law liable for both violations advances the purpose of federal immigration policy by deterring employers from hiring undocumented aliens for their most attractive quality: their willingness to work for less than the minimum wage. Lucas v. Jerusalem Café, LLC., 721 F.3d 927 (8th Cir. 2013).

Page 261.   Replace all of Note 7 after its first paragraph with:

Circuit courts split on the interpretation of the FLSA in the context of training programs. Some courts apply *Walling* or the six factors the DOL derived from *Walling*. See, e.g., Donovan v. Am. Airlines, Inc., 686 F.2d 267 (5th Cir. 1982) (relying on *Walling* to determine whether airline trainees were employees for the purposes of the FLSA); Hawkins v. Securitas Sec. Services USA, 2013 U.S. Dist. LEXIS 44914 (N.D. Ill. 2013) ("A trainee's entitlement to wages for time spent in training is governed by a six-part test developed by the Department of Labor and derived from Walling v. Portland Terminal Co."). Others consider the "economic realities" of the situation and look at the totality of the circumstances, sometimes considering the DOL guidelines. See, e.g., Kaplan v. Code Blue Billing & Coding, Inc., 504 Fed. Appx. 831, 834–35 (11th Cir. 2013) (stating that to determine whether a trainee is an employee a court "must consider "the economic realities of the relationship, including whether a person's work confers an economic benefit on the entity for whom they are working" and considering the DOL guidelines as "guidance"). Still others apply the primary benefit test, in which they ask whether the employer or the trainees principally benefited from the work the trainees did. See, e.g., Solis v. Laurelbrook Sanitarium & Sch., Inc., 642 F.3d 518 (6th Cir. 2011) (" the proper approach for determining whether an employment relationship exists in the context of a training or learning situation is to ascertain which party derives the primary benefit from the relationship"). The Ninth Circuit has developed its own approach in which it considers whether the putative employer received an advantage from the trainee's activities and whether there was an agreement for compensation. Nance v. May Trucking Co., 2014 U.S. Dist. LEXIS 5520, at *13–14 (D. Or. 2014) (to determine whether a trainee is an employee a court "consider[s] (1) whether Defendant received an immediate advantage from Plaintiffs' work at the orientation and (2) whether there was an express or implied agreement for compensation").

In the Southern District of New York, two judges applied the totality of the circumstance test to determine whether unpaid interns are employees and came to differing conclusions. Compare Xuedan Wang v. Hearst Corp., 293 F.R.D. 489, 493 (S.D.N.Y. 2013) motion to certify appeal granted, 2013 WL 3326650 (S.D.N.Y. 2013) (stating that "the Supreme

Court in *Walling* looked to the totality of circumstances of the training program to determine whether the plaintiffs were 'employees' under the FLSA," using the DOL's six factor test as a "framework for . . . analysis" and determining that there was a genuine issue of material fact about whether the interns were employees), with Glatt v. Fox Searchlight Pictures Inc., 293 F.R.D. 516, 532–34 (S.D.N.Y. 2013) on reconsideration in part, 2013 WL 4834428 (S.D.N.Y. 2013), 2013 WL 5405696 (S.D.N.Y. 2013) (applying the totality of the circumstances test, considering the DOL factors, and concluding that unpaid interns were employees for purposes of the FLSA). As a result, the questions of what test applies and whether unpaid interns are employees are currently before the Second Circuit.

The *Glatt* and *Wang* lawsuits are part of a flood of lawsuits from unpaid interns seeking back wages. These lawsuits could have significant consequences for unpaid internships. A pending lawsuit has already led magazine publisher Condé Nast to end its internship program entirely. Cara Buckley, *Sued Over Pay, Condé Nast Ends Internship Program,* N.Y. Times (Oct. 23, 2013).

The uncertain legality of unpaid internships is problematic. The problems are exacerbated by the large number of students who intern during college. The consulting company Accenture found that 72% of students who graduated from college in 2011 and 2012 had interned at some point during college. More than half of those internships were unpaid. Accenture, 2013 College Graduate Employment Survey 5. See also Busk v. Integrity Staffing Solutions, 713 F.3d 525 (9th Cir. 2013), cert. granted, 134 S.Ct. 1490 (2014). Plaintiffs worked for a company that provides warehouse space to clients such as Amazon. They brought federal and Nevada state class actions saying that they had been denied legally required compensation for the time it took them to pass through security clearance at end of their shifts and also for the time spent walking to the cafeteria for lunch. One issue the Supreme Court may address is whether a federal court can hear a state-law claim for which the state's opt-out class action procedure controls given that the federal FLSA law allows only opt-in class actions.

Page 262.   In the first paragraph of Note 7, replace "The Wage and Hour Division (WHD) of the Department Of Labor has derived a 6 factor test from the *Walling* decision" with the following sentence and then continue with the rest of the paragraph.

The Wage and Hour Division of the Department of Labor derived a 6-factor test from the *Walling* decision that provides guidance about the legality of trainee programs and in 2010 it extended that test to unpaid internships.

b.   EXEMPT EMPLOYEES

Page 262.   Please delete *In re Novartis Wage & Hour Litigation* **and replace with the following case.**

Christopher v. SmithKline Beecham Corp.
132 S.Ct. 2156 (2012).

■ JUSTICE ALITO delivered the opinion of the Court.

The Fair Labor Standards Act (FLSA) imposes minimum wage and maximum hours requirements on employers, but those requirements do not apply to workers employed "in the capacity of outside salesman." This case requires us to decide whether the term "outside salesman," as defined by Department of Labor (DOL or Department) regulations, encompasses pharmaceutical sales representatives whose primary duty is to obtain nonbinding commitments from physicians to prescribe their employer's prescription drugs in appropriate cases. We conclude that these employees qualify as "outside salesm[e]n."

* * *

Congress did not define the term "outside salesman," but it delegated authority to the DOL to issue regulations "from time to time" to "defin[e] and delimi[t]" the term. The DOL promulgated such regulations in 1938, 1940, and 1949. In 2004, following notice-and-comment procedures, the DOL reissued the regulations with minor amendments. The current regulations are nearly identical in substance to the regulations issued in the years immediately following the FLSA's enactment.

* * *

The general regulation sets out the definition of the statutory term "employee employed in the capacity of outside salesman." It defines the term to mean "any employee . . . [w]hose primary duty is . . . making sales within the meaning of [29 U. S. C. § 203(k)]" and "[w]ho is customarily and regularly engaged away from the employer's place or places of business in performing such primary duty." The referenced statutory provision states that " '[s]ale' or 'sell' includes any sale, exchange, contract to sell, consignment for sale, shipment for sale, or other disposition." Thus, under the general regulation, an outside salesman is any employee whose primary duty is making any sale, exchange, contract to sell, consignment for sale, shipment for sale, or other disposition.

The sales regulation restates the statutory definition of sale discussed above and clarifies that "[s]ales within the meaning of [29 U. S. C. § 203(k)] include the transfer of title to tangible property, and in certain cases, of tangible and valuable evidences of intangible property."

Finally, the promotion work regulation identifies "[p]romotion work" as "one type of activity often performed by persons who make sales, which may or may not be exempt outside sales work, depending upon the circumstances under which it is performed." Promotion work that is "performed incidental to and in conjunction with an employee's own outside sales or solicitations is exempt work," whereas promotion work that is "incidental to sales made, or to be made, by someone else is not exempt outside sales work."

* * *

Respondent SmithKline Beecham Corporation is in the business of developing, manufacturing, and selling prescription drugs. The prescription drug industry is subject to extensive federal regulation, including the now familiar requirement that prescription drugs be dispensed only upon a physician's prescription. In light of this requirement, pharmaceutical companies have long focused their direct marketing efforts, not on the retail pharmacies that dispense prescription drugs, but rather on the medical practitioners who possess the authority to prescribe the drugs in the first place. Pharmaceutical companies promote their prescription drugs to physicians through a process called "detailing," whereby employees known as "detailers" or "pharmaceutical sales representatives" provide information to physicians about the company's products in hopes of persuading them to write prescriptions for the products in appropriate cases. The position of "detailer" has existed in the pharmaceutical industry in substantially its current form since at least the 1950's, and in recent years the industry has employed more than 90,000 detailers nationwide.

Respondent hired petitioners Michael Christopher and Frank Buchanan as pharmaceutical sales representatives in 2003. During the roughly four years when petitioners were employed in that capacity, they were responsible for calling on physicians in an assigned sales territory to discuss the features, benefits, and risks of an assigned portfolio of respondent's prescription drugs. Petitioners' primary objective was to obtain a nonbinding commitment from the physician to prescribe those drugs in appropriate cases, and the training that petitioners received underscored the importance of that objective.

Petitioners spent about 40 hours each week in the field calling on physicians. These visits occurred during normal business hours, from about 8:30 a.m. to 5 p.m. Outside of normal business hours, petitioners spent an additional 10 to 20 hours each week attending events, reviewing product information, returning phone calls, responding to e-mails, and performing other miscellaneous tasks.

Petitioners were not required to punch a clock or report their hours, and they were subject to only minimal supervision.

Petitioners were well compensated for their efforts. On average, Christopher's annual gross pay was just over $72,000, and Buchanan's was just over $76,000.[7] Petitioners' gross pay included both a base salary and incentive pay. The amount of petitioners' incentive pay was based on the sales volume or market share of their assigned drugs in their assigned sales territories, and this amount was uncapped. Christopher's incentive pay exceeded 30 percent of his gross pay during each of his years of employment; Buchanan's exceeded 25 percent. It is undisputed that respondent did not pay petitioners time-and-a half wages when they worked in excess of 40 hours per week.

---

[7]   The median pay for pharmaceutical detailers nationwide exceeds $90,000 per year.

* * *

The DOL first announced its view that pharmaceutical detailers are not exempt outside salesmen in an amicus brief filed in the Second Circuit in 2009, and the Department has subsequently filed similar amicus briefs in other cases, including the case now before us. While the DOL's ultimate conclusion that detailers are not exempt has remained unchanged since 2009, the same cannot be said of its reasoning. In both the Second Circuit and the Ninth Circuit, the DOL took the view that "a 'sale' for the purposes of the outside sales exemption requires a consummated transaction directly involving the employee for whom the exemption is sought." Perhaps because of the nebulous nature of this "consummated transaction" test, the Department changed course after we granted certiorari in this case. The Department now takes the position that "[a]n employee does not make a 'sale' for purposes of the 'outside salesman' exemption unless he actually transfers title to the property at issue." Petitioners and the DOL assert that this new interpretation of the regulations is entitled to controlling deference.

* * *

In this case, there are strong reasons for withholding the deference that Auer v. Robbins, 519 U.S. 452 (1997), generally requires. Petitioners invoke the DOL's interpretation of ambiguous regulations to impose potentially massive liability on respondent for conduct that occurred well before that interpretation was announced. To defer to the agency's interpretation in this circumstance would seriously undermine the principle that agencies should provide regulated parties "fair warning of the conduct [a regulation] prohibits or requires."

This case well illustrates the point. Until 2009, the pharmaceutical industry had little reason to suspect that its longstanding practice of treating detailers as exempt outside salesmen transgressed the FLSA. The statute and regulations certainly do not provide clear notice of this. The general regulation adopts the broad statutory definition of "sale," and that definition, in turn, employs the broad catchall phrase "other disposition." This catchall phrase could reasonably be construed to encompass a nonbinding commitment from a physician to prescribe a particular drug, and nothing in the statutory or regulatory text or the DOL's prior guidance plainly requires a contrary reading. Even more important, despite the industry's decades long practice of classifying pharmaceutical detailers as exempt employees, the DOL never initiated any enforcement actions with respect to detailers or otherwise suggested that it thought the industry was acting unlawfully. We acknowledge that an agency's enforcement decisions are informed by a host of factors, some bearing no relation to the agency's views regarding whether a violation has occurred. But where, as here, an agency's announcement of its interpretation is preceded by a very lengthy period of conspicuous inaction, the potential for unfair surprise is acute.

* * *

Accordingly, whatever the general merits of Auer deference, it is unwarranted here. We instead accord the Department's interpretation a measure of deference proportional to the " 'thoroughness evident in its consideration, the validity of its reasoning, its consistency with earlier and late pronouncements, and all those factors which give it power to persuade.' "

* * *

We begin with the text of the FLSA. Although the provision that establishes the overtime salesman exemption does not furnish a clear answer to the question before us, it provides at least one interpretive clue: It exempts anyone "employed . . . in the capacity of [an] outside salesman." "Capacity," used in this sense, means "[o]utward condition or circumstances; relation; character; position." The statute's emphasis on the "capacity" of the employee counsels in favor of a functional, rather than a formal, inquiry, one that views an employee's responsibilities in the context of the particular industry in which the employee works.

* * *

Petitioners made sales for purposes of the FLSA and therefore are exempt outside salesmen within the meaning of the DOL's regulations. Obtaining a nonbinding commitment from a physician to prescribe one of respondent's drugs is the most that petitioners were able to do to ensure the eventual disposition of the products that respondent sells. This kind of arrangement, in the unique regulatory environment within which pharmaceutical companies must operate, comfortably falls within the catch-all category of "other disposition."

That petitioners bear all of the external indicia of salesmen provides further support for our conclusion. Petitioners were hired for their sales experience. They were trained to close each sales call by obtaining the maximum commitment possible from the physician. They worked away from the office, with minimal supervision, and they were rewarded for their efforts with incentive compensation. It would be anomalous to require respondent to compensate petitioners for overtime, while at the same time exempting employees who function identically to petitioners in every respect except that they sell physician administered drugs, such as vaccines and other injectable pharmaceuticals, that are ordered by the physician directly rather than purchased by the end user at a pharmacy with a prescription from the physician.

Our holding also comports with the apparent purpose of the FLSA's exemption for outside salesmen. The exemption is premised on the belief that exempt employees "typically earned salaries well above the minimum wage" and enjoyed other benefits that "se[t] them apart from the nonexempt workers entitled to overtime pay." It was also thought that exempt employees performed a kind of work that "was difficult to standardize to any time frame and could not be easily spread to other workers after 40 hours in a week, making compliance with the overtime provisions difficult and generally precluding the potential job expansion intended by the FLSA's time-and-a-half overtime premium." Petitioners each of whom earned an average of more than $70,000 per year and spent between 10 and 20 hours outside normal business hours each week performing work related to his assigned portfolio of drugs in his assigned sales territory are hardly the kind of employees that the FLSA was intended to protect. And it would be challenging, to say the least, for pharmaceutical companies to compensate detailers for overtime going forward without significantly changing the nature of that position. For these reasons, we conclude that petitioners qualify as outside salesmen under the most reasonable interpretation of the DOL's regulations. The judgment of the Court of Appeals is *Affirmed*.

■ JUSTICE BREYER, with whom JUSTICE GINSBURG, JUSTICE SOTOMAYOR, and JUSTICE KAGAN join, dissenting.

* * *

Unless we give the words of the statute and regulations some special meaning, a detailer's primary duty is not that of "making sales" or the equivalent. A detailer might convince a doctor to prescribe a drug for a particular kind of patient. If the doctor encounters such a patient, he might prescribe the drug. The doctor's client, the patient, might take the prescription to a pharmacist and ask the pharmacist to fill the prescription. If so, the pharmacist might sell the manufacturer's drug to the patient, or might substitute a generic version. But it is the pharmacist, not the detailer, who will have sold the drug.

To put the same fairly obvious point in the language of the regulations and of § 3(k) of the FLSA, the detailer does not "sell" anything to the doctor. Nor does he, during the course of that visit or immediately thereafter, "exchange" the manufacturer's product for money or for anything else. He enters into no "contract to sell" on behalf of anyone. He "consigns" nothing "for sale." He "ships" nothing for sale. He does not "dispose" of any product at all.

What the detailer does is inform the doctor about the nature of the manufacturer's drugs and explain their uses, their virtues, their drawbacks, and their limitations. The detailer may well try to convince the doctor to prescribe the manufacturer's drugs for patients. And if the detailer is successful, the doctor will make a "nonbinding commitment" to write prescriptions using one or more of those drugs where appropriate. If followed, that "nonbinding commitment" is, at most, a nonbinding promise to consider advising a patient to use a drug where medical indications so indicate (if the doctor encounters such a patient), and to write a prescription that will likely (but may not) lead that person to order that drug under its brand name from the pharmacy. (I say "may not" because 30% of patients in a 2–year period have not filled a prescription given to them by a doctor. And when patients do fill prescriptions, 75% are filled with generic drugs.

Where in this process does the detailer *sell* the product? At most he obtains from the doctor a "nonbinding commitment" to advise his patient to take the drug (or perhaps a generic equivalent) as well as to write any necessary prescription. I put to the side the fact that neither the Court nor the record explains exactly what a "nonbinding commitment" is. Like a "definite maybe," an "impossible solution," or a "theoretical experience," a "nonbinding commitment" seems to claim more than it can deliver. Regardless, other than in colloquial speech, to obtain a commitment to *advise* a client to buy a product is not to obtain a commitment to *sell* that product, no matter how often the client takes the advice (or the patient does what the doctor recommends).

* * *

Taken together, the statute, regulations, ethical codes, and Labor Department Reports indicate that the drug detailers do not promote their "own sales," but rather "sales made, or to be made, by someone else." Therefore, detailers are not "outside salesmen." And the detailers do not fall within that category. For these reasons, with respect, I dissent.

Page 274.   Please replace note 1 with the following note.

The Seventh Circuit considered overtime eligibility for another group of pharmaceutical sales representatives and avoided the issue of the "outside sales exemption" by holding that the representatives meet the requirements for the "administrator exemption." This means that the sales reps'" primary duty includes the exercise of discretion and independent judgment with respect to matters of significance." Schaefer-LaRose v. Eli Lilly & Co., 679 F.3d 560 (7th Cir. 2012).

Page 274.   Please add the following at the end of note 6.

The Obama administration has proposed amending the FLSA's companionship services exemption to grant minimum wage and overtime wage protection to homecare workers employed by third parties such as staffing agencies. The proposed amendments would limit the definition of "companionship services" to duties directly related to the provision of fellowship and protection rather than personal care services such as grooming, dressing, and driving to appointments. The Supreme Court unanimously decided that the statutory provision meant that the workers need not be paid for changing clothes. Justice Scalia discussed in detail the possible meanings of the word "clothes," because at least some of these workers had to wear protective gear: "a flame-retardant jacket, pair of pants, and hood; a hardhat; a 'snood'; 'wristlets'; work gloves . . . safety glasses, earplugs; and a respirator." Judge Richard Posner's decision in the court of appeals, reaching the result that the Supreme Court affirmed, had included a photograph of a male model wearing these items. Justice Scalia also discussed the meaning of "changing," saying that "layer[ing] garments" is covered as is taking off one item of clothing and replacing it with another. He said that glasses, earplug, and a respirator are not "clothes," but that adding those items takes little time so the additional seconds or minutes need not be compensated. Sandifer v. United States Steel Corp, 134 S.Ct. 870 (2014).

c.   WAGES

Page 277.   Please add the following note.

8.   Restaurant servers alleged that their employers showed service charges on customers' bills but did not give the servers the money. Their salaries were above minimum wage. New York law forbids an employer from retaining "any charge purported to be a gratuity." The state's highest court held that this provision applies not only to tips presented by the customer but also to a service charge shown on the bill that the customer is likely to think is a tip. Samiento v. World Yacht Inc., 883 N.E.2d 990 (N.Y. 2008).

See also Matamoros v. Starbucks Corp., 699 F.3d 129 (1st Cir. 2012), holding that Massachusetts' "Tips Act" does not permit Starbucks to share customer gratuities with "shift supervisors" as well as with baristas because the shift supervisors perform a small degree of supervisory work.

d. HOURS

Page 281.   Please add the following notes.

10. U.S. Steel workers sued the company for violating the FLSA by not paying for the time spent changing clothes at the plant and for walking to and from their work stations.   The company's and union's collective bargaining agreement did not provide compensation for that time.   29 U.S.C. §203(o) of the statute excludes from entitled time "any time spent in changing clothes or washing ... which was excluded ... by the express terms of ... a bona-fide collective bargaining agreement."   The court of appeals held that the statutory provision meant that the workers need not be paid for changing clothes nor for their walks to and from the workplace. Sandifer v. United States Steel Corp., 678 F.3d 590 (7th Cir. 2012) (Posner, J.), cert granted, 133 S.Ct. 1240 (2013).

11. West Yellowstone, Montana, employed a police force of four.   They worked 12-hour shifts but had to be on-call for the 12 hours preceding a shift.   When on call they had to stay within cell phone access and keep the ringer loud enough to wake them if they were asleep.   If called the officer would get a minimum of 2.5 hours of overtime pay.   A jury, influenced by evidence that Sergeant Stubblefield was in fact called out only 18 times in 609 on-call shifts (with similar numbers for two other officers) ruled for the town and the Montana Supreme Court refused to overturn the jury verdict. Stubblefield v. Town of West Yellowstone, 298 P.3d 419 (Mont. 2013).

f. ENFORCEMENT OF THE FLSA

Page 285.   Please add the following note.

5. The FLSA's anti-retaliation provision forbids employers from discharging or discriminating against any employee because, *inter alia*, the employee "filed any complaint" against such employer. Fair Labor Standards Act, 29 U.S.C. § 215(a)(3). In Kasten v. Saint-Gobain Performance Plastics Corp., 131 S.Ct. 1325 (2011), the Supreme Court considered whether the statutory phrase "filed any complaint" applies to oral as well as written complaints. On several occasions Kevin Kasten complained to his employers that the position of the timeclocks between the area where workers donned and doffed work-related protective gear violated the FLSA. Kasten argued that the oral complaints led the company to discipline him and eventually dismiss him. The Supreme Court held that the FLSA's anti-retaliation provision protects both oral and written complaints. Although the statutory text alone was inconclusive on the subject, Justice Breyer reasoned that both congressional intent to protect oral complaints and deference to an EEOC interpretation finding that oral complaints were covered weighed in favor of the holding. The Court limited protection to oral complaints which a reasonable, objective person would have understood as putting the employer on notice that the employee was asserting statutory rights under the Act. In a dissenting opinion, Justice Scalia, joined by Justice Thomas, argued that the plain meaning of the statutory phrase "filed any complaint" applied only to complaints filed with a government body and not complaints delivered from an employee to an employer. The majority declined to reach the issue addressed by the dissent, since the issue was not raised in the certiorari petitions.

6. Plaintiff, formerly a registered nurse at Pennypack Center in Philadelphia, sued on behalf of herself and "all other persons similarly situated." She said that petitioners violated the FLSA by deducting 30 minutes per shift for meal breaks even when the employees worked during those breaks. Defendant offered to settle the case for $7,500 in unpaid wages plus attorneys' fees and other costs. Plaintiff did not respond to defendant's offer. The Supreme Court, in an opinion by Justice Thomas, decided that because plaintiff had been offered full compensation and no other individuals had joined her suit, she no longer possessed a personal stake and her lawsuit was therefore moot. Justice Kagan, dissenting, wrote: "[A]n unaccepted offer of judgment cannot moot a case. When a plaintiff rejects such an offer . . . her interest in the lawsuit remains just what it was before. And so too does the court's ability to grant her relief." Genesis Healthcare Corp. v. Symczyk, 133 S.Ct. 1523 (2013) (5–4).

B. WHAT IS A JOB WORTH?

1. WAGE COMPARABILITY FOR INDIVIDUALS: THE QUEST FOR PAY EQUITY

b. TITLE VII OF THE CIVIL RIGHTS ACT OF 1964

Page 307. Please add the following note before the Sullivan reading.

NOTE

The Texas Supreme Court held that since the Texas Legislature has enacted nothing comparable to the Lily Ledbetter Act, a plaintiff suing pursuant to the Texas Commission on Human Rights Act, modeled after Title VII, must file a claim within 180 days of the date the employee learns what his or her pay will be. Prairie View A&M University v. Chatha, 381 S.W.3d 500 (Tex. 2012). Chief Justice Jefferson, dissenting, said: "This [decision] creates innumerable problems, not the least of which are the elimination of equitable defenses and a divergence between the Act and the statute it was enacted to promote. . . . I would hold that the 180-day period . . . is not a statutory prerequisite to suit."

CHAPTER 6

HEALTH BENEFITS

A. INTRODUCTION

Page 316.   Please add the following at the end of the first paragraph of Large Employer Penalty.

The employer mandate, scheduled to begin on January 1, 2014 was postponed until January 1, 2015. www.treasury.gov/connect/blog/Pages/ Continuing-to-Implement-the-ACA-in-a-Careful-Thoughtful-Manner-aspx.

Page 316.   Please add the following before the last full paragraph.

The Department of Health and Human Services (HHS) issued regulations in 2012 holding that the ACA provision requiring health plans to cover "preventive health services without cost sharing," 42 U.S.C. 300gg–13(a)(4), included all FDA-approved contraceptive methods and sterilization procedures, including the "morning-after pill." 77 Fed. Reg. 8725 (2012). There is a "religious employers" exemption, 45 C.F.R. § 147.130(a)(1)(iv)(A)–(B), but the exemption does not apply to for-profit businesses.

In Burwell v. Hobby Lobby, 134 S. Ct. 2751 (2014), the Supreme Court, five-to-four, held that "closely held," for-profit companies run on religious principles can challenge government actions pursuant to the Religious Freedom Restoration Act and that such companies can seek an exemption from the birth control mandate of the ACA. The Obama Administration previously had provided an accommodation to permit employees of religious-affiliated nonprofits to obtain insurance coverage without direct employer involvement, by authorizing insurers to provide the coverage directly. It is likely that this provision will be extended to religiously oriented, for-profit companies. Notwithstanding the decision in *Hobby Lobby*, laws in 28 states provide that health insurance policies covering prescription drugs are required to cover all FDA-approved contraceptive drugs and devices.

Page 317.   Please note the following.

The Free Choice Voucher provision was repealed in 2011.

Page 321.   Please add the following before B.

JUDICIAL CHALLENGE

The controversial Affordable Care Act (ACA) was subject to several judicial challenges alleging the statute is unconstitutional. The cases were consolidated in a much-anticipated Supreme Court decision in June 2012. In National Federation of Independent Business v. Sebelius, 132 S. Ct. 2566 (2012), the Supreme Court, five-to-four, in an opinion by Chief Justice Roberts, rejected challenges to the constitutionality of the ACA. There were two main issues. First, the challengers asserted that the individual mandate is not a valid exercise of congressional power under the Commerce Clause. Although a majority of the Court agreed that the Commerce Clause did not permit regulation of individuals who were doing nothing (i.e., not buying health insurance), a majority held that the individual mandate was a legitimate exercise of Congress' taxing power. Second, a majority of the Court held that the Medicaid expansion violates the Spending Clause of the Constitution by threatening states with the loss of their existing Medicaid funding if they decline to participate in the expansion. Nevertheless, the Court held that the constitutional violation is fully remedied by precluding the Secretary of Health and Human Services from withdrawing current Medicaid funding from any state electing not to participate in the expansion. Under the ACA states are eligible for 100 percent federal funding for three years to increase Medicaid eligibility to individuals with incomes below 133 percent of the federal poverty level ($30,657 for a family of four). After three years the federal payment drops to 90 percent.

Although the specific provisions applicable to employers were not the basis of the challenges to the ACA, employers certainly were interested in the outcome of the case. The effect of the Court's decision is to confirm the obligations of employers, including reporting of the value of health coverage on employees' Form W–2 (beginning 2013), limiting to $2,500 the amount of employer contributions to employees' flexible health care spending accounts (beginning 2013), and the employer mandate. The mandate for all employers, originally scheduled to take effect on January 1, 2014, was delayed until January 1, 2015. The mandate for mid-size employers (51–100 employees) was delayed until January 1, 2016.

D. FAMILY AND MEDICAL LEAVE

Page 353.   Please delete *Ragsdale* and replace with the following:

Balllard v. Chicago Park District

741 F.3d 838 (7th Cir. 2014).

■ FLAUM, Circuit Judge.

The Family and Medical Leave Act gives eligible employees a right to twelve workweeks of leave "[i]n order to care for the spouse, or a son, daughter, or parent, of the employee, if such spouse, son, daughter, or parent has a serious health condition." 29 U.S.C. § 2612(a)(1)(C). This case is about what qualifies as "caring for" a family member under the Act. In particular, it is about whether the FMLA applies when an employee requests leave so that she can provide physical and psychological care to a terminally ill parent while that parent is traveling away from home. For the reasons set forth below, we conclude that such an employee is seeking leave "to care for" a family member within the meaning of the FMLA.

I. Background

Beverly Ballard is a former Chicago Park District employee. In April 2006, Beverly's mother, Sarah, was diagnosed with end-stage congestive heart failure and began receiving hospice support through

Horizon Hospice & Palliative Care. Beverly lived with Sarah and acted as her primary caregiver; among other things, she cooked her mother's meals, administered insulin and other medication, drained fluids from her heart, bathed and dressed her, and prepared her for bed. In 2007, Sarah and a Horizon Hospice social worker met to discuss Sarah's end-of-life goals. Sarah said that she had always wanted to take a family trip to Las Vegas. The social worker was able to secure funding from the Fairygodmother Foundation, a nonprofit that facilitated these sorts of opportunities for terminally ill adults. The six-day trip was scheduled for January 2008.

Ballard requested unpaid leave from the Chicago Park District so that she could accompany her mother to Las Vegas. (The parties dispute many particulars of Ballard's request, including whether Ballard gave the Park District sufficient notice, but these issues are not germane to this appeal and we will ignore them.) The Park District ultimately denied the request, although Ballard maintains that she was not informed of the denial prior to her trip.

Ballard and her mother traveled to Las Vegas as planned, where they spent time together and participated in typical tourist activities. Beverly continued to serve as her mother's caretaker during the trip. In addition to performing her usual responsibilities, Beverly drove her mother to a hospital when a fire unexpectedly prevented them from reaching their hotel room, where Sarah's medicine was stored.

Several months later, the Chicago Park District terminated Ballard for unauthorized absences accumulated during her trip. Ballard filed suit under the FMLA. The Park District moved for summary judgment, arguing in part that Ballard did not "care for" her mother in Las Vegas because she was already providing Sarah with care at home and because the trip was not related to a continuing course of medical treatment. The district court denied the motion, explaining that "[s]o long as the employee provides 'care' to the family member, where the care takes place has no bearing on whether the employee receives FMLA protections." The Park District moved for an interlocutory appeal.

II. Discussion

We begin with the text of the statute: an eligible employee is entitled to leave "[i]n order to care for" a family member with a "serious health condition." 29 U.S.C. § 2612(a)(1)(C). The Park District does not dispute that Sarah Ballard suffered from a serious health condition. Instead, it claims that Beverly did not "care for" Sarah in Las Vegas. It would have us read the FMLA as limiting "care," at least in the context of an away-from-home trip, only to services provided in connection with ongoing medical treatment.

One problem with the Park District's argument is that § 2612(a)(1)(C) speaks in terms of "care," not "treatment." The latter term does appear in other subsections of § 2612, but Ballard does not rely on those provisions for her leave, and the Park District does not argue that they are implicated in this case. Furthermore, the Park District does not explain why participation in ongoing treatment is required when the employee provides away-from-home care, but not when she provides at-home care. Certainly we see no textual basis for that distinction in the statute.

Another problem is that the FMLA's text does not restrict care to a particular place or geographic location. For instance, it does not say that an employee is entitled to time off "to care *at home* for" a family member. The only limitation it places on care is that the family member must have a serious health condition. We are reluctant, without good reason, to read in another limitation that Congress has not provided.

Still, the FMLA does not define "care," so perhaps there is room to disagree about whether Ballard can be said to have cared for her mother in Las Vegas. We therefore turn to the Department of Labor's regulations to clear away any lurking ambiguity. There are no regulations specifically interpreting 29 U.S.C. § 2612(a)(1)(C). There are, however, regulations interpreting a closely related provision concerning health-care provider certification. Those regulations state:

What does it mean that an employee is "needed to care for" a family member?

(a) The medical certification provision that an employee is "needed to care for" a family member encompasses both physical and psychological care. It includes situations where, for example, because of a serious health condition, the family member is unable to care for his or her own basic medical, hygienic, or nutritional needs or safety, or is unable to transport himself or herself to the doctor, etc. The term also includes providing psychological comfort and reassurance which would be beneficial to a child, spouse or parent with a serious health condition who is receiving inpatient or home care.

* * *

29 C.F.R. § 825.116 (2008).

We see nothing in these regulations to support the Park District's argument, either. The first sentence defines "care" expansively to include "physical and psychological care"—again without any geographic limitation. The only part of the regulations suggesting that the location of care might make a difference is the statement that psychological care "includes providing psychological comfort and reassurance to [a family member] . . . who is *receiving inpatient or home care*." Even so, as the district court correctly observed, this example of what constitutes psychological care does not purport to be exclusive. Moreover, this example only concerns psychological care. The examples of what constitutes physical care use no location-specific language whatsoever.

Sarah's basic medical, hygienic, and nutritional needs did not change while she was in Las Vegas, and Beverly continued to assist her with those needs during the trip. In fact, as the district court observed, Beverly's presence proved quite important indeed when a fire at the hotel made it impossible to reach their room, requiring Beverly to find another source of insulin and pain medicine. Thus, at the very least, Ballard requested leave in order to provide physical care. That, in turn, is enough to satisfy 29 U.S.C. § 2612(a)(1)(C).

The Park District nevertheless argues that any care Ballard provided in Las Vegas needed

to be connected to ongoing medical treatment in order for her leave to be protected by the FMLA. But, like the statute itself, the regulations never use the term "treatment" in their definition of care. Rather, they speak in terms of basic medical, hygienic, and nutritional needs—needs that, as in this case, do not change merely because a person is not undergoing active medical treatment. And it would be odd to read an ongoing-treatment requirement into the definition of "care" when the definition of "serious health condition" explicitly states that active treatment is *not* a prerequisite.

In support of its ongoing-treatment argument, the Park District principally relies on out-of-circuit case law construing 29 U.S.C. § 2612(a)(1)(C). First, it cites a pair of Ninth Circuit cases holding that "caring for a family member with a serious health condition 'involves some level of participation in ongoing treatment of that condition.'" *Tellis v. Alaska Airlines, Inc.,* 414 F.3d 1045, 1047 (9th Cir.2005) (quoting *Marchisheck v. San Mateo Cnty.,* 199 F.3d 1068, 1076 (9th Cir.1999)). Tellis involved an employee who flew cross-country to pick up a car and drive it back to his pregnant wife; Marchisheck involved an employee who brought her son to the Philippines because she worried that his social environment in Los Angeles was unhealthy. Next, the Park District cites a First Circuit case about an employee who took leave to accompany her seriously ill husband on a "healing pilgrimage" to the Philippines. *Tayag v. Lahey Clinic Hosp., Inc.,* 632 F.3d 788 (1st Cir.2011). Before considering whether the pilgrimage qualified as medical care under the FMLA, the *Tayag* court noted that the employee "properly does not claim that caring for her husband would itself be protected leave" if the pair traveled "for reasons unrelated to medical treatment of [her husband's] illnesses."

We respectfully part ways with the First and Ninth Circuits on this point. The only one of these cases that purports to ground its conclusion in the text of the statute or regulations is *Marchisheck*. However, as explained above, we do not see how that conclusion follows. The relevant rule says that, so long as the employee attends to a family member's basic medical, hygienic, or nutritional needs, that employee is caring for the family member, even if that care is not part of ongoing treatment of the condition. Furthermore, none of the cases explain why certain services provided to a family member at home should be considered "care," but those same services provided away from home should not be. Again, we see no basis for that distinction in either the statute or the regulations.

At points in its briefing, the Park District describes Ballard's travel as a "recreational trip" or a "non-medically related pleasure trip." It also raises the specter that employees will help themselves to (unpaid) FMLA leave in order to take personal vacations, simply by bringing seriously ill family members along. So perhaps what the Park District means to argue is that the real reason Beverly requested leave was in order to take a free pleasure trip, and not in order to care for her mother. Whether that sort of argument is borne out by the record— which suggests that Sarah arranged the trip with her social worker as part of her end-of-life hospice planning, that Beverly consulted with

Sarah's doctor about what would be required on the trip, and that Beverly did in fact provide care in Las Vegas—is not for us to decide at this stage. However, we note that an employer concerned about the risk that employees will abuse the FMLA's leave provisions may of course require that requests be certified by the family member's health care provider. And any worries about opportunistic leave-taking in this case should be tempered by the fact that this dispute arises out of the hospice and palliative care context.

If Beverly had sought leave to care for her mother in Chicago, her request would have fallen within the scope of the FMLA. So too if Sarah had lived in Las Vegas instead of with her daughter, and Beverly had requested leave to care for her mother there. Ultimately, other than a concern that our straightforward reading will "open the door to increased FMLA requests," the Park District gives us no reason to treat the current scenario any differently. Yet even if we credit the Park District's policy concern, "[d]esire for what we may consider a more sensible result cannot justify a judicial rewrite" of the FMLA.

III. Conclusion

We AFFIRM the judgment of the district court.

QUESTIONS

The court notes that the Park District's main objection was that Ballard was seeking to take a recreational trip that was not medically necessary. Do you think part of the Park District's concern was about avoiding the "slippery slope" of FMLA leave takers? If so, is it realistic to assume there will be other requests for "recreational" leave?

CHAPTER 7

FREEDOM IN THE WORKPLACE

B. HARASSMENT

Page 397.   Please add the following note.

3A. Under *Ellerth and Faragher* employers are liable for harassment committed by a co-worker only if it was negligent in controlling the working conditions. If the harassment is committed by a supervisor, however, the employer is vicariously liable. In Vance v. Ball State University, 133 S.Ct. 2434 (2013), the Supreme Court, 5–4, in an opinion by Justice Alito, held that an employee is a supervisor for purposes of vicarious liability under Title VII only if he or she is empowered by the employer to take tangible employment actions against the victim, such as firing, demoting, or disciplining the employee. In dissent, Justice Ginsburg would have adopted the EEOC's definition of a supervisor, which included an individual authorized to direct the employee's daily work activities. The power to assign an individual's work duties, typically associated with being a supervisor, gives the harasser leverage over the individual, thereby diminishing the likelihood an internal complaint will be filed to alert the employer of the need to investigate and, where necessary, correct the situation or face liability under Title VII.

D. FREEDOM OF EXPRESSION

1. PUBLIC SECTOR

Page 427.   Please add the following notes.

3A. David Kristofek, a police officer, arrested a driver for traffic violations. When the arrested driver turned out to be the son of a former mayor of a nearby town, the police chief ordered Kristofek to let him go. Concerned about what he believed to be political corruption, Kristofek complained to fellow officer, his supervisors, and eventually the FBI. When the police chief learned of this conduct, he fired Kristofek. The district court granted the defendant's motion to dismiss on the ground that Kristofek's speech did not involve a matter of public concern because his speech was self-interested. On appeal, what result? See Kristofek v. Village of Orland Hills, 712 F.3d 979 (7th Cir. 2013) (held: public concern need not be the *sole* reason for speech; plaintiff stated a claim for relief even if the speech had a mixed motive).

4. In Jackler v. Byrne, 658 F.3d 225 (2d Cir. 2011), the Second Circuit clarified its analysis of *Garcetti* as expressed in *Weintraub*. According to the court, *Garcetti* requires that the subject of the employee's speech was a matter of public concern and that the employee was speaking "as a citizen" and not "solely" as an employee. It was on this latter point that the plaintiff in *Weintraub* failed, because his protest was as an employee and not as a citizen. By contrast, in *Jackler*, a probationary police officer alleged he was discharged for failing to file a false report about an incident involving police misconduct in an arrest. Even though his action arose in the line of duty it was protected because a civilian would be similarly protected. "We conclude that Jackler's refusal to comply with orders to retract his truthful Report and file one that was false has a clear civilian analogue and that Jackler was not simply doing his job in refusing to obey those orders from the department's top administrative officers and the chief of police."

CHAPTER 8

OCCUPATIONAL SAFETY AND HEALTH

Page 446. Please add these updated figures to the first paragraph.

According to the latest compilation of data by the Centers for Disease Control and Prevention, in 2012, a total of 4,383 U.S. workers died from work-related injuries. Although most deaths from occupational illness are not captured by the reporting system, for 2007, the estimate of total deaths from occupational illness was 53,445. In 2012, there were nearly 3 million nonfatal work-related injuries and illnesses in the private sector and 793,000 in state and local government. Also, in 2012, about 2.8 million work-related injuries were treated in emergency departments, with 140,000 hospitalizations. In 2007, the total economic cost for work-related deaths, injuries, and illnesses was $250 billion. Centers for Disease Control and Prevention, Workers' Memorial Day—April 28, 2014, 63(16) Morbidity & Mortality Weekly Rep. 346 (April 25, 2014).

CHAPTER 9

DISABLING INJURY AND ILLNESS

F. TORT ACTIONS AND "EXCLUSIVITY"

1. ACTIONS AGAINST THE EMPLOYER

Page 527.   Please add the following note.

3.   Employees who are not covered by workers' compensation, often including agricultural employees, are not barred from bringing negligence claims for work-related injuries. Adam Martensen was a farmhand who used an all-terrain vehicle (ATV) as he was repairing fences on a 400–acre pasture on his employer's ranch. One day, when the ATV overturned it pinned Martensen's right leg. He was unable to move or summon help. When he did not return from his work at the end of the day Martensen's employer considered searching for him, but decided it was unnecessary. A search party organized by Martensen's father the next day found him in 10 minutes. Martensen's leg was amputated above the right knee. According to the court, the existence of an employer-employee relationship can give rise to a duty to act. Martensen v. Rejda Bros., Inc., 283 Neb. 279, 808 N.W.2d 855 (2012).

PART IV

TERMINATING THE RELATIONSHIP

CHAPTER 10

DISCHARGE

C. TORT EXCEPTIONS TO AT-WILL EMPLOYMENT

2. PUBLIC POLICY

a. LEGAL DUTIES

Page 609.   Please add the following note.

4. In 2006, Debra Parks was fired by Alpharama, Inc. after having complained about Alpharma's policy of failing to inform doctors and the FDA that its drug Kadian could be harmful if taken in conjunction with other pain medications or with alcohol. Parks argued that a public policy exception should apply because the public has an interest in not being unknowingly poisoned. The Court of Appeals of Maryland declined to apply a public policy exception, noting that "Maryland has adopted a more conservative view of what is actionable, not wishing to involve the courts in borderline claims where the violation of public policy is not so clear." Parks v. Alpharma, Inc., 421 Md. 59 (2011). The Fourth Circuit essentially affirmed, holding that Parks failed to satisfy the notice prong of her retaliation claim. The court emphasized that the employer must be aware of an employee's conduct to be held to have unlawfully retaliated. U.S. ex rel. Parks v. Alpharma, Inc., 493 F. App'x 380 (4th Cir. 2012) (unpublished).

b. STATUTORY AND CONSTITUTIONAL RIGHTS

Page 615.   Please add the following notes.

11. Nathan Berry, employed by Liberty Holdings, was involved in an auto accident with Premier Concrete Pumping. Both Premier and Liberty were partially owned by the same person, Brent Voss. Berry successfully filed a personal injury lawsuit and nine months later was fired. Berry asserted that public policy protected him from being terminated for exercising his right to file lawsuits. The Iowa Supreme Court said that much like the right to consult with an attorney, the right to file lawsuits against an employer is not supported by public policy. The court said that the existence of a legal framework permitting an activity is insufficient to prove a state public policy in favor of the activity. More broadly, "legislative pronouncements that are limited in scope may not support a public policy beyond the specific scope of the statute." Berry v. Liberty Holdings, Inc., 803 N.W.2d 106 (Iowa 2011).

12. Joyce Martin had been working at Clinical Pathology Laboratories (CPL) for three years when she requested permission to leave work early to vote in the general election. CPL refused permission, but Martin nonetheless left work 15 minutes early to vote. Two days later, CPL terminated Martin's employment. Martin claimed public policy protection for her right to vote, citing the Texas Election Code, which prohibits employers from refusing to permit employees to be absent from work on election day for the purpose of attending the polls to vote. The Texas Court of Appeals, however, concluded that the criminal penalties of the Texas Election Code were sufficient and that the legislature did not intend to create a common-law exception to at-will employment: "Our general rule is that we, as an intermediate appellate court, will not adopt new common-law exceptions to the employment-at-will doctrine." Martin v. Clinical Pathology Laboratories, Inc., 343 S.W.3d 885 (Tex. App. 2011).

c.   PUBLIC HEALTH AND SAFETY

Page 619.   Please add the following note.

5.   Phyllis Delaney said she was dismissed for seeking four weeks off from work to donate a kidney to her brother. The Missouri court of appeals held that the state's public policy encourages organ donation and reversed a trial court decision dismissing Ms. Delaney's lawsuit. Delaney v. Signature Health Care Foundation, 376 S.W.3d 55 (Mo. Ct. App. 2012).

CHAPTER 11

EMPLOYEES' DUTIES TO THE EMPLOYER

A. BREACH OF CONTRACT BY AN EMPLOYEE

2. BREACH OF IMPLIED TERMS

Page 645.   Please add to the end of Note 3.

This is also the position of the Restatement (Third) of Employment Law, approved by the American Law Institute in 2014. Section 8.01 provides that only employees "in a position of trust and confidence" owe a fiduciary duty to their employers. The Comments explain that "Employees occupy such a position when they exercise managerial responsibilities for the employer or have substantial discretion and little direct oversight in carrying out their tasks, and especially when they have been entrusted with the employer's trade secrets."

Page 646.   Please add the following note.

6.   Rehab Solutions alleged that its in-house accountant, Mignon Willis, failed to fulfill many duties of her employment which eventually resulted in tax liens levied against Rehab's building. The Supreme Court of Mississippi held that theories of unjust enrichment and negligence do not support lawsuits by Rehab against Willis for nonfeasance of Willis's duties. Willis v. Rehab Solutions, PLLC, 82 So.3d 583 (Miss. 2012). The court cited the facts that Willis did not engage in illegal activity and that Rehab failed to properly oversee Willis.

7.   Should it make a difference if the former employee sets out on her own or if she joins a different company? In Fox v. Millman, 45 A.3d 332 (N.J. 2012), the defendant had worked for Target Industries, a plastic bag manufacturer, as a sales representative. When her employment was terminated, she took her former employer's customer list with her, despite the confidentiality agreement that she had signed. When she was hired by a new employer, Polymer Plastics, shortly thereafter, she gave them the customer list, which she presented as her own. When questioned by Polymer, she denied that she was under any confidentiality agreement with Target. Polymer made no further inquiries into the matter, such as contacting Target, and subsequently used the list to generate substantial profits. Polymer Plastics admitted that they knew that Millman had previously worked at Target, and at no other plastic manufacturing company, and that Polymer themselves required all of their employees to sign confidentiality agreements. Nonetheless, the New Jersey Supreme Court held that an employer does not have a duty to inquire as to whether or not materials received from a new employee are bound by a prior confidentiality agreement.

B. POST-EMPLOYMENT RESTRICTIONS

1. FUTURE EMPLOYMENT

Page 652.   Please add to the end of Note 3.

Florida court decisions on this subject were overturned by the Florida Legislature. According to the current Florida statute, Fla. Stat. § 542.335(1)(c), the party seeking enforcement has to show that the covenant was necessary to protect its legitimate interests.

Page 653.   Please add to the end of Note 6.

In New York, both considerations—the risk that employers will be overly broad or overly cautious—are taken into account. Courts will allow for partial enforcement of overly broad restrictive covenants, but only if the employer demonstrates "an absence of overreaching, coercive use of dominant bargaining power, or other anti-competitive misconduct." BDO Seidman v. Hirshberg, 712 N.E. 2d 1220 (N.Y. 1999). This is essentially the position of the Restatement as well, see §8.08 of the Restatement (Third) of Employment Law, approved by the American Law Institute in 2014.

Page 655.   Please add the following note.

12. A recent article in the New York Times discussed the trend towards a proliferation of non-compete agreements, even amongst hair stylists and summer camp counselors. *Noncompete Clauses Increasingly Pop Up in Array of Jobs,* http://www.nytimes.com/2014/06/09/business/noncompete-clauses-increasingly-pop-up-in-array-of-jobs.html?. Although there may not be hard data regarding exactly how much the usage on non-compete clauses has increased, a study conducted for The Wall Street Journal found that the number of published U.S. court decisions involving non-compete agreements rose 61% between 2002 and 2013. The study attributed this increase in large part to the increased enforcement of non-compete agreements against lower-level employees. *Litigation Over Noncompete Clauses Is Rising,* http://online.wsj.com/news/articles/SB10001 424127887323446404579011501388418552.

2. TRADE SECRETS

Page 661.   Please add the following notes.

6. In order to promote the utilization of inventions arising from federally supported research, the Bayh-Dole Act sets forth a three-tier system for patent rights ownership of "subject inventions." 35 U.S.C. §§ 200, 202–203 (2012). For "subject inventions," which include "any invention of the contractor conceived or first actually reduced to practice in the performance of work under a funding agreement," the Act awards patent rights first to the federal contractor, second to the federal government, and third to the inventor.

The National Institutes of Health provided Stanford with funding for research related to HIV measurement techniques. As part of his employment with Stanford, Dr. Mark Holodniy signed an agreement stating that he agreed to assign his interest in any invention to the university. Holodniy then began conducting research at Cetus, a California-based company, as part of his employment with Stanford. Holodniy signed an agreement stating that he was assigning his interest in any invention to Cetus. Later, Roche Molecular Systems, Inc. acquired Cetus and commercialized the HIV measurement technique developed by Holodniy and patented by Stanford.

Stanford sued Roche for patent infringement. The Supreme Court held that Roche had acquired an ownership interest in the patents from Holodniy's assignment of rights to Cetus and that this interest was not extinguished by the Bayh-Dole Act. The Court reasoned that when Congress had previously divested inventors of their rights in inventions, it had done so unambiguously. Here, the Act applied only to an "invention of the contractor"—for example, an invention which had been properly assigned to the contractor—and did not automatically divest an inventor of rights in an invention. Board of Trustees of the Leland Stanford Junior University v. Roche Molecular Systems, 131 S.Ct. 2188 (2011).

7. Many states have blacklisting statutes aimed at preventing employers from exchanging information about past employees with the intent of preventing those employees from obtaining future employment within the industry. Do employer suits to enforce non-compete agreements and to protect trade secrets fall within the scope of a state's blacklisting statute? Indiana's blacklisting statute prohibits any company from permitting its agents to blacklist a discharged employee or "attempt[ing] by . . . any means whatever, to prevent such discharged employee, or any employee who may have voluntarily left said company's service, from obtaining employment with any other person, or company . . . " Ind. Code § 22–5–3–2 (2012). The Supreme Court of Indiana ruled that a suit to protect alleged trade secrets does not fall within the scope of the state's blacklisting statute because the language of the statute did not support such a construction and an employee's interests in being free from frivolous litigation were better served by other remedies and defenses including the common law torts of malicious prosecution and abuse of process, motions to dismiss under federal and state rules of civil procedure, and anti-trust laws. Loparex, LLC v. MPI Release Technologies, LLC, 964 N.E.2d 806 (Ind. 2012).

CHAPTER 12

UNEMPLOYMENT

B. PLANT CLOSINGS

Page 681.   Please add the following notes.

8.   The Ninth Circuit held that an employee who leaves his or her job because the business was closing has not "voluntarily departed" and may be eligible for WARN Act relief just like an employee who suffers an "employment loss": departure because of a business closing, therefore, is "generally not voluntary, but a consequence of the shutdown and must be considered a loss of employment . . . " Collins v. Gee W. Seattle LLC, 631 F.3d 1001, 1006 (9th Cir. 2011). The court added that employees who would have retired, would have been discharged for cause, or voluntarily departed independently of a business closure are not considered to have suffered an employment loss.

9.   Kohler Company hired temporary workers in the middle of a strike and then dismissed them at the strike's conclusion without providing WARN Act notice. The court of appeals held that only workers fired and not replaced count for determining whether there was a mass layoff. Here 123 temporary workers were laid off and 103 striking workers were rehired to their jobs so the layoff was of only twenty, not enough to satisfy the WARN Act numerosity requirement. Sanders v. Kohler Co., 641 F.3d 290 (8th Cir. 2011).

10.   United Steel workers sued U.S. Steel for failing to provide WARN Act notice prior to a mass layoff in a Keewatin, Minnesota plant in December 2008, at the height of the financial crisis. Held: the statute's exception for unforeseeable business circumstances prevents this from being a statutory violation. (Nearly all the workers were rehired by December 2009.) The court wrote: "U.S. Steel thought it could survive the economic downturn until the unprecedented effects on the steel industry manifested themselves in late November 2008, thus requiring immediate action . . ." United Steel Workers of America Local 2670 v. United States Steel Corp., 683 F.3d 882 (8th Cir. 2012).

C. UNEMPLOYMENT INSURANCE

3. LEGAL ISSUES IN UNEMPLOYMENT INSURANCE

b.   SEPARATIONS

(ii) Discharge for Misconduct

Page 710.   Please add the following note.

13.   AnMed Health fired Pamela Crowe because she refused to comply with its policy requiring her to get a flu shot. Crowe's daughter had died at age 25, possibly from a disease triggered by a flu shot. Held, Crowe was not discharged for cause so is eligible for unemployment benefits. AnMed

Health v. South Carolina Dept. of Employment and Workforce, 743 S.E.2d 854, 2013 WL 2234037 (S.C. Court of Appeals, May 22, 2013).

CHAPTER 13

RETIREMENT

B. THE PRIVATE PENSION SYSTEM

2. ERISA

c. FIDUCIARY DUTIES UNDER ERISA

Page 763.   Please add the following notes.

6.   Concerning the equitable relief available when the fiduciary duty is violated, see Great-West Life & Annuity Ins. Co. v. Knudson, page 506 of casebook. See also CIGNA Corp. v. Amara, 131 S.Ct. 1866 (2011), holding that the Summary Plan Description is not an enforceable part of the ERISA plan; that ERISA does not give a federal court the authority to reform the terms of the plan as remedy; but that a court can grant "other appropriate equitable relief," including the benefits to which the plan says employees and prior employees are entitled.

7.   Plaintiffs failed to establish that Morgan Stanley Investment Management knew or should have known that certain mortgage-backed securities were pension investments that failed to meet their fiduciary responsibilities. A decline in market price (stemming from the real-estate bubble and subsequent financial crisis) of a type of security does not, by itself, give rise to a reasonable inference that it was imprudent to purchase or hold that type of security." The court applied "the duty of prudence . . . 'measured according to the objective prudent person standard developed in the common law of trusts.'" Pension Benefit Guaranty Corp. on behalf of Saint Vincent Catholic Medical Centers Retirement Plan v. Morgan Stanley Investment Management, Inc., 712 F.3d 705 (2d Cir. 2013) (2–1).

d. ARBITRARY AND CAPRICIOUS DECISIONS BY PENSION FUND TRUSTEES

Page 765.   Please add the following note.

3.   If an ERISA plan grants interpretive discretion to the plan administrator, is that discretion revoked if the administrator makes a wrong decision? The Supreme Court said no, rejecting the "one strike and you're out" approach that some lower federal courts had applied. Chief Justice Roberts wrote: "People make mistakes. Even administrators of ERISA plans. That should come as no surprise, given that [ERISA] is an 'enormously complex and detailed statute' . . ." Justice Breyer, dissenting, said the administrator had made three mistakes, but he did not make the point that "three strikes and you're out." Conkright v. Frommert, 559 U.S. 506 (2010) (5–3).

e.   FEDERAL PREEMPTION OF STATE LAW

Page 766.   Please add the following note.

2.   A U.S. statute applying to federal employees allows an employee to name a beneficiary for life insurance proceeds. A Virginia statute revokes a beneficiary designation from a former spouse where there was a change in the decedent's marital status. Virginia, home of many federal employees, established a cause of action rendering the former spouse liable to give an insurance benefit back to the party (often presumably a latter spouse or offspring) who would have received the money had not the federal law preempted Virginia's attempt to regulate the payments. The Supreme Court held that Virginia cannot interfere in this way with rules laid down by the national government. Hillman v. Maretta, 133 S.Ct. 1943 (2013).

C. SOCIAL SECURITY RETIREMENT BENEFITS

3.   GENDER DISCRIMINATION IN SOCIAL SECURITY

Page 785.   Please add the following at the end of note 3.

In 2012, the Supreme Court decided that whether or not posthumously conceived children qualify for Social Security survivor benefits depends on state intestacy law. Although one court of appeals had held that children conceived in vitro after the father's death are "children" within the definition of Social Security Act, Gillett-Netting v. Barnhart, 371 F.3d 593 (9th Cir. 2004), the Supreme Court held that "it was nonetheless Congress' prerogative to legislate for the generality of cases. It did so here by employing eligibility to inherit under state intestacy law as a workable substitute for burdensome case-by-case determinations whether the child was, in fact, dependent on her father's earnings." The Court then applied Florida law and found that a posthumously conceived offspring was not eligible for survivor benefits. Astrue v. Capato ex rel. B.N.C., 132 S.Ct. 2021 (2012).

4.   SOCIAL SECURITY POLICY

Page 788.   Please add the following note.

3.   In their 2013 report, the trustees of Social Security reported that the system can pay full benefits until 2035, when it will be able to pay about three-fourths of promised benefits. The average current monthly benefit is about $1,250, thus about $15,000 per annum. Most people age 65 and older get two-thirds or more of their income from Social Security. As of 2004, Social Security replaced about 42 percent of the typical retiree's pre-retirement earnings. Planned changes now in the law will reduce that number to about 31 percent by 2030.

D. RETIREE HEALTH CARE

Page 796.   Please add the following at the end of note 2.

But even though plans can be terminated unless they clearly say the contrary. when Human Resources personnel were not truthful with employees deciding whether to take a retirement deal, the company was obligated to reinstate those employees' retirement health benefits. In re

Unisys Corp. Retiree Medical Benefits ERISA Litigation, 579 F.3d 220 (3d Cir. 2009).

Page 797.   Please add the following note.

5.   Constitutional issues have recently arisen as state and local governments have sought to reduce the budget consequences of generous retiree health benefits.   The Michigan Court of Appeals found unconstitutional a 2010 statute requiring public school districts to withhold three percent of each employee's wages and remit the money as an "employer contribution" to the trust that funds retiree health care benefits. AFT Michigan v. State of Michigan, 825 N.W.2d 595 (Mich. Ct. Apps. 2012). Immediate review by Michigan Supreme Court denied, 822 N.W.2d 226 (Mich. 2012.)

Cincinnati reduced retiree healthcare benefits in 2009, adding a deductible of $200 and an out-of-pocket cap of $2,000. Held: these changes were not unconstitutional. Gamel v. City of Cincinnati, 983 N.E.2d 375 (Ohio Ct. App. 2012). But see Savela v. City of Duluth, 806 N.W. 2d 793 (Minn. 2011), holding that the collective bargaining agreements between Duluth and its employees guarantees to retirees the same health insurance benefits that the city provides to current employees.

Page 797.   Please add following the Notes and Questions.

Reese v. CNH America LLC

694 F.3d 681 (6th Cir. 2012).

■ SUTTON, Circuit Judge.

In litigation, as in film, sequels rarely satisfy. This case is no exception. Three years ago, we remanded this dispute to the district court for factfinding necessary to determine whether CNH America's proposed modifications to its retiree healthcare benefits are reasonable. The district court did not reach the reasonableness question and did not create a factual record that would permit us to answer the question on our own. As a result, we reverse and remand for further proceedings.

Our previous opinion makes it unnecessary to recount the protracted history of this litigation. There, we considered two questions: "Did [CNH] in the 1998 CBA agree to provide health-care benefits to retirees and their spouses for life? And, if so, does the scope of this promise permit CNH to alter these benefits in the future?" In answering the first question, we rejected CNH's claim that the CBA permitted the company to terminate the benefits, holding that eligibility for lifetime healthcare benefits had "vested."

In answering the second question ("What does vesting mean in this setting?"), we rejected the suggestion that the *scope* of this commitment in the context of healthcare benefits, as opposed to pension benefits, meant that CNH could make no changes to the healthcare benefits provided to retirees. Unlike pension obligations, we explained, healthcare benefits cannot readily be monetized at retirement or for that matter practically fixed. Doctors and medical-insurance providers come and go. Medical plans change from year to year. And fixed, unalterable medical benefits at all events are not what retirees want. Nothing, indeed, would make employers happier than to know that vesting in the healthcare-benefits context meant the *same thing* as vesting in the pension context. For then, a company faced with the obligation could account for what it had spent on each employee for healthcare benefits on the day of retirement, then commit to spend no less through the end of the retiree's (and spouse's) life. Nor would most employers be troubled if this commitment, like most defined-benefit pension plans, increased based on inflation as measured by the consumer-price index. The reality is that, even though we have relied on language tying healthcare benefits to pension benefits as a basis for determining that healthcare benefits have vested, vesting in the context of healthcare benefits provides an evolving, not a fixed, benefit.

The rub for retirees and employers alike is that healthcare benefits—what is provided and what it costs—have not been remotely static in modern memory. The reason has little to do with traditional causes of inflation and more to do with the expansion of the benefit: the remarkable growth in modern life-saving and comfort-improving medical procedures, devices and drugs. New and better medical procedures arise while others become obsolete. And it is the rare medical innovation that costs *less* than the one it replaces. Retirees, quite understandably, do not want lifetime eligibility for the medical-insurance plan in place on the day of retirement, even if that means they would pay no premiums for it. They want eligibility for up-to-date medical-insurance plans, all with access to up-to-date medical procedures and drugs. Whatever else vesting in the healthcare context means, all appear to agree that it does not mean that beneficiaries receive a bundle of services fixed once and for all. Companies want the freedom to change health-insurance plans. And beneficiaries want something more than a fixed, unalterable bundle of services; they want coverage to account for new and better, yet likely more expensive, procedures and medications than the ones in existence at retirement.

All of this was borne out by the parties' implementation of the relevant collective bargaining agreements—in at least two respects. As explained in our prior opinion, the 1998 CBA "created a Managed Health Care Network Plan for past and future retirees. In other words, it imposed managed care on all of them, which represented a reduction in the effective choices of coverage available for all retirees and the coverage actually provided to many, if not most, of them." "Pre-1998 retirees thus saw their coverage downgraded in at least one respect: Unlike the prior plan, under which they could choose any doctor without suffering a financial penalty, they generally had to pay more for choosing an out-of-plan doctor." Other cases reach the same conclusion.

Also confirming that the parties did not perceive the relevant CBAs as establishing fixed, unalterable benefits was the passage of the Medicare Prescription Drug, Improvement, and Modernization Act of 2003. No one batted an eye when the healthcare plans for which retirees were eligible were modified to account for the creation of Medicare Part D, the prescription-drug benefit for seniors.

In view of the distinction between the vesting of eligibility for a benefit and the scope of that commitment and in view of the parties' practice under the 1998 CBA of altering healthcare benefits under CBAs with materially identical language, we concluded that CNH could make "reasonable" changes to the healthcare plan covering eligible retirees. We listed three considerations: Does the modified plan provide benefits "reasonably commensurate" with the old plan? Are the proposed changes "reasonable in light of changes in health care"? And are the benefits "roughly consistent with the kinds of benefits provided to current employees"? * * *

The plaintiffs and the district court misread the panel opinion. In holding that "CNH . . . may reasonably alter" the plaintiffs' benefits, we recognized that CNH could alter them *on its own,* not as part of a new collective-bargaining process. * * *

To gauge whether CNH has proposed reasonable modifications to its healthcare benefits for retirees, the district court should consider whether the new plan provides benefits "reasonably commensurate" with the old plan, whether the changes are "reasonable in light of changes in health care" (including access to new medical procedures and prescriptions) and whether the benefits are "roughly consistent with the kinds of benefits provided to current employees." In doing so, the district court should take evidence on the following questions (and others it considers relevant to the reasonableness question):

- What is the average annual total out-of-pocket cost to retirees for their healthcare under the old plan (the 1998 Group Benefit Plan)? What is the equivalent figure for the new plan (the 2005 Group Benefit Plan)?

- What is the average per-beneficiary cost to CNH under the old plan? What is the equivalent figure for the new plan?

- What premiums, deductibles and copayments must retirees pay under the old plan? What about under the new plan?

- How fast are the retirees' out-of-pocket costs likely to grow under the old plan? What about under the new plan? How fast are CNH's per-beneficiary costs likely to grow under each?

- What difference (if any) is there between the quality of care available under the old and new plans?

- What difference (if any) is there between the new plan and the plans CNH makes available to current employees and people retiring today?

- How does the new plan compare to plans available to retirees and workers at companies similar to CNH and with demographically similar employees?

It is not lost on us that the reasonableness inquiry is a vexing one. But the difficulty of the inquiry flows at least in part from the vagueness of the commitment underlying this litigation. It is well to remember the language of the relevant commitment: "Employees who retire under the Case Corporation Pension Plan for Hourly Paid Employees after 7/1/94, or their surviving spouses eligible to receive a spouse's pension under the provisions of that Plan, shall be eligible for the Group benefits as described in the following paragraphs." What that means in the context of ever-changing medical-care developments, and ever-changing healthcare plans, is not easy. But if the parties cannot resolve the point on their own, we (and the district court) will do our best to resolve it for them. * * *

For these reasons, we reverse and remand for proceedings consistent with this opinion.

Bernice B. Donald, Circuit Judge, dissenting.

My review of the issues presented here leads me to the conclusion that the majority's approach to modifying the scope of the retirees' vested health care benefits, both past and present, involves a misapprehension of the relevant law. While reasonableness is a common standard in the law, I cannot agree that resorting to what is reasonable provides the proper analytical framework in the instant case. When faced with contract terms that result in unanticipated consequences for the parties, courts are naturally tempted to play the role of arbiter and seek to resolve the case equitably. This Court, however, is one of law and not equity. Because the resolution of this case, as well as the prior appeal, represents a departure from current law, I respectfully dissent.

When affirming in part the district court's first grant of summary judgment to Plaintiffs in the instant dispute, this Court held that the retirees "have a vested right to receive health care benefits for life." On this issue, *Reese I* was consistent with prior decisions of this Court holding that when an employer ties eligibility for welfare benefits to eligibility for pension benefits those welfare benefits vest for life.

At the same time, the Court reversed the district court's holding that "these [vested health care] benefits must be maintained precisely at the level provided for in the 1998 CBA." The Court remanded to the district court to determine "how and in what circumstances CNH may alter such benefits." Upon close reexamination, I have determined that our holding that CNH may *unilaterally* alter Appellees' vested health care benefits was in error, and the majority's resolution of the case fails to correct this error. * * *

Several decisions of this Court, as well as Supreme Court precedent, express the principle that, once a retiree's health care benefits have vested for life, an employer's unilateral modification of the scope of those benefits is a violation of the Labor Management Relations Act. . . . The retiree, moreover, would have a federal remedy under § 301 of the Labor Management Relations Act for breach of contract if his benefits were unilaterally changed. * * *

Thus, clearly established precedent in this Circuit leads to the conclusion that, because retirees' health care benefits vested for life, the level of those benefits must be deemed vested in scope and *not* subject to unilateral modification by CNH. Accordingly, the district court correctly applied the law of this Circuit when it held on remand that "even if changes can be made to retiree vested health care benefits, those changes must be reached through negotiation and agreement between the union and the employer." * * *

I recognize that the terms of the 1998 CBA, as interpreted according to Sixth Circuit precedent, pose a fundamental problem for the employer: how to fulfill its open-ended obligation to provide the health care benefits described in the CBA in spite of the rapid change and growth in the health care and health insurance industries. While